ı O

Best known today for the innovative satire and experimental narrative of
Tristram Shandy (1759–67), Laurence Sterne was no less famous in his time for
A Sentimental Journey (1768), an iconic text of the sensibility vogue and a
pioneering novel of consciousness, and for his controversial sermons. Born in
Ireland in 1713, Sterne spent much of his life as an obscure and professionally
thwarted clergyman in rural Yorkshire. But he brilliantly exploited the sensation
achieved with the first instalment of *Tristram Shandy*, to become, by his death in
1768, a fashionable celebrity across Europe. His subsequent influence on a range
of important literary movements and modes, from German romanticism to the
postmodern novel, has been pervasive. This Companion is the first collection of
essays to analyse the full range of Sterne's published output, including *A Political
Romance* and *The Sermons of Mr. Yorick*, in its historical and cultural context.
Specially commissioned chapters by leading scholars provide an authoritative and
accessible guide to Sterne's writings, their entanglement with traditions of satire
and the novel, their religious, philosophical, and scientific backgrounds, their
play on gender and national identity, their disruptions of print and visual culture,
and their surprising creative afterlives in modernist and postcolonial fiction.
Including a detailed chronology and guide to further reading, *The Cambridge
Companion to Laurence Sterne* offers a comprehensive new account of Sterne's
life and work.

THE CAMBRIDGE
COMPANION TO
LAURENCE STERNE

EDITED BY
THOMAS KEYMER

CAMBRIDGE
UNIVERSITY PRESS

CAMBRIDGE UNIVERSITY PRESS

Cambridge, New York, Melbourne, Madrid, Cape Town, Singapore, São Paulo, Delhi

Cambridge University Press
The Edinburgh Building, Cambridge CB2 8RU, UK

Published in the United States of America by Cambridge University Press, New York

www.cambridge.org
Information on this title: www.cambridge.org/9780521614948

First published 2009

Printed in the United Kingdom at the University Press, Cambridge

A catalogue record for this publication is available from the British Library

Library of Congress Cataloguing in Publication data
The Cambridge companion to Laurence
Sterne / edited by Thomas Keymer.
p.   cm.
Includes bibliographical references and index.
ISBN 978-0-521-84972-2 (alk. paper)
1. Sterne, Laurence, 1713–1768 – Criticism and interpretation.
I. Keymer, Tom.   II. Title.
PR3716.C26   2009
823'.6–dc22
2009005581

ISBN 978-0-521-84972-2 hardback
ISBN 978-0-521-61494-8 paperback

CONTENTS

ILLUSTRATIONS

CONTRIBUTORS

CHRISTOPHER FANNING is Associate Professor of English at Queen's University, Kingston, Ontario. He has published a series of essays about Sterne in his cultural and generic contexts (Scriblerian satire, the encyclopaedia, print culture, the sermon) in *Eighteenth-Century Fiction, Modern Philology, Philological Quarterly*, and elsewhere. He has also written on Mary Barber and Jonathan Swift.

ROBERT FOLKENFLIK'S publications on eighteenth-century narratives include *Samuel Johnson, Biographer* (1978), *The Culture of Autobiography: Constructions of Self-Representation* (1993), editions of *Tristram Shandy*, Swift's *Tale of a Tub* and Smollett's *Sir Launcelot Greaves*, and numerous essays about the novel genre. He is Professor Emeritus at the University of California, Irvine.

ELIZABETH W. HARRIES recently retired as Helen and Laura Shedd Professor of Modern Languages at Smith College, and is now at work on a study of narrative framing. Her book *The Unfinished Manner: Essays on the Fragment in the Later Eighteenth Century* came out in 1994, followed by *Twice upon a Time: Women Writers and the History of the Fairy Tale* (2001).

JUDITH HAWLEY, Professor of English at Royal Holloway, University of London, is general editor of the Pickering & Chatto series *Literature and Science, 1660–1834* (2003–4). She has written extensively about Sterne, bluestocking feminism, and other topics in the eighteenth-century and romantic period, and is currently working on a group biography of the Scriblerus Club.

THOMAS KEYMER is Chancellor Jackman Professor of English at the University of Toronto. His books include *Sterne, the Moderns, and the Novel* (2002), *Pamela in the Marketplace* (with Peter Sabor, 2005), and the Oxford World's Classics editions of Defoe's *Robinson Crusoe* and Johnson's *Rasselas*. He co-edits *Review of English Studies*, and is co-general editor of The Cambridge Edition of the Works and Correspondence of Samuel Richardson.

MELVYN NEW is Professor Emeritus of English at the University of Florida, and general editor of the Florida Edition of the Works of Laurence Sterne. His recent books include: with his former student, Derek Taylor, an edition of John Norris and Mary Astell's *Letters Concerning the Love of God* (2005); with W. G. Day, a text-book edition of *A Sentimental Journey and Bramine's Journal* (2006); and the Florida edition of Sterne's *Letters*, with Peter de Voogd (in press).

TIM PARNELL is Lecturer in English at Goldsmiths' College, University of London. He has edited *Tristram Shandy* (2000) and *A Sentimental Journey and Other Writings* (2003), and is co-editor, with J. A. Downie, of *Constructing Christopher Marlowe* (2000). His *Laurence Sterne: A Literary Life* is forthcoming from Palgrave Macmillan.

IAN CAMPBELL ROSS, Professor of Eighteenth-Century Studies in the School of English, Trinity College Dublin, is the author of *Laurence Sterne: A Life* (2001) and editor of the Oxford World's Classics edition of *Tristram Shandy* (1983; new edition 2009). He has published widely on eighteenth-century Irish and Scottish literature and is currently general editor of a new series of Early Irish fiction for Four Courts Press.

PETER DE VOOGD, Emeritus Professor of English Literature at the University of Utrecht, is founding editor of the *Shandean* and a former president of the International Association of Word & Image Studies. His publications include co-edited volumes on *Laurence Sterne in Modernism and Postmodernism* (1995), *The Reception of Laurence Sterne in Europe* (2004), and, with Melvyn New, the forthcoming *Letters of Laurence Sterne* in the Florida edition.

MARCUS WALSH is Kenneth Allott Professor of English Literature at the University of Liverpool. He has edited, with Karina Williamson, *The Poetical Works of Christopher Smart* (1980–96), and has written widely on Smart, Swift, Johnson, and Sterne, on the history and theory of editing, and on biblical interpretation and scholarship. His *Shakespeare, Milton, and Eighteenth-Century Literary Editing* was published in 1997, and he is currently editing *A Tale of a Tub*.

CAROL WATTS is Reader in Literature and Poetics in the School of English and Humanities, Birkbeck, University of London. She is the author of *Dorothy Richardson* (1995) and *The Cultural Work of Empire: The Seven Years' War and the Imagining of the Shandean State* (2007), and has also written extensively on poetics and film. Her publications as a poet include *brass, running* (2006).

DONALD R. WEHRS is Professor of English at Auburn University. He is the author of *African Feminist Fiction and Indigenous Values* (2001), *Islam, Ethics, and Revolt* (2008), and *Pre-Colonial Africa in Colonial African Narratives* (2008). He has published on Sterne, eighteenth-century fiction, Shakespeare, and other topics in *ELH*, *Modern Philology*, *New Literary History*, *Studies in English Literature 1500–1900*, and elsewhere.

ACKNOWLEDGEMENTS

A rich and energetic tradition of writing about Sterne reaches back into the eighteenth century, and we collectively thank the many scholars whose work is built on or bounced off in the chapters below. The editor is grateful to all contributors to the volume for their collegial participation and spirit, and especially to Tim Parnell for his good counsel. Thanks also to the anonymous readers for Cambridge University Press for their advice on the volume proposal, to Mario Giovane and Erin Parker for their assistance in preparing the manuscript for production, and to Linda Bree and her publishing colleagues for their expert guidance throughout.

CHRONOLOGY

1713   (24 November) Born in Clonmel, County Tipperary, the second of seven children of Roger Sterne, an impoverished army ensign, and his wife Agnes; spends peripatetic childhood with spells in Yorkshire, Dublin, and garrison towns in England and Ireland.

1723–4   Sent to live under the protection of his wealthy uncle Richard Sterne of Woodhouse, Yorkshire; attends grammar school at Hipperholme, near Halifax, where he probably boards.

1731   (31 July) Roger Sterne dies at Port Antonio, Jamaica, probably of malaria, shortly after his promotion to lieutenant.

1733   (November) Enters Jesus College, Cambridge, as a sizar (student subsidised by his college in return for menial services); suffers serious pulmonary haemorrhage during undergraduate years.

1737   (January) Graduates as Bachelor of Arts; (March) ordained as a deacon and appointed assistant curate in St Ives, Huntingdonshire.

1738   (February) Becomes assistant curate in Catton, Yorkshire; (August) ordained as a priest and, through the influence of his uncle, Jaques Sterne, a senior churchman, inducted as vicar of Sutton-on-the-Forest, Yorkshire.

1740   (July) Returns to Cambridge to receive Master of Arts degree.

1741   (January) Installed in York Minster as prebendary of Givendale; (30 March) marries Elizabeth Lumley (1714–73). At the behest of Jaques Sterne, writes an uncertain quantity of political journalism for the *York Gazetteer*, a Whig newspaper, and publishes a pro-Walpole election address, 'Query upon Query' (27 October), in the opposition *York Courant*.

1742   (January) Installed in York Minster as prebendary of North Newbald, a more lucrative preferment than Givendale; (July) breaks with Jaques Sterne and announces his withdrawal from factional writing (though later items have been attributed to him).

1743   (July) LS's poem 'The Unknown World' published in the *Gentleman's Magazine*.

1744   (March) Acquires a second living as vicar of Stillington, a parish adjoining Sutton, through his wife's influence; (November) acquires the Tindal Farm and adjacent land in Sutton, which he and Elizabeth manage with limited success until 1758.

1745   (1 October) Birth of LS's first daughter, Lydia, who dies within a day; other children may have died in infancy.

1745–6   Probably active again as a political writer during the Jacobite rebellion, as author of an anti-Catholic polemic in the *York Journal* (1 July 1746) and other items of uncertain attribution.

1747   (Good Friday) *The Case of Elijah and the Widow of Zerephath* preached as a charity sermon in St Michael-le-Belfry, York, and published shortly afterwards in York and London; (1 December) birth of a second daughter, Lydia (1747–80).

1750   (July) *The Abuses of Conscience* preached as an assize sermon at York Minster and published in York; (December) receives minor preferment from Lord Fauconberg as commissary of the Peculiar Jurisdiction of Alne and Tollerton.

1751   (July) Preferred by John Fountayne, a Cambridge acquaintance recently appointed Dean of York, to the commissaryship of the Peculiar Court of Pickering and Pocklington. Agnes Sterne committed to gaol for debt at about this time; she continues to harass and embarrass her son until her death in York (May 1759).

1756   Acquires land as a result of the Sutton Enclosure Act, but does not gain legal possession until 1762.

1758   (December) Abandons the agricultural venture and leases Tindal Farm to tenants; Elizabeth Sterne suffers mental breakdown at about this time.

1759   (January) *A Political Romance*, satirising Dean Fountayne's adversaries, published in York but withdrawn and destroyed under pressure from the Archbishop; only six copies now known to survive. Starts work on early drafts of *Tristram Shandy*, probably including the 'Rabelaisian Fragment', and contacts the London publisher Robert Dodsley; (December) *Tristram Shandy*, volumes 1 and 2, published in York.

1760   (March) Arrives in London and is lionised by metropolitan society; (April) second edition of *Tristram Shandy*, volumes 1 and 2, published in London by Robert and James Dodsley; (May) *The Sermons of Mr. Yorick*, volumes 1 and 2, published by the Dodsleys with a prestigious list of subscribers; (May) returns to Yorkshire to take up the living of Coxwold (which becomes his Yorkshire home – 'Shandy Hall') thanks to Fauconberg's patronage; (December) returns to London to see continuation of *Tristram Shandy* through the press.

1761   (January) *Tristram Shandy*, volumes 3 and 4, published by the Dodsleys; Sterne remains in London for six months, retiring to Coxwold (June) to resume *Tristram Shandy*, and returning to London (December) to see volumes 5 and 6 through the press with new publishers, Becket and Dehondt.

1762   (January) Travels to Paris, where he is welcomed into leading social and intellectual circles, but suffers another pulmonary haemorrhage; (July) joined in Paris by Elizabeth and Lydia, and the family heads south to spend the winter in Toulouse.

1763   Remains in the south of France, in fluctuating health, and the family settles in Montpellier for the winter.

1764   Returns alone to England via Paris, where (March) he preaches in the British ambassador's chapel before David Hume; moves back to Yorkshire for the summer, in poor health and financial trouble, to continue *Tristram Shandy*.

1765   (January) *Tristram Shandy*, volumes 7 and 8, published by Becket and Dehondt; remains in London for the winter, promoting the novels and drumming up subscriptions for further volumes of *Sermons*: (May) returns to Yorkshire, where he suffers another consumptive attack; (October) embarks on a second continental tour, crossing the Alps to visit Turin, Milan, Florence, and Rome in November and December.

1766   (January) Reaches Naples, where he stays until March; (April) *Sermons*, volumes 3 and 4, published by Becket and Dehondt; (June) returns via London to Coxwold.

1767   (January) A solitary ninth volume of *Tristram Shandy* is published by Becket and Dehondt; conducts a sentimental liaison in London with Eliza Draper (1744–78), the wife of an East India Company official; (April) Eliza's return to India prompts him to address to her his 'Bramine's Journal', the later part of which survives as the *Journal to Eliza* or *Continuation of the Bramine's Journal*; (May) returns to Coxwold, in ill health, to write *A Sentimental Journey through France and Italy*, where (October) Elizabeth and Lydia rejoin him.

1768   (January) Returns to London, dangerously ill, with volumes 1 and 2 of *A Sentimental Journey*, which Becket and Dehondt publish in February; (18 March) dies of consumption in his Old Bond Street lodgings, and is buried (22 March) at St George's, Hanover Square, before being reinterred in an outlying cemetery. His corpse is stolen, recognised on a Cambridge dissecting table by anatomy students, and quietly reburied in London.

1769   (June) *Sermons*, volumes 5 and 7, published by Becket; Elizabeth and Lydia return to France, where (1772) Lydia marries Jean-Baptiste-Alexandre-Anne Médalle.

1773   *Letters from Yorick to Eliza* published, apparently on Eliza Draper's authority, containing ten letters predating her return to Bombay.

1775   (October) Lydia Médalle travels to London to publish, with Becket, *Letters to the Late Rev. Mr. Laurence Sterne, To His Most Intimate Friends*; these volumes include LS's incomplete 'Memoirs', 'An Impromptu', and an expurgated text of the 'Rabelaisian Fragment'.

1904   First publication of the *Journal to Eliza*, in Wilbur Cross's edition of LS's *Works*.

1969   (8 June) Reburial of LS's remains in the churchyard at Coxwold following redevelopment of the St George's, Hanover Square, burial ground.

ABBREVIATIONS

CH	*Sterne: The Critical Heritage*, ed. Alan B. Howes (London: Routledge and Kegan Paul, 1974)
Letters	*Letters of Laurence Sterne*, ed. Lewis Perry Curtis (Oxford: Clarendon Press, 1935)
OED2	*Oxford English Dictionary*, 2nd edn, 23 vols. (Oxford: Clarendon Press, 1989–97)
PR	*A Political Romance*, intr. Kenneth Monkman (Menston: Scolar Press, 1971)
RF	Melvyn New, 'Sterne's Rabelaisian Fragment: A Text from the Holograph Manuscript', *PMLA* 88 (1972), 1083–92
Sermons	*The Sermons of Laurence Sterne*, ed. Melvyn New (Gainesville: University Presses of Florida, 1996) (references are to the sermon number, followed by the page number in the Florida edition; thus '*Sermons* 23.214' refers to sermon no. 23, p. 214)
Sermons Notes	Melvyn New, *The Sermons of Laurence Sterne: The Notes* (Gainesville: University Presses of Florida, 1996)
SJ/BJ	*A Sentimental Journey through France and Italy and Continuation of the Bramine's Journal: The Text and Notes*, eds. Melvyn New and W. G. Day (Gainesville: University Presses of Florida, 2002)
TS	*The Life and Opinions of Tristram Shandy, Gentleman: The Text*, eds. Melvyn New and Joan New (Gainesville: University Presses of Florida, 1978) (references are to Sterne's original volume and chapter numbers, followed by the page number in the Florida edition: thus '*TS* 5.16.446' refers to vol. 5, ch. 16 in the original, p. 446 in the Florida edition)
TS Notes	Melvyn New, with Richard A. Davies and W. G. Day, *The Life and Opinions of Tristram Shandy, Gentleman: The Notes* (Gainesville: University Presses of Florida, 1984)

Introduction

In the 250th anniversary year of *Tristram Shandy*, and with the tercentenary of his birth impending, Laurence Sterne remains at the heart of our thinking about narrative representation, the traditions of satire, and some of the most intriguing cultural phenomena of the eighteenth century: the sensibility vogue; the rise of celebrity authorship; transformations in the understanding of personal identity and selfhood. Yet Sterne's formidable achievement as an author was the work of less than a decade. He lived in obscurity as a provincial clergyman for a quarter of a century, and witnessed the suppression of his first sustained work of satire, *A Political Romance*, by church authorities, but shot to international fame with his comic masterpiece *Tristram Shandy*, the inaugural volumes of which appeared in the closing weeks of 1759. With four further instalments published over the next seven years (closing with a ninth volume of 1767, at which point *Tristram Shandy*, as one early reader beautifully put it, 'could not either be properly said to have been left finished or unfinished' (*CH* 236)), Sterne held a central position in the literary culture of his day until his death from consumption in 1768. *A Sentimental Journey through France and Italy*, his most popular and influential work in the decades to follow, had appeared just three weeks beforehand.

To many readers at the time, the innovative gestures and experimental techniques of Sterne's writing, alongside its insouciant defiance of established decorum, marked a decisive break with the literary past, or even seemed to usher in what the dominant novelist of the previous generation resentfully called a '*Shandy*-Age'.[1] This was an impression that Sterne worked hard to contrive, not least in the clever combination of teasing parody and creative transformation used in *Tristram Shandy* to evoke and trump the most prestigious models of satire and fiction from the previous half century. Especially in the early volumes of *Tristram Shandy*, Sterne drew ingeniously on the satirical repertoire of Swift and Pope, but redeployed it on a literary culture that had undergone radical change since *A Tale of a Tub* and the *Memoirs of Martinus Scriblerus*, notably with the maturing, in the hands of Richardson and Fielding, of the modern novel and its associated conventions of representation. In later volumes, serialisation provided Sterne with a vehicle flexible and capacious enough to take in other new texts and trends as they emerged over the years of publication, endlessly renewing the novelty of *Tristram Shandy* and its status as a barometer of cultural fashions. Emphatically a work of its extended moment, Sterne's text could even absorb and recycle the attacks of his earliest adversaries, extending the intertextual loop to the point where, as one commentator wrote of the third instalment, 'you have now turned the Tables upon them, and ... have taken and pursued Hints that were chalked out by your Parodists'.[2]

Yet there is also a sense in which, like Tristram in the marketplace at Auxerre, Sterne occupies several different times at once. After decades of disparagement and relative eclipse in the Victorian era, he came into his own again in the early twentieth-century heyday of modernism, when his witty interrogation of the capacity of language and narrative to represent concrete worlds, transparent meanings, seamless chronologies, and coherent selves seemed to speak in new ways to theorists and practitioners of the novel. For the Russian formalist critic Viktor Shklovsky, *Tristram Shandy* had dismantled in advance the enabling forms and conventions of nineteenth-century realism, and at about the same time Virginia Woolf, drawn more to the creative alternative that followed this parodic rejection, hailed *A Sentimental Journey* as a stream of consciousness novel *avant la lettre*. 'No writing seems to flow more exactly into the very folds and creases of the individual mind, to express its changing moods, to answer its lightest whim and impulse', Woolf wrote.[3] Yet there is also something defiantly retrograde about Sterne's writing, even from an eighteenth-century perspective and to critics who dispute the narratological approach inaugurated by Shklovsky and Woolf, his interrogation of fictional realism is merely the chance by-product of his immersion in a formally disrupted tradition of satire that is emphatically pre-novelistic. His early reputation as 'the English Rabelais', and as having written 'an original composition, and in the true Cervantic vein' – both opinions are from the influential commentator William Warburton (*CH* 56), who never unpacked the contradiction – speak to the embeddedness of *Tristram Shandy* in Renaissance sources. From D. W. Jefferson's classic essay of 1951 on '*Tristram Shandy* and the Tradition of Learned Wit', to the commentary volumes of the standard Florida Edition of the Works of Laurence Sterne (1978–), much criticism and scholarship has been devoted to identification and retrieval of the persistently early-modern ambience of Sterne's writing.

Spanning all these periods are the philosophical contexts foregrounded in another influential study of the postwar years, John Traugott's *Tristram*

Shandy's World, which has generated a wealth of commentary on Sterne's ambiguous engagement with Lockean psychology and linguistics, and on his relationship to traditions of philosophical scepticism that reach back to Montaigne in the sixteenth century, and forward to the Enlightenment circle of the Baron d'Holbach, in which Sterne was embraced on his visits to Paris.[4] Other versions of the philosophical approach, albeit seemingly played out now, have made the case for Sterne's anticipation of twentieth-century phenomenology and existentialism; more recently, secularising emphases have been vigorously contested by scholarship aiming to reassert the importance of mainstream Anglican theology in Sterne's thinking. Even Tristram's famous declaration that 'we live amongst riddles and mysteries' (*TS* 4.17.350) has now been recuperated as a more or less verbatim quotation by Sterne from a Restoration sermon of unimpeachable Pauline credentials.[5]

The present volume is not a survey of Sterne's fluctuating critical reputation, nor of changing scholarly approaches, but the chapters that follow are all written in light of the complex traditions of exploration and debate that have surrounded Sterne's writing in the past few decades, and they also break new ground, introduce unexploited sources, and offer fresh perspectives, in ways designed to shape the agenda for future enquiry and research. Topics include the relationship between Sterne's writings and his ecclesiastical and celebrity careers; the entanglement of *Tristram Shandy* with Rabelaisian and Swiftian traditions of satire, and with the developing genres of autobiography and the novel; the religious, philosophical, and scientific backgrounds of Sterne's writings, including the theological implications of his sermons and the ambiguous sentimentalism of *A Sentimental Journey*; their teasing and provocative play on questions of politics, from gender roles to national identity, specifically in relation to Sterne's Anglo-Irish background; his ingenious exploitation of the mechanisms of print culture, both on the page and in practice, and the visual culture of representations and artefacts that later embraced the novels; and the creative energies channelled or unleashed by Sterne's writing in modernist and postcolonial fiction.

NOTES

1. Samuel Richardson, in his revised sixth edition of Daniel Defoe, *A Tour thro' the Whole Island of Great Britain*, 4 vols. (1761), III, 249.
2. *An Admonitary Letter to the Rev. Mr. S- - - - -, Upon the Publication of His Fifth and Sixth Volumes of Tristram Shandy* (1761), 5.
3. Viktor Shklovsky, 'The Novel as Parody: Sterne's *Tristram Shandy*', in his *Theory of Prose*, trans. Benjamin Sher, intr. Gerald L. Bruns (Elmwood Park, IL: Dalkey

Archive Press, 1991), 147–70; Virginia Woolf, *The Common Reader, Second Series*, ed. Andrew McNeillie (London: Hogarth Press, 1986), 78–85.

4. D. W. Jefferson, '*Tristram Shandy* and the Tradition of Learned Wit', *Essays in Criticism* 1 (1951), 225–48; John Traugott, *Tristram Shandy's World: Sterne's Philosophical Rhetoric* (Berkeley, CA: University of California Press, 1954).

5. Melvyn New, 'The Odd Couple: Laurence Sterne and John Norris of Bemerton', *Philological Quarterly* 75 (1996), 361–85; see also *Sermons Notes* 218–19.

I

IAN CAMPBELL ROSS

Laurence Sterne's life, milieu, and literary career

'Tristram Shandy is still a greater object of admiration, the Man as well as the Book.'[1] Thomas Gray's comment on Laurence Sterne's extraordinary literary and social success was written in April 1760, little more than three months after the publication of the first two volumes of *The Life and Opinions of Tristram Shandy, Gentleman* (1759–67). That Sterne had so quickly become not only a literary celebrity but one synonymous with the witty hero of his novel was astonishing enough. Still more remarkable was the fact that, by the spring of 1760, the celebrity author was equally well known in a second guise: as the good-natured Parson Yorick, whose character would survive his demise in the opening volume of *Tristram Shandy* to become the purported author of Sterne's second great fiction, *A Sentimental Journey through France and Italy* (1768). In the eight years of extraordinary fame he was to enjoy before his own untimely death, the Revd Laurence Sterne kept himself in the public gaze by impersonating now Tristram, now Yorick – as suited his mood, his audience, or the moment – in an act of ludic self-fashioning without precedent in English letters.

Sterne was born on 24 November 1713 in Clonmel, Ireland. His place of birth was fortuitous, for his parents had only recently arrived in the small County Tipperary town. Sterne's father, Roger, a junior army officer, had been posted with his regiment to Ireland from Dunkirk at the end of the War of the Spanish Succession; his mother, Agnes, daughter of an army provisioner, travelled with her husband. Though born into a prosperous family of Yorkshire gentry, Roger Sterne had left home in obscure circumstances that saw him financially insecure throughout the remainder of his life. Laurence's early years were mostly passed in a series of short stays in barracks, or as a temporary guest of Irish relatives, including Brigadier-General Robert Stearne, who entertained his poor relations at Tullynally Castle, County Westmeath, for almost a year, before the family was obliged to move on once more.

In 1723 or 1724, Roger Sterne left his wife and one surviving daughter – four other children died in infancy – to take Laurence to the house of his wealthy brother, Richard, at Woodhouse, near Halifax, Yorkshire. There, the boy would be accepted out of family duty rather than affection. Father and son would never see each other again, though Sterne remembered him fondly – 'My Father was a little Smart Man...most patient of Fatigue and Disappoint^ts of wch it pleased God to give him full Measure ... but of a kindly sweet Disposition'[2] – in the memoir he wrote for his own daughter nearly thirty years later. Eventually ordered to Jamaica with his regiment, Roger Sterne died there of fever in 1731.

As the army was one recourse for the Sternes, the Church of England was another. Sterne's great-grandfather, Richard, had been Archbishop of York for almost twenty years until his death in 1683. Laurence was apparently destined for the Church from an early age. A pupil at a boarding school at Hipperholme, run by the Revd Nathan Sharpe, he was described as 'a boy of genius' by his teacher, who 'was sure I should come to preferment' – a prediction the middle-aged writer delightedly repeated in his memoir for Lydia, though only once it had been fulfilled.[3] Leaving Yorkshire in 1733 for the University of Cambridge, Sterne graduated with a bachelor's degree four years later. It was here that he first experienced the worst symptoms of the consumption, or pulmonary tuberculosis, that would dog him for the remainder of his life; as a student he suffered his first severe haemorrhage in his lungs, later recalling that 'I bled the bed full' (*Letters* 180).

Despite early separation from his family, serious illness, and constant financial insecurity, Laurence Sterne did possess one significant advantage when he entered the Church of England, for he could count among his relations another uncle, brother to Roger and Richard, who was already a successful ecclesiastical lawyer. The Anglican Church could be as frustrating a career as the army for those who lacked the financial resources or patronage necessary to rise in the ranks, and it was through the influence of the Revd Dr Jaques Sterne, later Archdeacon of York and Precentor of York Minster, that his nephew initially prospered. Following brief periods as a curate in Huntingdonshire and Yorkshire, Laurence Sterne took priest's orders in 1738 and immediately acquired his first living as vicar of Sutton-on-the-Forest, near York.

Dr Sterne's support, though, came at a price. The Established Church was heavily politicised, and Jaques Sterne was an enthusiastic supporter of the Whig party, led by Sir Robert Walpole, Prime Minister since 1721. Laurence Sterne's preferment to a decent church living was to be repaid by assisting his uncle in supporting the Whig cause in Yorkshire. This he did, for a while, writing political propaganda in the *York Gazetteer*, a Whig paper recently founded to counteract the influence of the Tory *York Courant*. In general and by-elections in 1741 and 1742, Laurence Sterne put forward his best arguments in support of Whig candidates, while attacking and, if necessary, smearing his political opponents. Such partisan writing did not go unchallenged and, though he wrote anonymously, Sterne soon found his identity discovered and himself subjected to abusive comment in the *Courant* and locally published pamphlets. By the summer of 1742, he had had enough, publicly apologising for the abuse he had heaped on the Tory candidates and their supporters. His withdrawal from Whig politics had its consequences. In January 1741, he had gained ecclesiastical preferment in the form of a prebendaryship in York Minster, valuable to him for the stipend it brought with it; in December, he had exchanged this stall for the wealthier prebend of North Newbald. By abandoning politics, Sterne immediately forfeited all further assistance from his now alienated uncle, who became a lifelong enemy.

Sterne's only escape lay in his parish. In 1741, he had married Elizabeth Lumley, with a background in the Yorkshire gentry, and together they devoted themselves to improving the vicarage house and garden, while avoiding the expensive temptations of city life in York. Through a connection of Elizabeth's, Sterne acquired a second parish, Stillington, adjacent to Sutton. Even two livings proved insufficient to the tastes of the couple, who found themselves frequently in debt, despite attempts at thrift and a long, though eventually unsuccessful, attempt to augment their income by farming. When the Jacobite Rebellion led by the Young Pretender, Charles Edward Stuart, broke out in 1745, Sterne devoted his energies to supporting the Hanoverian cause, contributing financially to the defence of the city and county of York, and attempting (unsuccessfully) to badger a male servant into serving with the forces of George II. Although it is doubtful he was the author of several anti-Jacobite pamphlets that have been speculatively attributed to him, Sterne did pick up his pen once more, in the summer of 1746, following the Jacobite defeat at Culloden in April, with an unpleasant attack on York's Roman Catholic community.[4]

For almost two decades, though, Sterne seemed to have few literary ambitions. A single poem, 'The Unknown World', achieved anonymous publication in the *Gentleman's Magazine* for July 1743, and, as a clergyman, Sterne often wrote sermons that, delivered with the appearance of complete spontaneity, gained him local fame. Not that his talents in the pulpit went entirely unremarked in York, where prebendal duties obliged him to preach his turn in the Minster, for two sermons achieved publication. These were the charity sermon, *The Case of Elijah and the Widow of Zerephath* (1747), and an assize sermon, *The Abuses of Conscience* (1750), which in 1759 Sterne audaciously incorporated into the first instalment of *Tristram Shandy*. For the rest, Sterne showed scant enthusiasm for the parish round, though he enjoyed the legal roles in the magistrates' and church courts that came with his position. Socially, he found himself at odds with the local magnate in Sutton, an unhappy circumstance partly redeemed by his friendship with Stephen Croft, the squire at Stillington, and, perhaps, with the group of eccentrics that met at Skelton Castle ('Crazy Castle'), the Yorkshire home of a university friend, John Hall-Stevenson.

Although capable of generous acts of private charity, Sterne was widely considered by strait-laced neighbours as ill-suited to the cloth, not only for occasional neglect of his clerical duties but, above all, for his ill-concealed and eventually notorious sexual liaisons with servants (his wife once discovered him in bed with their maid) and prostitutes in York. Though contracted for love, the Sternes' marriage was not a successful one, and the contemporary scandal associating her husband's infidelity with the temporary imbalance of mind that led Elizabeth, in the late 1750s, to believe herself Queen of Bohemia may not be without foundation. To add to domestic disharmony, Sterne had long had an uneasy relationship with his widowed mother. Agnes's constant attempts to squeeze money out of her needy son – a situation turned to the clergyman's disadvantage by his vindictive uncle – did not, perhaps, entirely justify Sterne's determination to keep his mother at the greatest possible distance. A partial reconciliation, at least, was eventually effected shortly before Agnes's death in 1759.

In that year, Laurence Sterne was forty-five years old. His marriage was unhappy (though he was fond of the couple's only surviving daughter, Lydia), the farming venture he hoped would make him money was on the point of collapse, and Sterne had seen no significant clerical preferment for over a decade and a half. Yet, within the space of a few months, his entire life changed, and from the obscurity of a country parish he emerged into the glare of a literary celebrity that he would continue to enjoy for the remainder of his life.

The origins of Sterne's celebrity are to be found in the unpromising circumstances of ecclesiastical politics. Denied advancement in the Church after quarrelling with his uncle, Sterne had hoped for better things when an influential former college acquaintance, the Revd John Fountayne, was appointed Dean of York Minster in 1747. Besides supporting Fountayne in meetings of the Minster chapter, Sterne (an accomplished Latinist) wrote for him the *concio ad clerum* or discourse to the clergy that Fountayne was required to preach in Cambridge in 1751, in part fulfilment of his doctorate in divinity. Initially, Fountayne seemed willing to reward Sterne, appointing him to the Commissaryship of the Peculiar Court of Pickering and Pocklington, in preference to the ambitious church lawyer, Dr Francis Topham. The remuneration was negligible, however, and Sterne's hopes of a significant increase in income were dashed when Fountayne indicated that he thought his debt now paid in full. Though resentful, Sterne let the matter rest there until 1758, when a quarrel broke out between Fountayne and Francis Topham. A pamphlet war ensued, in which Sterne again sought to promote his own interests by supporting Fountayne. His contribution was *A Political Romance*, printed in January 1759. In an allegorical 'History of a Good Warm Watch-Coat', Sterne satirised the ecclesiastical dispute as a petty squabble, turning the archdiocese of York into a country parish – and compounded the humour by adding a 'key', in which competing members of a political club in the city offer inflated accounts of the history, which they understand as a political allegory of European significance. Sterne did not entirely spare even himself, introduced in the transparent guise of Lorry Slim (he was a tall, notably gaunt figure), but he also less wisely satirised the conduct of both the previous and present archbishops of York.[5] In London for the parliamentary session, the Archbishop summoned Fountayne and Topham to the capital and warned them to stop bringing York into disrepute. Additionally, he ordered the burning of the entire edition of *A Political Romance* – and while a few copies survived, even Sterne himself did not apparently possess one. The blow was hard, for the author was proud of his work and had insisted it be priced at a shilling, worth double the sixpenny-pamphlets that preceded it (*PR* 51).

Sterne did not allow the suppression of the *Romance* to put an end to his literary ambitions, however. '[W]hy truly I am tired of employing my brains for other people's advantage', he declared (*Letters* 84). Now he determined he was capable of writing successful comic fiction for his own benefit, and on a much larger scale. In the space of a few months, he had written enough of a new work to approach the eminent London bookseller, Robert Dodsley. The original plan was for a bawdy encyclopaedic satire that owed much to Sterne's love of Rabelais and Swift; part of it probably survives as the 'Rabelaisian Fragment' (see ch. 2 of this work). Though unconvinced, Dodsley offered suggestions for making the book more marketable. These Sterne embraced so enthusiastically that, having written what we now know as volumes 1 and 2 of *Tristram Shandy*, he borrowed money to have it printed and published in York. Concerning himself with the size of the book, its paper and type, and reading proofs with great thoroughness, he declared: 'it shall go perfect into the World'.[6]

The first instalment of *The Life and Opinions of Tristram Shandy, Gentleman* appeared in York in December 1759. The title pages of the two volumes were dated 1760, and lacked any indication of the place of publication, a strategy designed to disguise the work's provincial origins. Unlike the more general, Scriblerian-influenced satire that Sterne had originally intended, the new work was cast as a modern fictional autobiography. Though the events of Tristram's life are mostly far removed from Sterne's, author and hero were quickly identified with each other, and the work draws quietly on elements of the author's own biography: the sympathetic portrayal of Uncle Toby owes something both to Sterne's father and to the military career of Brigadier-General Robert Stearne; the ludicrous Dr Slop caricatures the York physician Dr John Burton, a political enemy from the distant days of the Jacobite Rebellion; and Parson Yorick is a real, if very partial, self-portrait.

That Sterne was writing a comic work was evidently known in York, even beyond the author's immediate circle. Encouraged by its local reception but anxious to secure wider circulation, Sterne engaged in an ingenious stratagem to secure *Tristram Shandy*'s success in London. He wrote a letter praising his book, which he persuaded a visiting singer – Catherine Fourmantel, then his mistress – to copy out as her own and send to the actor, playwright and influential arbiter of taste, David Garrick. Though Garrick most likely saw through the deception, he read the book and promoted it, thereby helping to ensure its metropolitan as well as provincial success.

And a success it certainly was. The small, York-printed first edition sold rapidly. When Sterne reached London in early March 1760, he was understandably delighted to find that no copy of the book could be had there 'for Love or money'.[7] A second edition was needed, and although the Dodsleys had not been willing to pay £50 for Sterne's fiction a few months before, they now paid £250 for the copyright, in addition to the £50 Sterne had earned from copies already sold. A second edition of volumes 1 and 2 of *Tristram Shandy* – with a print run perhaps ten times larger than the first edition's – was on sale by 2 April. Besides a number of smaller changes, this edition had two significant additions. The first was a dedication of the work to the Prime Minister himself, William Pitt; the second, two illustrations by the leading artist of the day, William Hogarth. In an age when ambitious authors regularly attempted to secure the most prestigious dedicatees for their work, Sterne had earlier sought local aristocratic patronage, so that the Marquess of Rockingham, then lord-lieutenant of the North and East Ridings of Yorkshire, took no fewer than eight sets of the York edition. A future prime minister, Rockingham would be one of many who took Sterne socially under his protection in the spring of 1760. Having spent the previous twenty-five years in near-total obscurity, Sterne now found himself lionised in London society, and his letters make clear the delight with which he accepted the visits and invitations that came his way from nobility – 'from morning to night my Lodgings ... are full of the greatest Company' (*Letters* 102) – and even royalty. The second edition, meanwhile, sold quickly, and two more London (as well as four Dublin) editions were required by the end of 1760.

Nor was this all. Sterne had ended volume 2 of *Tristram Shandy* with a promise of a further instalment in a year's time. The public who so eagerly bought *Tristram Shandy*, and the many spin-offs – imitations, parodies, ballads, moral critiques – generated by it, could not wait so long. Accordingly, Sterne and his publishers exploited their success by offering writings of a different kind. In volume 2 of *Tristram Shandy*, Sterne had expressed his hope that 'The Abuses of Conscience', read aloud by Corporal Trim to much comic as well as moral effect, would please readers. If so, he intimated, other such homilies might be had. Accordingly, he now gathered together fifteen sermons, which, in early March, he had advertised as being shortly for sale in York. The Dodsleys, however, had elaborate plans for marketing their celebrity author's new works in London. To add to Sterne's prestige, they sought subscribers for the two volumes, and the eventual subscription list of some 660 names, put together in a matter of weeks, was extraordinarily impressive. It included dukes and duchesses, over a dozen earls (including Lord Chesterfield and Sterne's Yorkshire neighbour, Lord Fauconberg, who gave the clergyman-author the living of a third Yorkshire parish, Coxwold, where the Sternes would settle), seven bishops, politicians of quite different persuasions, and leading cultural figures, including the poet laureate William Whitehead, David Garrrick, the bluestocking Elizabeth Montagu, and the fashionable portraitist Joshua Reynolds, alongside Hogarth. What appealed to such men and women must surely, Sterne and his publishers implied, be worth the while of less socially elevated readers. And so it proved. A second edition was called for within two months.

By the time it appeared, Sterne had at last, and with reluctance, turned his back on London to return to his wife and daughter, not to mention his three parishes, in Yorkshire. Six months previously, he had been a needy and obscure figure; by the spring of 1760, he was the most fashionable author in England, a literary celebrity whose writings had brought him both wealth and fame. 'I wrote not [to] be *fed*, but to be *famous*', he had declared.[8] Uneasily aware of the stigma that still attached to writing for money, Sterne played down his desire to profit financially by his success, but the ingenuity and assiduity he displayed in creating a market for his work gives the lie to his publicly professed indifference to monetary reward.

In any case, it was soon obvious to Sterne that he must choose between making his own way in the increasingly commercialised world of publishing or risking a speedy return to obscurity. The first two volumes of *Life and Opinions* had been published anonymously. In an age when the novel – that 'new species of writing' – was still the object of suspicion, *Tristram Shandy*'s satirical bawdry did not escape censure, even as the work captivated readers by means of its whimsical humour and memorable, affectionately drawn characters. When the public demanded to know the author's identity, the revelation that he was a clergyman shocked many. Before publication, Sterne had been anxious on this score: 'till you read my Tristram, do not, like some people, condemn it', he told a female correspondent (*Letters* 84). Now he cited Rabelais and Swift as clerical forebears with a penchant for irreverent wit – a defence unconvincing to those who thought such predecessors no fit models for a priest of the Established Church. Today, it might seem as if the subsequent publication of two volumes of sermons would have reassured Sterne's critics. But it did nothing of the kind, and even some readers who had enjoyed *Tristram Shandy* thought Sterne's playful title, *The Sermons of Mr. Yorick*, simply scandalous. Again, Sterne was not unaware of the risks he ran. In the end, he drew back from publishing under his preferred title of *The Dramatic Sermons of Mr. Yorick, By Tristram Shandy, Gentleman* – a yoking together of the Word of God, the playhouse, a jester, and a facetious fictional hero that seemed recklessly designed to offend as many readers as possible.

If Sterne was alert to the dangers, he seems to have been taken by surprise by the intensity of both the acclaim and the censure accorded him. What distinguished Sterne for many contemporaries was the surprising coupling of a laudable morality with whimsical bawdy. One writer declared in 1760 that Sterne possessed an 'infinite share of wit and goodness, things ... which are very seldom, indeed, found in any degree together'. It was, the same writer added, 'one of the odd qualities of this very odd person, to join contradictions'.[9] Samuel Johnson would later observe, apropos of *Tristram Shandy*, that 'Nothing odd will do long',[10] but that both the author and his work did indeed last is attributable in part to Sterne's sharp recognition that his literary and personal success lay precisely in joining contradictions. At least since the writing of *A Political Romance*, with its portrait of Lorry Slim, he had been aware of the advantage of creating a fictional persona for himself. In writing *Tristram Shandy*, he had offered two, teasingly diverse self-representations, appearing both as the buffoonish but good-natured Parson Yorick, and as the witty, ill-starred Tristram. Almost immediately, Sterne saw possibilities for appropriating these two *personae* in his own life. In broad-minded literary and social circles, he became Tristram Shandy – and there are many anecdotes to suggest Sterne, when 'Shandy[ing] it' (*Letters* 157), indulged recklessly in sexual innuendo and (a perhaps assumed) religious scepticism. When anxious to escape moral censure, display his sensibility, or play the conscientious clergyman, he would present himself in company as Mr Yorick. It was by playing one role off against the other, often with exceptional skill in tricky circumstances, that Sterne managed, throughout the remainder of his life, to retain the (sometimes uneasy) approbation of moralists, while continuing to amuse those novel readers whose tastes still ran to a broad, suggestive humour, even as such tastes were slowly losing ground to the vogue for sentimental fiction.

Once settled into his new home at Coxwold, some distance north of Sutton, Sterne's main task, parish duties aside, was to make a start on the continuation of *Tristram Shandy*. In his fiction, as in his personal correspondence, he frequently insisted on his spontaneity ('I begin with writing the first sentence——and trusting to Almighty God for the second' (*TS* 8.2.656)), but the writing proved hard work. By December 1760, however, he had two more volumes ready for the Dodsleys, who published them the following month. Sterne now had little time for mere provincial success; he was bored with Coxwold and family life – relations with his wife were poor again – and made haste to get back to London, immediately taking up the giddy social round he so enjoyed, especially when he was himself the centre of attention. Not all the attention he received was welcome. The continuation of *Tristram Shandy* provoked critical reaction much as before, divided between those who revelled in its satiric comedy and those who felt that Sterne allowed too much indecency to creep into a work that, shorn of its excesses, would have had a stronger moral claim on readers.

Though his book again sold well, Sterne could not simply ignore negative reactions to his work or himself; presented at court, he was snubbed by the young King George III.[11] Moreover, the widespread (and perhaps not inaccurate) view that Sterne had deliberately set out to provoke his critics – in his bawdy 'Slawkenbergius's Tale', for example – had unwelcome repercussions of a different kind. Between the publication of volumes 3 and 4 and that of volumes 5 and 6 in December 1761, Sterne lost the publishers who had done so much to help him market his book successfully. The reasons for Sterne's break with the Dodsleys remain unclear, but seem likely to stem from Sterne's unwillingness to tone down those elements in his work that provoked reserve or disgust in some readers.[12] At all events, the remaining five volumes of *Tristram Shandy* appeared under the London imprint of T. Becket and P. A. Dehondt.

Sterne's refusal entirely to abandon his bawdy manner may, in the end, be as much attributable to literary and commercial shrewdness as to a simple delight in being able to assert his own will, after so many years of subordination within the hierarchical world of the Established Church. In late 1761, however, he had more pressing matters on his mind. Much of *Tristram Shandy* had been written in severe ill-health: one of the most poignant manifestations of the autobiographical strand in his comic fiction is the tubercular cough that racks both Tristram and Sterne alike. Fearing himself close to death, Sterne drew up a will and crossed the Channel to seek refuge in the milder climate of the south of France. Pausing en route in Paris, he was surprised to find himself almost as much a celebrity in literary circles there as in London. Flattered, Sterne extended his stay for over six months, enjoying the company both of wealthy and generous aristocrats and of notably sceptical Enlightenment writers, including Diderot and the Baron d'Holbach. As Joshua Reynolds's portrait of him (now in the National Portrait Gallery, London) had confirmed his celebrity in England in 1760, so now he sat for Louis Carogis (Carmontelle), whose other famous subjects included David Garrick, David Hume and, in 1763, the infant prodigy Mozart. In Paris, Sterne again took care to present himself to best advantage, at times taking the part of 'Chevalier Shandy', at others playing the 'bon enfant' Yorick. The role-playing that some found irritating in Sterne was more than self-indulgent posturing, however. The invalid Sterne himself recognised the intimate connection between mental and physical wellbeing, writing to Garrick that 'by mere Shandeism sublimated by a laughter-loving people, I fence as much against infirmities, as I do by the benefit of air and climate' (*Letters* 163).

Yet neither Shandeism nor public acclaim could effect a recovery. Waiting only for his wife and daughter to join him, Sterne journeyed south and west to Toulouse, where he spent the winter of 1762–3. As usual, he was initially delighted with his new surroundings, but the dullness of the company, compounded by his own poor French – 'I splutter French so as to be understood' (*Letters* 178) – and the need to economise drove him, in the following spring, to seek refuge in Montpellier, a favourite resort for English invalids, but one that eventually disappointed him. Leaving Elizabeth and Lydia in France, Sterne started for England in May 1764. In Yorkshire, he had to attend to parish affairs unwisely left in the care of a barely-competent curate. More importantly, he had urgent need to write a continuation of *Tristram Shandy*, for sales of volumes 5 and 6 had been slow. Now, Sterne made use of his recent experience abroad as the basis of Tristram's description of his own travels in search of health – volume 7 opens with a scintillating account of the hero's encounter with Death – that take him, via Paris and the Rhône valley, through the south-west of France to Toulouse.

Published in January 1765, the fourth instalment of the novel regained for Sterne an appreciative audience, and provided a much-needed addition to his bank-balance. Inevitably, not all was praise, and reviewers again (though often more in sorrow than real anger) reproved the author for his ribaldry. The humour of Tristram's travels was much admired, however, and the heightened sentiment that increasingly characterised the work (Sterne had already given the public one greatly admired sentimental set-piece, in

Le Fever's story in volume 6) was accorded the highest acclaim. As though to show he still valued the aristocratic patronage that commercial success had partly rendered unnecessary, he had dedicated volumes 5 and 6 to Viscount Spencer and his wife, also copying out a fair version of the Le Fever episode to present to Lady Spencer as a gift[13] – though the dedication was artfully designed to reassure genteel female readers that they too might not be ashamed to read *Tristram Shandy*. The delicacy of Sterne's writing in volume 8 was also much praised, many reviewers choosing to overlook the sexual innuendo in the account of Widow Wadman's courtship of Uncle Toby, moved as they were by the author's indisputable gift for pathos.

Delicacy was not the dominant note in Sterne's contemporary attempts to secure his financial future. Though the proceeds from the new instalment of *Tristram Shandy* temporarily relieved his needs, he was anxious to profit from being back in the public eye. His new publishers had been asking for a further selection of sermons for months, and though Sterne frequently protested that they would soon be ready, he had little enthusiasm for the task of preparing them for the press. He was enthusiastic, however, about acquiring 'as splendid & numerous a List of Nobility &c——as ever pranced before a book, since subscriptions came into fashion' (*Letters* 252). Accordingly, there were few friends or acquaintances whose names – and money – Sterne did not solicit. 'I should grieve not to have your name amongst those of my friends——& in so much good company as it has a right to be in—so tell me to set it down' (*Letters* 252–3), he told one correspondent. Published in January 1766, the two slim volumes contained only twelve sermons – three fewer than the 1760 volumes and four fewer than Sterne had promised Becket – and one of those was 'The Abuses of Conscience', now making its third appearance in print. Though the subscription list was, for the most part, as prestigious as Sterne had hoped, no bishop added his name this time, while subscribers included the well-known sceptics Diderot, d'Holbach, and Voltaire (the last an extravagant admirer of 'The Abuses of Conscience'). As with the first volumes, Sterne's propensity to wit, evident in a number of sermons, together with their attribution to Yorick, led some reviewers and other readers to feel uneasy about the extent to which they could be considered sermons at all. This was not a universal view, and Sterne's orthodoxy had been accepted by the compilers of *The Practical Preacher* (1762), a four-volume anthology of sermons by the most admired protestant divines. Others were less certain and, where they did not reject them entirely (as did Sarah Scott or Samuel Johnson, for instance), preferred to consider Sterne's sermons as moral essays. Yet even William Cowper, who thought the sermons devoid of Christian revelation, considered the writer 'a great master of the pathetic', better qualified than any contemporary author to convert readers to the cause of virtue.[14]

By the time volumes 3 and 4 of the *Sermons* appeared, Sterne himself was again abroad. In October 1765, he had left England on the first leg of a visit to France and Italy. After a short stay at Calais (a visit he would recall in *A Sentimental Journey*), Sterne headed to Paris, where he stopped long enough to visit old friends. From there, he travelled via Lyon to Turin and Milan (scene of the only Italian episode in *A Sentimental Journey*). Moving south, he paused for a few days at Florence, where he met the artist Thomas Patch, who subsequently painted Sterne as Tristram encountering Death. The cold of the Tuscan winter quickly drove Sterne further south, by way of Rome to Naples, where he arrived in early 1766. Always a traveller who preferred socialising to sightseeing, he found himself in his element in the gay world of Neapolitan society: 'We have a jolly carnival of it——nothing but operas—— punchinellos——festinos and masquerades' (*Letters* 269). Abandoning plans to visit Germany and the Low Countries, Sterne paid a visit instead to Elizabeth and the now almost twenty-year-old Lydia, who had decided to make their home in France. He stayed no more than a week before turning north once more, towards England.

This time, Sterne did not dally in London but headed home to Coxwold. He was anxious to write the next instalment of *Tristram Shandy*, but now the urgency was due not to lack of funds but to the desire to start a new work, inspired by his continental travels. Although 'A thousand nothings, or worse than nothings' (*Letters* 281) initially delayed him, the continuation of his novel was soon under way: 'I am in my peaceful retreat, writing the ninth volume of Tristram' (*Letters* 284), he reported contentedly. He was evidently not working to a tight plan, since he was able to insert a brief episode sympathetic to the anti-slavery cause that had been encouraged, if not wholly suggested, by a letter – beginning 'I am one of those people whom the vulgar and illiberal call "Negurs"'[15] – that he received from a black servant of literary inclination, Ignatius Sancho. Sterne's main involvement in politics of any kind now lay over a quarter of a century in the past, but the Whig allegiances he held then never deserted him, and, despite his love of social acclaim from whatever quarter, his political sympathies remained liberal throughout his life.

Having started well with his continuation of *Tristram Shandy*, Sterne found himself blocked by the early autumn of 1766. Distressingly short of money, he badly needed funds to send to his wife, who had fallen ill and seemed, to the anxious Lydia, close to death. Meanwhile, his duties at Coxwold were augmented by the time-consuming needs of a major land enclosure scheme in his Stillington parish. Writing was hard, he told his friend John Hall-Stevenson, and what he did manage only 'so so' (*Letters* 290). When the fifth instalment of *Tristram Shandy*, again dedicated to William Pitt, appeared in late January 1767 (to the usual mixture of extravagant praise and indignant censure), it consisted of a single volume, instead of the usual two. That Sterne's mind was on his next work is suggested both by this truncation and by the notoriously teasing ending to volume 9, when Yorick, asked by Tristram's mother 'what is all this story about?', gives the reply 'A COCK and a BULL ... And one of the best of its kind, I ever heard' (*TS* 9.33.809) – a conclusion in which there is no conclusion, leaving readers ever since to speculate whether Sterne expected to return to his most famous work.[16]

That he did not intend to continue in the short term is certain. As far back as July 1766, Sterne had mentioned plans for a four-volume work, and by the winter of 1766–7, this had become so firm in his mind that he not only referred to it by its eventual title, *A Sentimental Journey*, but was busily soliciting subscriptions. When volume 7 of *Tristram Shandy* was published in January 1765, Ralph Griffiths of the *Monthly Review* had complimented him on understanding 'the true art of travelling, better than any other I ever knew or heard of' (*CH* 165), and Sterne evidently knew the value of his work in this vein, whose originality appears throughout the volume, not least in his proto-Romantic 'PLAIN STORIES' (*TS* 7.43.648). The new work would offer an extended account of a journey through France and Italy by Mr Yorick – a 'sentimental' rather than 'idle', 'inquisitive', 'lying', 'proud', 'vain', or 'splenetic' traveller (*SJ/BJ* 15). This last was a category occupied, in Sterne's mind, by his fellow-novelist Tobias Smollett, whose often querulous but well-received *Travels through France and Italy* had appeared in 1766, and whom Sterne would famously lampoon as 'Smelfungus'.[17]

At the same time as he began work on *A Sentimental Journey*, Sterne met Elizabeth Draper, the twenty-two-year-old wife of an East India Company official, in England on a visit to settle the couple's children at school. The sentimental friendship they shared in person and through correspondence – including the *Journal to Eliza* or *Bramine's Journal*[18] – dominated much of the remaining months of Sterne's life. Though his many flirtatious relationships with young women were notorious, no affair consumed his attention so completely or with such important literary repercussions as that with Eliza. In his earliest known letter to her, in January 1767, Sterne was already expressing extravagant admiration of a young woman who seems, initially, to have been flattered by the attentions of so great a celebrity. The two quickly adopted pet names for each other, inspired by Eliza's Indian background: Sterne was the 'Bramin' and Eliza the 'Bramine'. The intense friendship the pair enjoyed – or Sterne imagined – was overshadowed by the knowledge that their time together would be short, since Eliza was shortly due to return to India. The awareness of the transient nature of their relationship – though Sterne would often fantasise about a future marriage between them – was heightened by a recurrence of Sterne's illness. Casting caution aside, he addressed Eliza in letters couched in terms of passionate infatuation at odds with all social propriety. Asking for 'artless' letters in return, Sterne begged Eliza: 'Let them speak the easy carelessness of a heart that opens itself, any how, and every how, to a man you ought to esteem and trust. Such, Eliza, I write to thee,—and so I should ever live with thee, most artlessly, most affectionately, if Providence permitted thy residence in the same section of the globe' (*Letters* 306).

When Elizabeth Draper eventually set sail for India in April 1767, Sterne extracted a promise that they would write to each other during their enforced separation. Sterne's journal is extraordinary in its detailed revelation of the state of a mind consumed with sentimental passion and a frail body increasingly ravaged by tuberculosis. It is remarkable too for revealing Sterne's creative control of his representation of this mind and body, both as he enjoyed periods of remission from his illness, and as Eliza sailed further away. At times painfully raw, the *Journal*'s seemingly spontaneous narrative is carefully shaped – its chronology at moments demonstrably faked – so that the whole ebbs and flows teasingly between self-revelation and self-concealment.

By the end of his life, Sterne had become a master at fictionalising his autobiography, and at using autobiographical experiences as the basis of his fiction. 'I have brought y^r name *Eliza!* and Picture into my work—where they will remain—when You & I are at rest for ever', Sterne wrote in the *Journal*, and in *A Sentimental Journey* ('*By Mr. Yorick*') he does indeed allude obliquely to the author's friendship with Elizabeth Draper, and to a miniature portrait of her he had commissioned (*SJ/BJ* 202, 3). Yet despite this, and despite the fact that the work drew closely on Sterne's own experiences of continental travel in 1762–4, and again in 1766–7, it can be relied on as a guide to neither. Published by Becket and Dehondt on 27 February 1768, little more than a fortnight before the author's death, *A Sentimental Journey* once more had an impressive list of 334 subscribers – fewer than Sterne had hoped to attract, but still testimony to the entrepreneurial skills of the seriously ill writer, and to the deep affection he continued to inspire.

Sterne's death, coming so shortly after publication, doubtless encouraged reviewers to emphasise the pathos of the author's final book, and for the rest of the century *A Sentimental Journey* remained, along with his sermons (extended in 1769 by two posthumous volumes), his most admired work. All the same, and despite Sterne's own description of the *Journey* as his 'work of redemption',[19] the sentiment that many exclusively chose to see is more than matched by a sly, ever-present sexual subtext that culminates in the ambiguous closing sentence of the first part (volumes 3 and 4 were never written). The Yorick of *A Sentimental Journey* was an ambivalent figure but – especially when considered as self-representation – an influential one. Following his death in his London lodgings, on 14 March 1768, when Sterne could 'Shandy it' no more, it was in terms of his sentimental self-characterisation that contemporaries preferred to remember – and eulogise – him. 'Alas poor Yorick!' one reviewer wrote simply, while another declared that 'Our Sentimentalist having lately made a journey to that country *from whose bourne no traveller returns*, his memory claims at least as much indulgence as our duty to the public permitted us to allow him when alive'.²⁰ As the bawdy humour of *Tristram Shandy* became increasingly alien to polite taste in the later eighteenth century, a compilation of the most admired sentimental episodes from his writings, *The Beauties of Sterne* (1782), became an enduring bestseller.

Born at the end of a journey through the Irish countryside, Sterne was not permitted in death to rest easy. Interred in St George's burial ground in London on 22 March, he was surreptitiously resurrected, appearing – to the astonishment of one onlooker who had known him in life – on the anatomist's table at his old university at Cambridge. Hastily returned to the cemetery, Sterne's corpse lay there until the burial ground was threatened by redevelopment in 1969, when one of his greatest twentieth-century admirers recovered his skull and relocated it in the churchyard of St Michael's, Coxwold, where it remains.²¹

NOTES

1. Thomas Gray, *Correspondence of Thomas Gray*, eds. Paget Toynbee and Leonard Whibley, 3 vols. (Oxford: Clarendon Press, 1935), II, 670.
2. *Sterne's Memoirs: A Hitherto Unrecorded Holograph Now Brought to Light in Facsimile*, ed. Kenneth Monkman (Coxwold: The Laurence Sterne Trust, 1985), 13.
3. *Letters* 3–4. For the writing of his memoirs in two stages (the first in 1758, the second in 1767), see Monkman's introduction and notes to *Sterne's Memoirs*, xii–xiv, xxxi; also Ian Campbell Ross, *Laurence Sterne: A Life* (Oxford: Oxford University Press, 2001), 34–5 and 437 (n. 57).
4. See *York Journal; or, Protestant Courant* (1 July 1746), quoted by Kenneth Monkman, 'Sterne, Hamlet, and Yorick: Some New Material', in *The Winged Skull: Papers from the Laurence Sterne Bicentenary Conference*, eds. Arthur H. Cash and John M. Stedmond (London: Methuen, 1971), 112–235. For the dubious attribution to Sterne of further pamphlets from this period, see Kenneth Monkman, 'Sterne and the '45 (1743–8)', *Shandean* 2 (1990), 45–136.
5. For the identification, see Ian Campbell Ross and Noha Saad Nassar, 'Trim (-trim), Like Master, Like Man: Servant and Sexton in Sterne's *Tristram Shandy* and *A Political Romance*', *Notes and Queries* 36 (1989), 62–5.
6. See *The Correspondence of Robert Dodsley, 1737–1764*, ed. James E. Tierney (Cambridge: Cambridge University Press, 1988), 37.

7. John Croft, 'Anecdotes of Sterne Vulgarly Tristram Shandy', in *The Whitefoord Papers*, ed. W. A. S. Hewins (Oxford: Clarendon Press, 1898), 227.

8. 'To Dr *****' (*Letters* 90); this letter was almost certainly intended for publication.

9. *Tristram Shandy's Bon Mots, Repartees, Odd Adventures, and Humorous Stories* (1760), 3–4.

10. James Boswell, *Life of Johnson*, ed. R. W. Chapman, rev. J. D. Fleeman (Oxford: Oxford University Press, 1970), 696.

11. See Jonas Dennis, *A Key to the Regalia* (1820), 102–3n.

12. See also, for James Dodsley's reported claim in 1765 that he had been 'a loser by [Sterne's] works', Melvyn New, 'A New Sterne Letter and an Old Mystery Closer to Solution', *Shandean* 17 (2006), 80–4.

13. See Melvyn New, 'A Manuscript of the Le Fever episode in *Tristram Shandy*', *Scriblerian* 23 (1991), 165–74.

14. *The Letters and Prose Writings of William Cowper*, eds. James Kinsley and Charles Ryskamp, 3 vols. (Oxford: Clarendon Press, 1979), I, 135. For a recent view of Sterne's religious position, see Carol Stewart, 'The Anglicanism of *Tristram Shandy*: Latitudinarianism at the Limits', *British Journal for Eighteenth-Century Studies* 28 (2005), 239–50.

15. *Letters of the Late Ignatius Sancho, an African*, ed. Vincent Carretta (Harmondsworth: Penguin, 1998), 73.

16. Writing to William Combe, Sterne claimed that 'I miscarried of my tenth Volume by the violence of a fever, I have just got thro' (*Letters* 294).

17. *SJ/BJ* 37. For a reconsideration of Sterne and Smollett as travellers, see Ian Campbell Ross, 'When Smelfungus met Yorick: Sterne and Smollett in the South of France, 1763', in *Tobias Smollett, Scotland's First Novelist: New Essays In Memory of Paul-Gabriel Boucé*, ed. O M Brack, Jr (Newark, NJ: University of Delaware Press, 2007), 74–93.

18. The letters that make up the journal may be read either in sequence, interspersed with other of Sterne's correspondence (*Letters* 322–400), or as a separate work, *Continuation of the Bramine's Journal* (*SJ/BJ* 167–225).

19. Richard Griffith and Elizabeth Griffith, *A Series of Genuine Letters, between Henry and Frances*, 6 vols. (London, 1786), V, 83.

20. *CH* 200 (Ralph Griffiths in the *Monthly Review* for April 1768), 197 (*Critical Review* for March 1768, echoing *Hamlet*, III.i.80–1).

21. See Kenneth Monkman, continued by W. G. Day, 'The Skull', *Shandean* 10 (1998), 45–79.

2

MARCUS WALSH

Scriblerian satire, *A Political Romance*, the 'Rabelaisian Fragment', and the origins of *Tristram Shandy*

The first two volumes of *Tristram Shandy* burst upon a surprised and marvelling world in 1759, from the pen of a clergyman almost unpublished before that date, and virtually unknown outside York ecclesiastical circles. What dragons' teeth had been sown to bear such an apparently full-grown progeny? What rough beast or shaggy dog was slouching, from Sterne's church living at Sutton-on-the-Forest, toward London to be born?

We know a good deal about the literary traditions that influenced *Tristram Shandy*, or from which *Tristram Shandy* was conjured. They include (especially for Sterne's first two volumes) the writings of the French sixteenth-century humanist and humorist François Rabelais, author of *Gargantua and Pantagruel*; Jonathan Swift's first satiric masterpiece, *A Tale of a Tub* (1704), and its associated attack on enthusiastic religious dissent, *A Discourse Concerning the Mechanical Operation of the Spirit*; and the satires of the Scriblerus Club, particularly *The Memoirs of Martinus Scriblerus*, on early eighteenth-century abuses of learning.[1] Our understanding of what such texts meant to Sterne, and how he set about re-forging these materials into something new and rather different, may be a little advanced by looking at two earlier and fragmentary pieces of writing from his hand: *A Political Romance* and the 'Rabelaisian Fragment'.

A Political Romance was written as a contribution to a political dispute that arose in the diocese of York. Some initial disentangling of the skeins of that dispute is necessary. One Dr Francis Topham, a York lawyer, held a number of legal offices in the Church, but had expectations or promises of several more, which fell vacant on the death of Dr William Ward in 1751. Amongst these, he was granted the commissaryship of the Exchequer and Prerogative Court. To his disappointment, however, Topham was denied the commissaryship of the Peculiar Court of Pickering and Pocklington (which the Dean, John Fountayne, gave instead to Sterne himself), and the commissaryship of the Court of the Dean and Chapter (which was granted to the lawyer William Stables). Topham, having given vent to his anger at a public sessions dinner in York, where Sterne was present, nursed his grievance until 1757. In that year, following the appointment of the new Archbishop, Dr John Gilbert, he canvassed both Dean Fountayne and Dr Gilbert for a renewed grant of the patent for the commissaryship of the Exchequer and Prerogative Court, to include not only his own life, but that of his son, Edward, then seven years of age. At a meeting of the three men, in November 1758, Archbishop Gilbert refused to accede to Topham's ingenious and unusual, though not unprecedented, proposal. Topham was furious, at what he thought to be yet another breach of promise. He went public, in *A Letter Addressed to the Reverend the Dean of York* (1758); Dean Fountayne, with the assistance of Sterne, promptly published *An Answer to a Letter Address'd to the Dean of York* (1758); Topham retorted in *A Reply to the Answer to a Letter Lately Address'd to the Dean of York* (1759); and Sterne effectively concluded the pamphlet war (the Dean having already, in his *Answer*, promised to take no further part in the wrangle) with *A Political Romance*, published in January 1759 – price one shilling.[2]

Sterne's diminishing allegory of this storm in an ecclesiastical teapot was in its earlier and unpublished form set in the imaginary village of Cocksbull, and was reportedly entitled 'The history of a good warm watch-coat, with which the present possessor is not content to cover his own shoulders, unless he can cut out of it a petticoat for his wife, and a pair of breeches for his son' – the 'watch-coat' representing, of course, the patent for the commissaryship of the Exchequer and Prerogative Court.[3] The commissaryship of Pickering and Pocklington was allegorised as 'an *old-cast-Pair-of-black-Plush-Breeches*', and Francis Topham reduced to 'one *Trim*, who is our Sexton and Dog-Whipper' (*PR* 1). Trim later gathers to himself the further offices of mole- and, with a typically Sternean suggestion, coney-catcher;[4] the Dean and Archbishop are translated to the relatively higher dignities of parish-clerk and parson.

Even before *A Political Romance* was published, Sterne was working on another project: no less than a first essay at what would very soon become *Tristram Shandy*. Our main evidence for the form this first version took is a letter of April 1760, from an unidentified correspondent to an unidentified recipient, written on the basis of an evening spent with Sterne the previous summer:

> A System of Education is to be … thoroughly discussed. For forming his future Hero … a private Tutor … the great and learned Dr. W[arburton]: Polemical Divines are to come in for a slap. An Allegory has been run up on the Writers on the Book of Job. The Doctor is the Devil who smote him from Head to Foot, and G[re]y P[ete]rs and Ch[appel]ow his miserable Comforters.[5]

This account suggests that Sterne had written a new version of that central Scriblerian mock treatise, *The Memoirs of Martinus Scriblerus*, and had made a satiric intervention in a noisy and long-running contemporary squabble about the interpretation of the Bible – a dispute that will require further exposition later in this chapter. The elements of the allegory described in the anonymous letter are William Warburton's controversial reading of the Book of Job in his *Divine Legation of Moses Demonstrated* (1737–41), the rebuttals of various scholars including Richard Grey (1744), Charles Peters (1751), and Leonard Chappelow (1752), and Warburton's robust counter-attacks in *Remarks on Several Occasional Reflections* (1744) and later editions of the *Divine Legation*. However, what remains of this first attempt towards *Tristram Shandy*, now known as the 'Rabelaisian Fragment', shows little trace of the allegory on Job.[6] Its key elements are a proposal, uttered in a chapter room at York, by a character called Longinus Rabelaicus, for a textbook on the writing of sermons; and a noisy, and inventively obscene, narrative of the efforts of a character called Homenas, in the next room, to plagiarise a sermon on his own account.

Laurence Sterne was born two generations later than Jonathan Swift. There are many distinctions to be drawn between the young Irish clergyman dividing his time between his church offices in Dublin and Kilroot and Sir William Temple's residence at Moor Park, and aiming at a bishopric, and the sentimental and already middle-aged parson riding the dirty lanes of remote North Yorkshire, and hoping for belated literary renown. Yet there are already similarities of method and attitude between the early works of Swift and these two early and fragmentary works of Sterne. The clothes allegory of *A Political Romance*, for instance, that 'History of a good warm watch-coat', is in some respects similar to, and may well be borrowed from, Swift's *Tale of a Tub*, where a father (who stands for God) bequeaths each of his three sons a coat (which stands for the Christian religion). Indeed, in his letter printed at the end of *A Political Romance*, Sterne forbids his bookseller (that is, publisher) to 'add or diminish one Comma or Tittle, in or to my *Romance*' (PR 50), words that echo the father's warning to his sons in Swift's *Tale* 'not to add to, or diminish from their Coats'.[7] Both authors are indebted to the extravagance, the invention, and the indecency of Rabelais. In a letter to an unnamed recipient, in the summer of 1759, Sterne writes, with a not wholly ingenuous regard to the modesty of both his language and his career aspirations, that 'I deny I have gone as farr as Swift—He keeps a due distance from Rabelais—& I keep a due distance from him' (*Letters* 76). In the 'Rabelaisian Fragment' there are many echoes, however, of Rabelais's characteristic bawdry, and resonances too of the cheerfully obscene suggestions scattered throughout Swift's *Tale* and *Discourse Concerning the Mechanical*

Operation of the Spirit. In his first draft of the 'Fragment', for instance, Sterne had made Homenas steal his sermon from the prolific sermonist Dr John Rogers, so that the act of plagiarism has him (with a play on a slang term later favoured by James Boswell) 'Rogering it as hard as He could drive'. The doubleness is reinforced by the bawdy, and blasphemous, exclamation to Rogers that follows: '*Dearly Beloved Roger, the Scripture moveth thee & me in sundry Places*' (RF 1089, 1090).

But there are deeper and more consequential resemblances of method and thought between Sterne and his predecessor. Swift was fascinated by the fragmentary, and the borrowed or stolen fragment in particular was both a frequent form and a frequent target of his wit. The Hack persona who authors Swift's *Tale* is a great snapper-up of unconsidered trifles, a cabbager of other men's scraps. He boasts of having made for himself a 'laborious Collection of Seven Hundred Thirty Eight *Flowers*, and *shining Hints* of the best *Modern* Authors, digested with great Reading, into my Book of *Common-places*' (*Tale* 209; cf. 148); from that imaginary commonplace book, with its extracts from Homer and Lucretius, Burton and Bacon, Horace and Herodotus, Dryden and Ned Ward, fairy tales and romances, church histories and joke books, chapbooks and fables, Tom Brown and Sir Thomas Browne, the Hack constructs his great work, sometimes acknowledging and often hiding his sources. In Swift's *Battel of the Books*, first published with the *Tale* in 1704, the army of the Modern books all too often fights with weapons stolen from wherever they can be found; the great critic Bentley, for instance, is accused of wearing critical armour – his *Dissertation upon the Epistles of Phalaris*[8] – 'patch'd up of a thousand incoherent Pieces' (*Tale* 250).

For Swift the professional churchman, however, borrowing or plagiarism, turning others' leaves rather than working from one's own knowledge and thinking, was both ineffectual and reprehensible. In a key statement, in his *Letter to a Young Gentleman, Lately Entered into Holy Orders* (1720), he warns specifically against faggoting sermons out of the brushwood sources that were helpfully raked together in commonplace books:

> Commonplace-books … have been long in use by industrious young Divines …
> they generally are Extracts of Theological and Moral Sentences, drawn from
> Ecclesiastical and other Authors, reduced under proper Heads; usually begun,
> and perhaps, finished, while the Collectors were young in the Church, as being
> intended for Materials, or Nurseries to stock future Sermons … I could wish that
> men of tolerable Intellectuals would rather trust their own natural Reason,
> improved by a general Conversation with Books, to enlarge on Points which
> they are supposed already to understand … Whoever only reads, in order to
> transcribe wise and shining Remarks … will be … misled out of the regular Way

of Thinking, in order to introduce those Materials which he has been at the Pains to gather: And the Product of all this, will be found a manifest incoherent Piece of Patchwork.[9]

Homenas, the young clergyman of Sterne's 'Rabelaisian Fragment', is similarly a borrower from published divines; not, however, of scattered citations, but wholesale. At the centre of Sterne's 'Fragment' is a dramatic act of plagiarism. Homenas, obliged soon to preach a sermon on a subject of which he knows nothing, resorts to stealing ('nimming') a volume of the writings of an eminent turn-of-the-century divine, Dr Samuel Clarke:

> HOMENAS who had to preach next Sunday ... —knowing Nothing at all of the Matter—was all this while at it as hard as He could drive ... finding Himself unable to get either forwards or backwards—with any Grace——d—n it," says He ... "Why, may not a Man lawfully call in for Help, in this, as well as any other human Emergency?" So without any more Argumentation, except starting up and nimming down from the Top Shelf but one, the second Volume of Clark tho' without any felonious Intention in so doing, He had begun to clapp me in ... Five whole Pages, nine round Paragraphs, and a Dozen and a half of good Thoughts all of a Row ... (*RF* 1089)

Though the writer absolves him of 'felonious Intention', Homenas knows there will be consequences if he is taken in the fact: 'Now—quoth *Homenas* to Himself, "Tho' I hold all this to be fair and square Yet, if I am found out, there will be the Deuce & all to pay.—"' Punishment for his act of literal and literary aspiration is physical and immediate: '*Homenas was got upon Dr. Clark's back, Sir*—— ... *He has broke his Neck, and fractured his Skull and beshit himself into the Bargain, by a fall from the Pulpit two Stories high*' (1089). His clerical audience at once sees through Homenas's passing off Clarke's words and wit as his own, to the permanent damage of his reputation:

> Alass poor *Homenas*!— ... *Homenas* will never preach more while Breath's in his Body!——No, Faith. I shall never again, be able to tickle it off as I have done ... — *Pray*, Mr. Such a one, *Who held forth last Sunday*? Doctor CLARK, *I trow*, says one. *Pray what Doctor* CLARK, quoth a second? *Why*, HOMENAS's *Doctor* CLARK, quoth a third. *O Rare* HOMENAS! cries a fourth ... 'twil be all over with me before G-d,— (1089–90)

Even while they abjure such wholesale plagiarism, however, both Swift and Sterne make teasing detailed resort, as a conscious and essential part of their ironic method, to overt allusion, covert allusion, and occasional local verbal theft. Both make claims to originality, in words that simultaneously invalidate their claims. In the 'Apology' that prefaces the fifth edition (1710) of *A Tale of a Tub*, a work densely fraught with the spoils of raids upon others' compositions, Swift insists that 'through the whole Book he has not borrowed one single Hint from any Writer in the World' (*Tale* 13). He would reassert his independence and originality in his *Verses on the Death of Dr. Swift* – in lines that were themselves adapted from John Denham's *On Mr. Abraham Cowley*: 'To steal a hint was never known, | But what he writ, was all his own.'[10] Only the informed reader could at once recognise the quotation and appreciate the joke.

Sterne too was an inveterate user of other men's words, and in composing his own sermons he borrowed from many Restoration and early eighteenth-century divines, including both John Rogers and Samuel Clarke, the sources of Homenas's plunderings in different versions of the 'Fragment'.[11] Like Swift, he delighted to play allusive games with his knowing or unknowing readers. The name 'Homenas' is that of the Bishop of Papimany in the fourth book of *Gargantua and Pantagruel*, and indeed the whole 'Fragment' is recognisably loaded with the language of the standard seventeenth-century translation of Rabelais by Sir Thomas Urquhart and Peter Motteux (1653–94).[12] If Sterne went on to lament the recycling of knowledge in *Tristram Shandy*, it would be in words borrowed, without explicit acknowledgement, from Robert Burton's *Anatomy of Melancholy* (1621–51): 'Shall we for ever make new books, as apothecaries make new mixtures, by pouring only out of one vessel into another?'[13] Just as Swift's contemporaries argued that the wit of the author of the *Tale* is 'not his own in many Places' (*Tale* 13), so Sterne would later in the century be identified as a borrower, and then accused as a plagiarist, by John Ferriar.[14] Neither charge sticks. 'Nimming' Homenas 'clapps' in whole pages and round paragraphs; in Swift and Sterne, borrowings are ironically transformed. Whereas Homenas fears above all things to be 'found out' in his fraud, for Swift and Sterne, quotation, echo and allusion are not acts of deceit, but creative (and often subversive) instruments of communication with, and interrogation of, their readers.

It is an irony of literary history that both Sterne and Swift have latterly, and sometimes incautiously, come to be called 'novelists'. Neither man was in fact much inclined to take stories seriously. The *Tale of a Tub*, Swift's earliest major publication, begins (after we've already negotiated about a third of it) with a fairy tale – 'Once upon a Time, there was a Man who had Three Sons' – and degenerates within a page into a romance – 'they travelled thro' several Countries, encountred a reasonable Quantity of Gyants, and slew certain Dragons' (*Tale* 73–4). Sterne's Tristram accuses his readers, already corrupted by the narrative linearities of romantic or novelistic fictions, of 'a vicious taste…of reading straight forwards, more in quest of the adventures, than of the deep erudition and knowledge which a book of this cast, if read over as it should be, would infallibly impart with them' (*TS* 1.20.65). Swift had been at least equally explicit, and a good deal less courteous, on the subject of the concupiscent reader, discovering in human nature 'several *Handles*', of which '*Curiosity* is one, and of all others, affords the firmest Grasp: *Curiosity*, that Spur in the side, that Bridle in the Mouth, that Ring in the Nose, of a lazy, an impatient, and a grunting Reader' (*Tale* 203).

Both Swift and Sterne take ample and several revenges upon such equine, bovine, and porcine readers. They offer us, in the apposite words of Randle Cotgrave's *Dictionarie of the French and English Tongues* (1611), '*Contes de la Cicogne*: Idle histories; vaine relations; tales of a tub, or, of a rosted horse'. (These last two phrases of Cotgrave's definition take in both Swift's allegory of the early Church and Sterne's 'Rabelaisian Fragment': 'I'll be shot quoth *Epistemon* if all this Story of thine of a roasted Horse is simply no more than S——SAUSAGES?, quoth *Panurge*' (*RF* 1088).) Instead of comedies or trage-dies, ending with marriages or deaths, they give us digressions, shaggy-dog stories, lost and unfinished tales. Swift's digressions are everywhere emulated in *Tristram Shandy*, and rather openly so in *A Political Romance*: 'This *Reading-Desk*, as you will observe, was but an Episode wove into the main Story by the Bye;—for the main Affair was the *Battle of the Breeches* and *Great Watch-Coat*' (*PR* 26-7). The title at least – and something of the mode – of *A Discourse upon the Mechanical Operation of the Spirit...A Fragment*, presented by Swift as a recovered letter, is echoed in 'A Fragment in the Manner of Rabelais', presented by Sterne as a found manuscript. It is picked up during the course of *A Sentimental Journey* in a further Shandean *objet trouvé*, another 'Fragment', of a narrative written 'in a Gothic letter', in 'the old French of Rabelais's time', on a sheet of waste paper used by La Fleur to carry Yorick a 'little print of butter' (*SJ/BJ* 134). This pathetic story is lost when La Fleur uses it to wrap a bouquet upon the boulevards of Paris (140), an abruption not wholly unlike the ending of Swift's fragmentary dissertation on religious dissent, *The Mechanical Operation of the Spirit*, which ceases in mid-argument on the grounds that 'the Post is just going' (*Tale* 289).

If they queried the predictabilities and completions of story, Swift and Sterne were yet more suspicious of the totalisations and regularities of imposed rules, institutes, universal systems, cyclopaedias and enchiridions. The bull's eye of Swift's satire is the systematising of knowledge, mathema-tical, musical, physico-logical, physico-theological, physico-mechanical. The Hack who writes the *Tale of a Tub* provides many universal prescriptions, and promises more in his list of 'Treatises wrote by the same Author', a list that includes, significantly, 'A Critical Essay upon the Art of *Canting*, Philosophically, Physically, and Musically considered' (*Tale* 2). If that promise were not already fulfilled in Swift's fragment on *The Mechanical*

Operation of the Spirit, it becomes so in Sterne's 'Rabelaisian Fragment', where Longinus Rabelaicus's 'thorough-stitch'd System of the KERUKOPÆDIA' sets forth 'all that is needful to be known ... of the Art of making all kinds of your theological, hebdomadical, rostrummical, humdrummical what d'ye call-ems'. 'What d'ye call ems', of course, are sermons, which Sterne's Triboulet says he would not wish to hear 'chanted', nor his Gymnast wish to hear 'canted'. Longinus Rabelaicus is himself implicated in the satire of system makers, in his wish that 'all the scatter'd Rules of the KERUKOPÆDIA, could be but once carefully collected into one Code, as thick as *Panurge*'s Head, and the Whole *cleanly* digested—(Shite! says *Panurge* ...) and bound up ... by way of a regular Institute, and then put into the Hands of every Licenced Preacher in great Britain & Ireland' (*RF* 1088–9).

Above all, Swift and Sterne are suspicious of systems of interpretation, and especially of systems of allegorical and typological reading. Swift associates such systems repeatedly with the methods of Grubstreet writers, and with historical wrestings of the meaning of Holy Writ. 'The *Grubæan* Sages', we are told, 'have always chosen to convey their Precepts and their Arts, shut up within the Vehicles of Types and Fables'. The main narrative of Swift's Hack is the allegory of the three brothers, Peter, Martin, and Jack, who represent the three various and warring elements of the Christian church. The Hack's allegory of stage-itinerant, pulpit and scaffold 'contains a great Mystery, being a Type, a Sign, an Emblem, a Shadow, a Symbol, bearing Analogy to the spacious Commonwealth of Writers, and to those Methods by which they must exalt themselves to a certain Eminency above the inferiour World' (*Tale*, 66, 61). Peter (that is, the Roman church) makes the Bible mean what he wishes, by insisting, for instance, that the expression 'Silver Fringe' must be 'understood in a *Mythological*, and *Allegorical* sense'. The adventures of Jack (that is, the dissenters), the Hack is convinced, 'will furnish Plenty of noble Matter for such, whose converting Imaginations dispose them to reduce all Things into *Types*; who can make *Shadows*, no thanks to the Sun; and then mold them into Substances, no thanks to Philosophy; whose peculiar Talent lies in fixing Tropes and Allegories to the *Letter*, and refining what is Literal into Figure and Mystery'.

The *Tale* offers itself as a text for just such converting interpretation. The Hack invites each of the princes of Christendom to take 'seven of the *deepest Scholars* in his Dominions and shut them up close for *seven* Years in *seven* Chambers, with a Command to write *seven* ample Commentaries on this comprehensive Discourse' (*Tale* 88, 189–90, 185). And, indeed, the allegories of the *Tale of a Tub* at once provoked, perhaps beyond Swift's wishes, explanatory *scholia*. William Wotton, one of Swift's principal victims, replied in his detailed *Observations upon the Tale of a Tub* (1705), which would be hijacked by Swift himself into the parodic footnotes of the fifth edition of the *Tale*. The publisher Edmund Curll took the opportunity to turn a not very honest penny in his *Complete Key to the Tale of a Tub* (1710), for which Jonathan Swift's own cousin, Thomas Swift, apparently contributed (without Jonathan's knowledge or approval) a set of broadly uninformative notes.

Inheriting the profound and general Anglican mistrust of allegorising and multiple reading, Sterne had, as already noted above, a more recent and particular provocation in William Warburton's elaborate reading of the Book of Job, in an Appendix published in the second volume (1741) of *The Divine Legation of Moses Demonstrated*.[15] Warburton argued that the foundation of the Jewish state under Moses depended not on a promise of future rewards and punishments, but on a private promise from God to Moses of an extraordinary or 'equal' providence, by which present rewards and punishments were directly related to obedience to the law. The Book of Job posed the particular problem that the notion of equal providence is both identified and questioned; notably, in Job's own words: 'Wherefore do the wicked live, become old, yea, are mighty in power?' (Job 21:7). Warburton therefore was obliged to read Job not as historical truth, but as allegory, and in doing so he (predictably) gave rise to a controversy with more orthodox Anglican divines, which lasted for more than twenty years. Representatively, John Tillard objected that he was 'not capable of conceiving any thing in Religion, but what is easy, plain, and natural, and can never believe that God would puzzle his Creatures with intricate Questions and abstruse Difficulties, made ten times more so by Mr. W's Explication'. On the contrary, he insisted,

> *First*, that there can be no Prophecy, double Sense, Allegory, *&c.* but what must be understood to be so by the Person, who speaks and delivers them, or by the Persons to whom they are spoke and deliver'd, as soon as, or before any particular Application is made of them, otherwise Enthusiasts and designing Persons may make any thing a Prophecy, or any Expression to have a double Sense, *&c. Secondly*, All Prophecies, figurative Expressions, *&c.* can have besides a literal Meaning, but one figurative or secondary Sense, and when that is determin'd, or once applied, it may occasion infinite Confusion to allow it to extend farther.[16]

Tillard's suspicions of proliferating figurative and allegorical interpretations, and his insistence on plain authorial intentions, specifically answer the strategies of Warburton's *Divine Legation*. They are also recognisably related to Swift's mainstream Anglican rejection of 'Tropes and Allegories' and his insistence on Scripture's 'plain, easy Directions' (*Tale* 190). Similarly, Sterne's *A Political Romance*, though it addresses and participates in the particular Warburtonian theological controversy, belongs to a longstanding discourse of Anglican insistence on direct and rational interpretation of the comprehensible scriptural text, and is a general parody of allegorising interpretative methods.

That parody is spelt out and developed at deliberate length in *A Political Romance*'s own incorporated 'Key', in ways that herald Sterne's play with interpretation and meaning in *Tristram Shandy*. The 'Key' is printed, not at the foot of each page, where in the fifth edition of Swift's *Tale* the unfortunate Wotton had found himself scattered, but in seventeen pages of commentary by Sterne, subjoined and published with the *Romance* itself. Sterne would later in the same year consider that *Tristram Shandy* itself offered 'great Room' for commentary, and in a letter to his publisher Robert Dodsley, he contemplates sending it 'into the World—cum Notis Variorum', as though emulating the distinctive mock apparatus of a Scriblerian text (*Letters* 75).

The *Romance* is made the subject of analysis in the 'Key', not by the seventy-two scholars of the Septuagint, or Swift's 'seven ... *deepest Scholars*' (*Tale* 185), but by 'a small Political Club' in the city of York, whose members produce a variety of readings of the *Romance*, all allegorical in one way or another. The President begins by 'discover[ing] plainly, That the Disturbances therein set forth, related to those on the *Continent*', the character Trim being the King of France, Trim's wife the Empress, and so on (*PR* 31). Though it seems that 'This Hypothesis of the President's explain'd every Thing in the *Romance* extreamly well', a 'Gentleman' insists 'That Mr. President was altogether wrong in every Supposition he had made' (34–5), much as Swift, in his 1710 'Apology', had insisted that Wotton 'is entirely mistaken, and forces Interpretations which never once entered into the Writer's Head' (*Tale* 12). This gentleman then offers an alternative reading, which is equally political, and equally allegorical, and 'had too much Ingenuity in it to be altogether slighted' (*PR* 36), only himself to be answered by the interpretation offered by a tailor, who recognises in the '*Pair of Breeches*' a figuration of the island of Sicily, and 'an honest Shoe-maker', who finds the kingdom of Italy shadowed by the '*Jack-Boot*' of the *Romance* (38).

The interpretations offered so far are not only multiple and contradictory, but also 'clear and decisive' (*PR* 39), much like the readings of the seven scholarly commentators envisaged by Swift's Hack; but there are yet more to follow. A lawyer, evidently influenced by Swift's Hack's obsession with 'the profound Number THREE' (*Tale* 57), determines that the *Romance* is 'incontestably ... *Tripartite*', and expounds it as a (mock) 'Panegyrick upon the *Humility* of *Church-Men*'; to which a parson, equally wishing to claim the satire for his own party, responds by calling it a 'Panegyrick upon the *Honesty* of *Attornies*'; and when an apothecary laughs with the parson's rejoinder, the lawyer finds that, after all, the '*Cob-web*' that, in the *Romance*, is used to staunch the Parson's cut finger, 'is a fine-spun Satyre, upon the flimsy Nature of one Half of the Shop-Medicines, with which you make a Property of the Sick' (*PR* 40–3). So Sterne's 'Key' turns the *Romance* at last into a playful allegory of subjective and self-interested misinterpretation, using words that clearly look forward to *Tristram Shandy*, with its hobby-horsical readers, its opinions and transactions, and the 'dark veil' of the black page (*TS* 3.36.268), beneath which meanings lie shrouded:

> —Thus every Man turn'd the Story to what was swimming uppermost in his own Brain;—so that, before all was over, there were full as many Satyres spun out of it,—and as great a Variety of Personages, Opinions, Transactions, and Truths, found to lay hid under the dark Veil of its Allegory, as ever were discovered in the thrice-renowned History of the Acts of *Gargantua* and *Pantagruel*.
>
> (*PR* 45)

Not one key, in fact, but many keys: *quot homines, tot sententiae*; so many men, so many minds. The proliferation of meanings that emerge in York's Political Club is just the outcome that Rome had predicted when the Bible was exposed to common readers; just the threat that Protestants had found in Roman misapplications (like Swift's Peter's) of Church tradition to the interpretation of Scripture; just the risk that Anglican theorists had warned against when dissenters made personal property of the Bible, and (like Swift's Jack) found 'a Way of working it into any Shape he pleased'. For Swift, the Testament, the Father's Will, is no subject for allegorising or typological misprision, but consists of 'certain plain, easy Directions', readily found by readers who 'have … Candor to suppose good Meanings, [or] Palate to distinguish true Ones' (*Tale* 190, 4–5). For Sterne, too, Warburtonian allegorising, or any such scholastic solipsism, is a dangerous business. Meanings are to be valued by truth, not number. The last word of the discussion at the hermeneutic Political Club is given to 'a Whitesmith' – a metalworker; a worker or finisher in tin or steel – 'who was the only Member in the Club who had not said something in the Debate'. His closing declaration asserts the value of true interpretation while leaving it still beyond reach: 'But let me tell you, Mr. President, says he, That the *Right Key*, if it could but be found, would be worth the whole Bunch put together' (*PR* 47).

NOTES

1. *The Memoirs of the Extraordinary Life, Works, and Discoveries of Martinus Scriblerus* was written chiefly by John Arbuthnot, with other members of the Scriblerus club (Alexander Pope, John Gay, Jonathan Swift, Thomas Parnell, and Robert Harley, Earl of Oxford), between 1714 and 1727, and first published in the second volume of *The Works of Mr. Alexander Pope, in Prose* (1741).

2. For more detailed discussions of the quarrels, see Arthur H. Cash, *Laurence Sterne: The Early and Middle Years* (London: Methuen, 1975), 242–77, and Kenneth Monkman's introduction to *A Political Romance* (Menston: Scolar Press, 1971).

3. Of the six original copies of *A Political Romance* now known to survive, one contains a unique cancellandum (a page reprinted and replaced in other copies) identifying the location as 'Cocksbull near Canterbury' (Edward Simmen, 'Sterne's *A Political Romance*: New Light from a Printer's Copy', *Papers of the Bibliographical Society of America* 64 (1970), 419–29). The original title was reported ten years later by an author who claimed to be Sterne's close friend (but was not, as is sometimes assumed, John Hall-Stevenson): see the preface to *Yorick's Sentimental Journey, Continued*, 2 vols. numbered III–IV (1769), III, viii.

4. *PR* 23. A coney is a rabbit, but also a woman; for the bawdy implication, see *OED2*, s.v. Coney, sense 5a and, especially, 5b.

5. Cash, *Laurence Sterne: The Early and Middle Years*, 279–80, quoting a document first published in the *St James Chronicle* for April 1788.

6. The manuscript, now in the Pierpont Morgan Library, New York (M.A. 1011), has been edited by Melvyn New, with introduction, textual apparatus and notes, as 'Sterne's Rabelaisian Fragment: A Text from the Holograph Manuscript', *PMLA* 87 (1972), 1083–92.

7. *A Tale of a Tub*, eds. A. C. Guthkelch and D. Nichol Smith, 2nd edn (Oxford: Oxford University Press, 1958), 81 (hereafter cited as *Tale*). The scriptural original, for both Swift and Sterne, is Revelation 22:18–19: 'If any man shall add unto these things, God shall add unto him the plagues that are written in this book: | And if any man shall take away the words of the book of this prophecy, God shall take away his part out of the book of life.'

8. First published as an appendix in William Wotton, *Reflections upon Ancient and Modern Learning*, 2nd edn (1697), and separately published in a much expanded form in 1699.

9. *The Prose Works of Jonathan Swift*, eds. Herbert Davis *et al.*, 14 vols. (Oxford: Blackwell, 1939–68), IX, 75–6.

10. *Complete Poems of Jonathan Swift*, ed. Pat Rogers (Harmondsworth: Penguin, 1983), 854 (*Verses on the Death of Dr. Swift*, lines 317–18). Denham's lines read: 'To him no Author was unknown, | Yet what he wrote was all his own' (*On Mr. Abraham Cowley His Death, and Burial amongst the Ancient Poets* (1667), 2 (lines 29–30)).

11. See below, ch. 5; also Lansing Van der Heyden Hammond, *Laurence Sterne's Sermons of Mr. Yorick* (New Haven, CT: Yale University Press, 1948).

12. As Melvyn New points out: see *RF* 1085; also 1092 (nn. 15, 20, 21, 23).

13. *TS* 5.1.408; see *TS Notes* 338–9.

14. In 'Comments on Sterne', in *Memoirs of the Literary and Philosophical Society of Manchester* (Warrington, 1793), IV, 45–86, and Ferriar's later *Illustrations of Sterne* (1798), 56–92, 98–9. See H. J. Jackson, 'Sterne, Burton, and Ferriar: Allusions to the *Anatomy of Melancholy* in Volumes V to IX of *Tristram Shandy*', *Philological Quarterly* 54 (1975), 457–70, and Jonathan Lamb, 'Sterne's System of Imitation', *Modern Language Review* 76 (1981), 794–810, both reprinted in *Laurence Sterne*, Longman Critical Readers, ed. Marcus Walsh (London: Longman, 2002), 123–37, 138–60.

15. For more extended discussion, see Martin C. Battestin, *The Providence of Wit* (Oxford: Clarendon Press, 1974), 197–200; Melvyn New, 'Sterne, Warburton, and the Burden of Exuberant Wit', *Eighteenth-Century Studies* 15 (1982), 245–74; Jonathan Lamb, 'The Job Controversy, Sterne, and the Question of Allegory', *Eighteenth-Century Studies* 24 (1990), 1–19.
16. John Tillard, *A Reply to Mr. Warburton's Appendix, in his Second Volume of the Divine Legation of Moses* (1742), 167.

3

JUDITH HAWLEY

Tristram Shandy, learned wit, and Enlightenment knowledge

> Thus,---thus my fellow labourers and associates in this great harvest of our learning, now ripening before our eyes; thus it is, by slow steps of casual increase, that our knowledge physical, metaphysical, physiological, polemical, nautical, mathematical, ænigmatical, technical, biographical, romantical, chemical, and obstetrical, with fifty other branches of it, (most of 'em ending, as these do, in *ical*) have, for these two last centuries and more, gradually been creeping upwards towards that Ακμὴ of their perfections, from which, if we may form a conjecture from the advances of these last seven years, we cannot possibly be far off.
>
> (*TS* 1.21.71–2)

Tristram Shandy writes with a keen sense of his particular moment in intellectual history: the arts and sciences, he proclaims, are about to reach their acme or peak. While he luxuriates in the belief that labourers in the field of knowledge will soon reap a bumper harvest, compilers of encyclopaedias found the speed of advancement in the arts and sciences a source of anxiety, as well as a cause for celebration. Thus Ephraim Chambers in the first edition of his *Cyclopaedia* (1728) alludes to the 'Multitude of Improvements in the several Parts, especially of Natural Knowledge, made in these last Years', but adds a caveat.[1] Paradoxically, because knowledge is advancing too fast, there is now too much material to learn; progress will grind to a halt unless compilers such as himself reduce it to manageable proportions. Similarly, and more nonsensically, Tristram deduces that when knowledge peaks, people will stop writing; 'the want of all kind of writing will put an end to all kind of reading', and knowledge will go into decline again, creating opportunities for writers once more (*TS* 1.21.72). This kind of muddle reveals Sterne smiling at his narrator, disavowing his pretensions.

Pompously declaring that he writes 'as a man of erudition ... even my similes, my allusions, my illustrations, my metaphors, are erudite' (*TS* 2.2.98), Tristram refers in the course of his work to the seven liberal arts that formed the backbone of European education for hundreds of years (grammar, logic, rhetoric, arithmetic, geometry, music, and astronomy), frequently revealing his ignorance as he does so.[2] Although Tristram's confidence in the ripeness of learning is clearly misplaced, and his classification of knowledge is at best eccentric, *Tristram Shandy* does incorporate a parodic survey of the branches of knowledge. In its whimsical and haphazard way, Sterne's fiction covers the field from ancient to modern, Renaissance to Enlightenment. Each of Tristram's 'icals' is represented in a work he calls, albeit perversely, his 'cyclopaedia of arts and sciences' (2.17.141). To begin at the end of his catalogue of learning, knowledge 'obstetrical' is obviously at the heart of the book. But lesser branches are not neglected. For example, allusions to Stevinus's sailing chariot and the competition to devise a mechanism for measuring longitude at sea might qualify as knowledge 'nautical' (2.14.134–6, 3.29.255, 8.33.721). Knowledge 'biographical' and 'romantical' are represented by scattered references to popular works such as *Don Belianis of Greece* (2.19.180), *Guy, Earl of Warwick* (6.32.555), or *Valentin and Orson* (6.32.555), to say nothing of allusions to canonical literature from Homer to Shakespeare. As far as polemical knowledge goes, we might invoke the 'Memoire presenté a Messieurs les Docteurs de Sorbonne' (1.20.67–9) or Ernulphus's 'Curse' (3.10.200–3.11.211), or several slighting references to the polemical divinity of Bishop Warburton and others (1.19.57, 3.31.257, 5.28.462–3), as well as the countless combative debates, both real and fictional, that jangle throughout the text. For metaphysical knowledge, we need look no further than the investigation into the seat of the soul (2.19.169–81), or Tristram's explorations of the problems inherent in Locke's theories of association and language.[3] As for 'aenigmatical' knowledge, that lies hidden under the marbled page (3.36.269–70) – if not, Sterne implies, on every page.

It is the physical, physiological, mathematical and technical branches of knowledge that grow most vigorously under Tristram's hands. Knowledge 'physical' might mean either medicine (physic) or physics (natural philosophy). Given that the damaged body bulks so large in *Tristram Shandy*, and that, in Walter's opinion, love is a disease, medicine is a vital concern in the Shandy household. Generation and foetal development, anatomy and surgery, and practical medicine in the form of diet, regimen, and the rival merits of hot spirits and cold bathing, all find their place here. Sterne was familiar with contemporary arguments that man was a form of machine. In the late seventeenth and early eighteenth centuries, iatromechanical philosophers applied mathematics and mechanics to the theory of medicine. Doctors such as Archibald Pitcairne (1652–1713), Richard Mead (1673–1754, the butt of one of Sterne's bawdy jokes (*TS* 1.7.12)), and Herman Boerhaave (1668–1738) proposed that the body was little more than a machine composed of tubes, pumps and levers operated by hydraulics. Later in the century, physicians and physiologists elaborated the idea, and argued that more subtle – but still mechanical – networks of nerves and fibres conveyed sympathetic vibrations between the mind and the body.[4]

Mechanical philosophy sometimes seems to govern the Shandy household. The bedtime rituals of Walter and Elizabeth, and of the Widow Wadman, are regular as clockwork. Tristram's family (*TS* 5.6.427), his book (1.22.80–1, 7.1.575), humanity in general (4.8.333), and nature herself (6.17.525) are described as machines that need oiling and constant management for their delicate mechanisms to work smoothly and productively.[5] Although he is not named in *Tristram Shandy*, Isaac Newton is the natural philosopher or scientist associated most closely with the mechanical view of the universe. In his ground-breaking *Principia* (1687), Newton proposed that one force – the force of gravity – governed motion on earth and in the heavens.[6] To many, including orthodox thinkers in the Church of England, his theories were a source of optimism because they explained the universe as a well-regulated machine, operating according to rational laws rather than being governed by a chaotic and unpredictable Nature. While Newton did not remove God from the machine (his universe requires the constant presence of the deity to keep it running), his work also provided fuel for philosophers, such as La Mettrie, who wished to argue that both the macro- and the microcosm were merely material and mechanical.

The mechanical seems at odds with the organic, and we might expect Tristram – apparently a free spirit – to be hostile to this Newtonian view of universal order. Certainly, he claims to understand almost nothing of mechanisms (*TS* 7.30.626) and, like Yorick, expresses an invincible dislike of, and opposition to, gravity (1.11.28). Yet there is no getting away from the tendency of all things in his narrative to fall, whether Trim's hat, unweighted sash windows, or military projectiles. Indeed, Tristram seems to hold that the operations of mind and body are largely mechanical. His father and uncle behave like a pair of clockwork toys, responding in programmed ways in conversation with each other. Whenever anyone uses the words 'curtain' or 'siege' in whatever context, it is as if a switch is thrown in Toby's mind, transporting him back to the battlegrounds of King William's wars. In response, Walter fumes, rages, storms and exerts 'mechanical functions' (3.41.283) as if he were an automaton.

At the very start of his *Life and Opinions*, when describing how his mother connects Walter's performance of his two monthly duties (copulation and clock-winding), Tristram explains how the mind associates apparently disparate ideas: 'which strange combination of ideas, the sagacious Locke… affirms to have produced more wry actions than all other sources of prejudice whatsoever' (*TS* 1.4.7). He alludes here to the empirical philosopher John Locke, author of *An Essay Concerning Human Understanding*, first published in 1690 but as influential throughout the eighteenth century as Freud was in the twentieth. Roughly speaking, Locke argued that all ideas are originally derived from physical sensations; the mind reflects on particular sensations and produces ideas; ideas become associated in the mind through chance or custom, as well as rational connection. When one idea comes to mind, associated ideas, or even a train of ideas, will follow:

> This strong Combination of *Ideas*, not ally'd by Nature, the Mind makes in it self either voluntarily, or by chance, and hence it comes in different Men to be very different, according to their different Inclinations, Educations, Interests, *etc*. Custom settles habits of Thinking in the Understanding, as well as of Determining in the Will, and of Motions in the Body; all which seems to be but Trains of Motion in the Animal Spirits, which once set a going continue in the same steps they have been used to, which by often treading are worn into a smooth path, and the Motion in it becomes easy and as it were Natural.[7]

If this passage seems familiar to readers of *Tristram Shandy*, that is because Sterne reworks it, with comic exaggeration, in his opening chapter (*TS* 1.1.1–2). Locke simply sets his animal spirits 'a going'; more jovially, Tristram finds, on setting them 'a-going', that 'away they go cluttering like hey-go-mad'. Sterne's relationship to Locke is often thought to be that of a parodist more than a disciple, and *Tristram Shandy* contains many hints that he thought Locke's theories questionable or even insane. Yet the link between association and madness is inherent in Locke already. Because it brings ideas together by chance rather than logical connection, association is a departure from reason, Locke argues, and thus a form of madness. Moreover, it is not a means of discovery but a source of confusion, and is thus comparable to the mental obscurity caused by the instability or ambiguity of language. Sterne, whose humour depends so much on wordplay and witty conjunctions, never endorses the hard-line rationalism of Locke, but revels in its comic potential.

In cases such as these, key Enlightenment ideas are incorporated in complex ways, and to complex ends, in *Tristram Shandy*. Nor can this brief survey take in all of Sterne's allusions to Enlightenment knowledge, including geography and travel writing (*TS* 5.2.415–17, 7.9.588, 5.28.461, 7.4.580, 7.18.601–2), natural history (5.34.472–5.35.475), and the fine arts (2.9.121, 3.5.192). Moreover, *Tristram Shandy* makes links between different branches of knowledge that are more than mere eccentric associations. Sterne's satire on Toby's hobby-horse, the science of fortifications, is at once a spoof of technical jargon and a sensitive study of the psychological defence mechanisms of this paradoxically gentle old warrior. Indeed, fortification is a sub-branch of natural philosophy. It combines mechanical, mathematical and technical knowledge (parabolas, hyperbolas, cycloids, conic sections, salient angles) and the vulnerably human (groins, knees, and other delicate body parts). It also depends in some respects on Newtonian mechanics, for it was

Newton who codified and elaborated the analysis of moving bodies, and gave mathematical demonstrations of the parabolic lines traced by projectiles in their journey from gun to target.

Yet Sterne's cornucopian, heteroclite text is also cluttered with intellectual materials that are markedly less new. At the end of the eighteenth century, John Ferriar complained that Walter Shandy had 'all the stains and mouldiness of the last century about him'.[8] And not just the seventeenth century, for Walter's learning acquaints him with a cast of characters stretching back to the dark ages and the classical era before them. In *Tristram Shandy*, Aristotle rubs shoulders with the Bacons (Francis and Roger), with Cato and Cicero, Dioscurides, Euclid, Ficino, and many others through Spon, Xenophon, and Zoroaster. Swarms of superannuated Dutch grammarians, rhetoricians, and professors of law, both civil and ecclesiastical, shamble across the mental landscape of Shandy Hall.

What is remarkable here is both the range of knowledge invoked in *Tristram Shandy* – the vast historical sweep and the breadth of coverage of the circle of arts and sciences – and the fact that these branches of knowledge should have been grafted to a novelistic rootstock. Awareness of Sterne's interest in the emergent conventions of the novel has recently revived (see below, ch. 4), but it remains no less important to read him in company with Erasmus, Rabelais, Cervantes, and Swift, as well as with Richardson or Fielding. Variously called, with different degrees of exactitude, Menippean satire, the Anatomy, or the tradition of learned wit, the satirical genre to which *Tristram Shandy* partly belongs shows greater concern for academia than for adventure. In Sterne's hands, it places Cluverius and Didius, Burgersdicius and Kysarcius, Crakanthorp and Phutatorius alongside one another, teasing the reader to distinguish the real-life pedants (in this case the historian Cluwer, the philosopher Burgersdijk, and the theologian Crakanthorp, forgotten scholars of the early seventeenth century) from Sterne's own satirical inventions.

In his classic essay of 1951, D. W. Jefferson identified Sterne's debt to medieval scholasticism, or rather to writers who played games with this tradition. 'There is something in the scholastic approach to intellectual issues—a speculative freedom, a dialectical ingenuity—which lends itself to witty development', Jefferson argued: 'And there is something in the empiricist's approach—a puritanical restriction on speculation, a plodding regard for truth—which is alien to wit. We do not look for jokes among the serious students of Newton and Locke, but a person brought up in the old tradition of wit might well find that some of the new ideas of Newton and Locke suited his purpose.'[9] For Jefferson, Sterne thus applies the disruptive traditions of Rabelais and Renaissance satire to the new empirical philosophy of his own era. In the misplaced 'Author's Preface' of volume 3, for example, Tristram sets out to dismantle the Lockean assumption that 'your men of least wit are reported to be men of most judgement', and he does so with Rabelaisian equipment. His discussion of wit and judgement is topical, Locke's ideas still being current, but the humour is old, enlisting Rabelaisian bodily comedy to dismiss Locke's argument as so much 'farting and hickuping' (*TS* 3.20.227). To symbolise his way of writing from within the tradition of learned wit, Sterne almost literally inserts Tristram into Rabelais's text, and continues beyond it himself. He borrows a list of humble objects from Rabelais, draws attention to his borrowing by means of inverted commas, but then places a phrase of his own – 'or a cane chair' – within the quotation itself: '"for what hinderance, hurt or harm, doth the laudable desire of knowledge bring to any man, if even from a sot, a pot, a fool, a stool, a winter-mittain, a truckle for a pully, the lid of a goldsmith's crucible, an oyl bottle, an old slipper, or a cane chair"' (3.20.235).

The fact that Tristram sits in just such a chair as he writes then gives rise to his celebrated proposal 'to illustrate this affair of wit and judgment, by the two knobs on the top of the back of it'. In pursuing this line of satire, however, Tristram's misplaced preface is not so much a critique of Locke *per se* as a counter attack on critics who had accused Sterne of having too much wit and too little judgement for a clergyman, notably by publishing his sermons under the comic pseudonym of Yorick. Similarly, Sterne's repeated riffs on gravity are not a serious attempt to refute Newton, but rather an attack on heavy-handed pedantry, based on a happy coincidence of terminology; Sterne links the graveness of pedants with Newton's law of gravity to suggest that both bring things down.[10]

Sterne also reduces some of his thinkers to mere cardboard figures, in keeping with the tendency of Menippean satire, in the influential analysis of Northrop Frye, to deal less with rounded characters 'than with mental attitudes'. As Frye continues, 'Pedants, bigots, cranks, parvenus, virtuosi, enthusiasts, rapacious and incompetent professional men of all kinds, are handled in terms of their occupational approach to life as distinct from their social behaviour'.[11] Menippean satire (deriving from the writings of the cynic philosopher, Menippus, in the third century BC) is a genre of intellectual satire that, according to Eugene Kirk, is 'essentially concerned with right learning or right belief'.[12] It mocks intellectual arrogance and pretension, exposes abuses in learning, and sports with both the matter and the manner of the learned, sometimes in a spirit of satirical hostility, sometimes simply in play. Characteristic of the genre is the use of extreme distortions of argument and various kinds of low genres, mock forms, and, centrally, exuberant mixtures of low and high register.

Greatly advanced by the Greek satirist Lucian, the genre survived in the Middle Ages and flourished anew with the Renaissance rediscovery of the learning of the Ancients. The religious controversies of the seventeenth century gave the genre new energy. Because Menippean satire itself upholds no one ideological position, it could be put to the task of mocking Jesuits, Puritans, Royalists, or anyone else. Sterne's digressiveness is given particular currency by Locke's theory of associations, and is crucial to the creation of his multi-layered, multi-faceted central characters. But it is also, like his use of arcane terminology, his inclusion of heterogeneous discourses, or his caricatures of particular professional points of view, a sign of his emulation of his Menippean masters: the lectors of learned wit, from Lucian to Swift.[13]

However, Jefferson's association of Sterne's witty treatment of learning with the habits of mind and rhetorical techniques of medieval scholasticism is also somewhat misleading. It implies that eighteenth-century readers would have recognised a marked disjunction between Sterne's comic techniques and his intellectual content. Yet Sterne did not need to revert to the Middle Ages for his knowledge of sophistry and formal disputation: he was trained up in these methods as a student at Cambridge. Moreover, both the character and the contents of *Tristram Shandy* reflect Sterne's undergraduate studies, which were at once dustily scholastic and cutting edge. He attended Cambridge during a period of curricular transition in which, according to Victor Morgan, 'one can discern some relics of the medieval arts course still in its breadth, its emphasis on grammar, rhetoric and logic, with mathematics and astronomy having a crucial role – and with philosophy (in something more like the modern sense) as a higher plane in the arts course'. However, Aristotle had already disappeared from the science curriculum, to be replaced by a line of mathematicians beginning with Euclid and culminating in Newton, while 'the natural sciences provided the bone structure of "philosophy"'.[14] The new science, in effect, had been grafted on to the old. By 1750, the trivium and quadrivium had largely been replaced by a course of study dominated by mathematics and culminating in the 'Senate House Examination', but in the 1730s, when Sterne was at Cambridge, the methods of intellectual analysis, even the form in which assessment and examination took place, were essentially still the old scholastic form of logical analysis and formal Latin debate.[15]

Although Sterne studied at the comparatively backward Jesus College (also the college, at other points in the century, of the philosopher David Hartley, and of Coleridge), it is likely that he worked from *Advice to a Young Student* (1730), a study guide prepared by Daniel Waterland, tutor and later Master of the intellectually progressive Magdalene College. Waterland – to whom Yorick dismissively refers in *Tristram Shandy* (*TS* 6.11.514) – assumed that most students were intended for a career in the Church, but did not recommend that they concentrate on divinity until their fourth year of study, after they had laid down a firm foundation in philosophy and classical learning. Students, he instructed,

> must be acquainted with Mathematicks, Geography, Astronomy, Chronology, and other Parts of Physicks; besides Logick, Ethicks, and Metaphysicks; all which I comprehend under the general Name of *Philosophy* ... To *Classical* Learning, I refer the Study of Languages, and of Oratory, History, Poetry, and the like; and all these are preparatory to *Divinity*, or subservient to it.[16]

With this combination of modern natural philosophy and ancient learning as the bedrock of a Cambridge education, budding vicars evidently had to study a great many 'icals'. Many of the authors who crop up in *Tristram Shandy*, including fourteen of the eighteen genuine authors referred to in the opening volume, appear on Waterland's reading lists, and would thus have been common currency in the conversation of an educated gentleman or clergyman. The Ancients, such as Homer, Aristotle, Plato, Pliny, and Tacitus, mingle with the Moderns: Newton, Locke, Whiston, Keil, Cheyne, Rapin, Burgersdijk, Pufendorf, and Malebranche.[17]

Although Newton's natural philosophy and its theological implications were controversial in the eighteenth century, he was readily recruited to bolster the Church of England, imperilled as its adherents felt it to be by a range of heterodox opinion.[18] However theologically naïve it may seem to us now, it was widely held that Newtonian mechanics could underpin the notion of a providentially ordered universe without hazarding the concept of a supernatural divine principle. That is why Waterland and others argued that Newtonian natural philosophy and Lockean empiricism should form one of the chief props of a clergyman's education, the other being the classics for the training thereby provided in logic, rhetoric, and ethics.

When students had laid down these foundations, they were instructed to read sermons (rather than divinity *per se*) for the sake of both doctrine and style. Rhetoric and style were an important part of a student's armoury, vital to the preacher, and these too inform Sterne's learned wit. Not only his sermons but also his satires are coloured by the habits of study recommended by Waterland, who urges undergraduates to improve their rhetorical skills by keeping 'a *Quarto* Paper-Book for a Commonplace to refer any Thing curious to; any Elegancies of Speech, any uncommon Phrases, or any remarkable Sayings'.[19] It is highly likely that Sterne kept such a commonplace book, or collection of sayings, and dipped into it when he needed striking phrases. Here too he maintains a link between recent developments in education and ancient rhetorical tradition. When Waterland advises students to endeavour 'not to copy out, but to imitate and vary the most shining Thoughts, Sentences, or Figures which you meet with in your reading', he refers back to the classical teachings of Cicero and Quintilian, as elaborated by Erasmus in his *De duplici copia verborum ac rerum*.[20] According to this tradition, writing is a process of rewriting one's predecessors through invention, elaboration, variation, supplementation, embellishment, amplification, and digression.

Sterne converts *res* into *verba*, or, to put it another way, demonstrates how a knowledge of things could be converted into linguistic fertility while subjecting new scientific knowledge to old literary techniques. This copiousness is exemplified throughout *Tristram Shandy*, not least in Tristram's celebrated discussion of his work as written 'against the spleen' (*TS* 4.22.360), which juxtaposes a traditional humoral theory of the body ('the *gall* and other *bitter juices*') with a modern mechanical account of bodily processes ('the succussations of the intercostal and abdominal muscles'). At the same time, in describing 'a more frequent and a more convulsive elevation and depression of the diaphragm', Sterne's style at this point combines a representation of opposing mechanical forces with a demonstration of classical rhetorical balance.

The same combination of scientific language and Renaissance wit is at the heart of 'Shandeism', an approach to life that Tristram defines in a passage sandwiched between allusions to Rabelais and Cervantes: 'True *Shandeism* ... opens the heart and lungs, and like all those affections which partake of its nature, it forces the blood and other vital fluids of the body to run freely thro' its channels, and makes the wheel of life run long and chearfully round' (*TS* 4.32.401). The best medicine for a run-down man machine, Shandeism is implicitly related to Rabelais's Pantagruelism, the indefinable spirit that derives from his anti-hero Pantagruel.[21] The agent of joy in Rabelais is wine; in Sterne it is the laughing, free-spirited craziness implied by the name Shandy, a Yorkshire dialect word meaning crack-brained or wild. Both Sterne and Rabelais associate the health of the spirit with the state of the body. Yet Sterne's verbal source here is not Rabelais himself but a recently published medical text, James Mackenzie's *History of Health, and the Art of Preserving It* (1758). He reworks a passage in which Mackenzie discusses the effect of the passions on health in general and digestion in particular, arguing that fear, grief, envy, and hatred 'retard the circular motion of the fluids' to harmful effect: 'MODERATE joy and anger, on the other hand, *and those passions and affections of the mind which partake of their nature*, as chearfulness, contentment, hope, virtuous and mutual love, and courage in doing good, invigorate the nerves, accelerate the circulating fluids, promote perspiration, and assist digestion.'[22]

Other borrowings from Mackenzie are lightly peppered throughout *Tristram Shandy*; they are of interest not only because they give us an image of the valetudinarian Sterne consulting a recent medical handbook, but also, more significantly, because Mackenzie attempts to reconcile the prescriptions of the ancients with the mechanical anatomy of the moderns. As he writes at one point, 'here we may with pleasure remark a surprising agreement and harmony between the successful practice of the antients ... and the mechanical theory of the moderns, founded upon the wonderful structure of our solids, and the perpetual rotation of our fluids, with which the ancients were unacquainted'.[23] For Tristram (a writer who goes out of his way to reconcile contrary motions and differing accounts (*TS* 1.14.41, 1.22.81), this harmonisation of modern mechanics and ancient humours holds obvious attractions.

Having seen that *Tristram Shandy* belongs to the tradition of learned wit, and that Sterne brings together ancient and modern learning not just to satirise one from the perspective of the other, but because his education and instincts combined them, we must also consider the distinctiveness of his contribution to that tradition – or even his distinctiveness from it. Granted, Sterne employs many of the techniques of Menippean satire, including wrong-headed debates such as the Visitation Dinner (4.26–7) or the controversies that ravage Strasbourg in the encyclopaedic 'Slawkenbergius's Tale'. He avails himself of the bawdy puns of his master Rabelais, and models the life story of his hapless hero on that satirical creation of the Pope-Swift circle, Martinus Scriblerus (see above, ch. 2); both have fathers who test their barmy theories about naming, noses, nurture, and education on their sons. But Sterne's learned bagatelle is more than just a rummage through the lumber-rooms of learning, or a squib on academic debates, or even a specific attack on mechanism and materialism. What makes *Tristram Shandy* so richly satisfying is that life and opinions, personal feelings and intellectual projects, are so closely interwoven. Yes, they are sometimes at odds, illustrating the 'comic clash between the world of learning and that of human affairs' that Jefferson identified as Sterne's primary theme.[24] This clash is instantiated in the speed with which Tristram outgrows the *Tristrapaedia*, the manual his father laboriously composes for his education:

> ——every day a page or two became of no consequence.——
> ——Certainly it was ordained as a scourge upon the pride of human wisdom,
> That the wisest of us all, should thus outwit ourselves, and eternally forego our
> purposes in the intemperate act of pursuing them.   (*TS* 5.16.448)

Yet Sterne rarely sets up as 'scourge' of the proud himself. Rather, he acknowledges that, as minds 'cloathed with bodies, and governed by our imaginations' (5.7.432), we are all bound to outwit ourselves. Intellectual pursuits and academic hobby-horses are, as Christopher Ricks puts it, 'shown to minister to permanent human needs'.[25] Thus Sterne's Menippean set-pieces are situated in a subtle human context. The characters, who are little more than 'mental attitudes', walk the boards of the psychic theatre of the more rounded Shandy males, and Sterne demonstrates how essential are academic interests to the make-up of his characters.

A sign of the degree to which the branches of learning form part of the 'human needs' of Sterne's characters is that they figure in the work as scattered images, as well as in depictions of pedants and specialists. In an effort to comprehend and represent what makes people tick, Sterne draws out and weaves together their ideas in the form of extended metaphors and verbal patterns, making poetry out of Locke's theory of associations. In particular, he finds imaginative ways of depicting the process of thought itself. In one typical parlour colloquy with his brother, Walter tries to explain Locke's complex ideas of duration and its simple modes by means of concrete examples. As usual, the conversation runs on parallel tracks, and there is no meeting of minds:

> Now, whether we observe it or no, continued my father, in every sound man's head, there is a regular succession of ideas of one sort or other, which follow each other in train just like——A train of artillery? said my uncle *Toby*.—A train of a fiddle stick!—quoth my father,—which follow and succeed one another in our minds at certain distances, just like the images in the inside of a lanthorn turned round by the heat of a candle.—I declare, quoth my uncle *Toby*, mine are more like a smoak-jack.——Then, brother *Toby*, I have nothing more to say to you upon the subject, said my father.   (*TS* 3.18.225)

This passage, indeed this whole chapter, follows Locke's *Essay* closely. Locke wondered 'whether it be not probable that our *Ideas* do, whilst we are awake, succeed one other in our Minds at certain distances, not much unlike the Images inside of a Lanthorn, turned round by the Heat of a Candle'.[26] As with his adaptation from Rabelais in the 'Author's Preface', Sterne adds to the source and constructs his comic edifice on its foundations. By inserting his train in the middle of Locke's ideas, Sterne prepares for his joke: Toby, distracted by the analogy, reverts to his military obsession, and thus Locke's theories about time and the succession of ideas are defeated by proof of his theory of the association of ideas. Completing the defeat is the similarly distracting analogy through which Walter, following Locke, likens the mind to a magic lantern that, warmed by the heat of its imagination, projects images as it revolves. Yet Toby finds his own mind to be so smudged and obscured by smoke from his over-heated brain that it is best compared to a smoke-jack: 'an apparatus for turning a roasting-spit, fixed in a chimney and set in motion by the current of air passing up this' (*TS Notes* 233). Tristram likes this image so much that he elaborates on it further, associating it with his forebears Rabelais and Cervantes (*TS* 3.19.225, 3.20.226); Locke, in the mean time, retreats from view.

There are numerous further images of mental space. A string of allusions connects the head and the womb, and thus links two chief themes of *Tristram Shandy*: mental and physical creativity. When Walter explains his technique for generating knowledge by means of auxiliary verbs, he describes it in mechanical terms that bring together Toby's military machines and Dr Slop's obstetrical ones: 'The force of this engine, added my father, is incredible, in opening a child's head.——'Tis enough, brother *Shandy*, cried my uncle *Toby*, to burst it into a thousand splinters' (*TS* 6.2.492). Typically, Walter is insensitive to the associations his metaphor has, and thinks figuratively of opening a child's head to receive new ideas. The vulnerable Toby recalls the way in which his hands were crushed by Slop's use of them to demonstrate his newly invented forceps, and shudders to think what might have happened to his nephew's headpiece (cf. 3.16.220, 2.7.118). Despite the fact that Sterne holds up mechanical ways of thinking to inspection by parodying them, he also demonstrates their explanatory effectiveness. He knocks Locke, yet at the same time not only employs Locke's theory of associations in his characterisation, but also embodies Locke's concept of the train of ideas in the very principle of order governing his text. *The Life and Opinions of Tristram Shandy* seems designed to demonstrate a series of paradoxes beginning with the magnificent conundrum that, despite the work opening with a *coitus interruptus*, Tristram is conceived; despite the many interruptions to the narrative, stories are told; despite Sterne's debt to the masters of learned wit, he creates an original work. New life emerges from old.

To such a fidgety, digressive, and apparently self-propelled narrator as Tristram, Newton's first law of motion – 'Every body continues in its state of rest, or uniform motion in a right line, unless it is compelled to change that state by forces impressed upon it' – is anathema. Being a man of spirit, Tristram 'will have fifty deviations from a straight line to make ... which he can no ways avoid' (*TS* 1.14.41). Yet Newton's third law, that 'to every action there is always an equal and opposite reaction', would make more sense to Tristram.[27] For every attempt to make himself go in a straight line, there is an opposing impulse to deviate. Both are necessary; both are inevitable. On the one hand, Sterne presents us with images of mechanical mensuration in which thoughts are trammelled in 'tracks and trains ... and by treading the same steps over and over again, they presently make a road of it, as plain and as smooth as a garden-walk' (1.1.2); on the other, he provides examples of ideas striking out in a new direction.

Walter, who in some respects runs like clockwork, also thinks freely: he is 'capable of entertaining a notion in his head, so out of the common track' (1.19.57) that he would confound the reader. What is at stake here is not so much a direct opposition between the mechanical and the organic, nor between the fixed and the free. Moreover, there is no opposition between natural philosophy and theology. Just as the relationship between ancient and modern forms of writing and learning is complicated by the fact that both were combined in the curriculum of Sterne's day, and just as Sterne creates something new by absorbing and adapting his predecessors, so the minds of his characters are at once influenced by external forces, and determined to blaze their own trails. Tristram emphasises the originality of his father's thinking, but suggests that this thinking departs from and builds on the work of others, rather than coming out of nowhere: 'here he took a road of his own, setting up another *Shandean* hypothesis upon these corner-stones they had laid for him' (2.19.175). It is an uncharacteristically mixed metaphor, combining an image of routes and movement with one of constructions rising out of fixed positions. It is thus a highly appropriate figure for Sterne's own method of combining tradition and innovation, learning and wit.

NOTES

1. Ephraim Chambers, *Cyclopædia: or, An Universal Dictionary of Arts and Sciences* (1728), i. This simultaneous celebration and lament is voiced by other encyclopaedists: see also the Prefaces to *A Supplement to Dr. Harris's Dictionary of Arts and Sciences* (1744), 1; John Barrow, *A New and Universal Dictionary of Arts and Sciences* (1751), 32.

2. Tristram's references to authorities on the various liberal arts include the following: *Grammar*: Lily (*TS* 7.18.601), Schoppe (1.19.60); *Logic*: Burgersdijk (1.19.60), Crakanthorp (1.19.60), Lull (5.42.484), Ramus (1.19.60), Pellegrini (5.42.484); *Rhetoric*: Aristotle (1.19.60), Cato (5.6.428), Cicero (5.3.419, 5.3.422–5, 8.24.681), Isocrates (1.19.60), Quintilian (1.19.60), Voss (1.19.60); *Geometry*: Archimedes (1.19.58), Torricelli (2.3.103); *Music*: Scarlatti (3.5.192); *Astronomy*: Galileo (2.3.103), Copernicus (1.21.76).

3. On Locke's argument that the association of ideas is a form of madness, see Michael V. De Porte, *Nightmares and Hobbyhorses: Swift, Sterne and Augustan Ideas of Madness* (San Marino: Huntington Library, 1974).

4. Sources for most of Sterne's descriptions of the nervous system have not been traced, but see James Rogers, 'Sensibility, Sympathy, Benevolence: Physiology and Moral Philosophy in *Tristram Shandy*', in *Languages of Nature: Critical Essays on Science and Literature*, ed. Ludmilla Jordanova (London: Free Association Books, 1986), 117–58. Medical thinkers and writers cited include Bacon (*TS* 5.34.472–5.35.475), Borro (2.19.174), Descartes (2.19.173), Drake (9.26.791),

Floyer and Baynard (6.36.563), de Graaf (9.26.791), van Helmont (5.35.475), Mackenzie (2.1.95), Taliacotus (3.38.276), Paré (3.35.267, 3.38.276–8), and Wharton (9.26.791).

5. Among the actual machines mentioned are the Shandy family clock (*TS* 1.1.2), Stevinus's sailing chariot (2.14.135), the pentograph (1.23.85), the ballista, the battering-ram and Toby's curious draw-bridge (3.24.247–9), and the great clock of Lippius (7.30.625).

6. First published in Latin as *Philosophiae Naturalis Principia Mathematica* (1687), and usually referred to as the *Principia*, Newton's great work was issued in revised editions in 1713 and 1726, and translated into English as *Mathematical Principles of Natural Philosophy* (1729). Because much of the work consisted of complex mathematical calculations, few could read it; its chief ideas were disseminated through commentaries, extracts and paraphrases.

7. John Locke, *An Essay Concerning Human Understanding*, ed. Peter H. Nidditch (Oxford: Clarendon Press, 1975), 396 (2.33.§6), quoted in *TS Notes* 42–3.

8. John Ferriar, *Illustrations of Sterne* (1798), 57.

9. D. W. Jefferson, '*Tristram Shandy* and the Tradition of Learned Wit', in *Tristram Shandy: Contemporary Critical Essays*, ed. Melvyn New (New York, NY: St Martin's Press, 1992), 8, first published in *Essays in Criticism* 1 (1951), 225–48.

10. See Sigurd Burckhardt, '*Tristram Shandy*'s Law of Gravity', *ELH* 28 (1961), 70–88.

11. Northrop Frye, *Anatomy of Criticism: Four Essays*, foreword by Harold Bloom (Princeton, NJ: Princeton University Press, 2000), 309. Frye's influential classification of *Tristram Shandy* as Menippean satire has been contested by Howard D. Weinbrot, who finds in Sterne a disqualifying preference for fun over gloom, with 'an un-Lucianic later-eighteenth-century benevolence that nullifies Menippean satire' (Weinbrot, *Menippean Satire Reconsidered: From Antiquity to the Eighteenth Century* (Baltimore, MD: Johns Hopkins University Press, 2005), 11).

12. Eugene P. Kirk, *Menippean Satire: An Annotated Catalogue of Texts and Criticism* (New York, NY: Garland Publishing, Inc., 1980), xi; see also the same author's essay (as Eugene P. Korkowski), '*Tristram Shandy*, Digression, and the Menippean Tradition', *Scholia Satyrica* 1.4 (1975), 3–15.

13. For overt invocations of Tristram's literary heroes, see, for example, *TS* 3.19.225, 3.36–7, 5.3.418, 5.26.457, 8.34.727, 9.24.780, and the title page mottoes for volumes 5 and 6; also *Letters* 76–7, 79, 87, 99–101, 116, 120, 132, 233–4, 294, 304–6, 319.

14. Victor Morgan, *A History of the University of Cambridge, Volume II, 1546–1750*, with a contribution by Christopher Brooke (Cambridge: Cambridge University Press, 2004), 341.

15. For a description of the likely form of Sterne's examinations, see Arthur H. Cash, *Laurence Sterne: The Early and Middle Years* (London: Methuen,1975), 52.

16. Daniel Waterland, *Advice to a Young Student* (1730), 7. Waterland drew up this practical scheme of study in about 1706; it circulated in manuscript form, and was published without his permission in 1729, whereupon he authorised the anonymous edition of 1730 (rev. 1755).

17. Of the fifty-five authors listed by Waterland under the headings of 'Philosophical' and 'Classical', twenty-one are referred to in *Tristram Shandy*. See Judith Hawley, '"Hints and Documents": A Bibliography for *Tristram Shandy*', *Shandean* 3

(1991), 9–36, and 4 (1992), 49–65; also, for fuller details of the authors cited, *TS Notes*. For Sterne's awareness that his 'Cervantic' wit would appeal to an undergraduate audience 'at the Universities', see *Letters* 87.

18. For a representative sample of the vast literature on the religious and political significance of Newtonianism, see *Studies in the History and Philosophy of Science* 35 (2004), a special issue on Newton and Newtonianism, edited by Scott Mandelbrote.

19. Waterland, *Advice*, 10.

20. Waterland, *Advice*, 11. First published in 1512, Erasmus's *De duplici copia verborum ac rerum* ('On Abundance of Words and Ideas') was republished at least 150 times in the sixteenth century. On the Renaissance tradition of copious discourse, see Terence Cave, *The Cornucopian Text: Problems of Writing in the French Renaissance* (Oxford: Clarendon Press, 1979).

21. See *TS Notes* 334, and cf. *Letters* 139.

22. James Mackenzie, *The History of Health, and the Art of Preserving It*, 3rd edn (Edinburgh, 1760), 389 (emphasis added). Mackenzie is cited in *TS Notes* as a source for *TS* 2.1.95, 4.307, 4.31.394, 5.34.472–3; he also provides material for 1.10.18, 1.20.66, 2.3.101, 2.17.145–6, 2.19.175, 4.32.401–2, 5.33.471, 5.35.474 and 9.1.736 (Judith Hawley, 'Laurence Sterne and the Circle of Sciences: A Study of *Tristram Shandy* and Its Relation to Encyclopaedias' (diss., Oxford, 1990), 133–75).

23. Mackenzie, *History of Health*, 330.

24. Jefferson, '*Tristram Shandy* and Learned Wit', 30.

25. Christopher Ricks, introductory essay in Laurence Sterne, *Tristram Shandy*, ed. Melvyn New (London: Penguin, 1997), xv.

26. Locke, *Essay*, 184 (2.14.§9).

27. The first and third law are quoted from *Newton: Texts, Backgrounds, Commentaries*, eds. I. Bernard Cohen and Richard S. Westfall (New York, NY: Norton, 1995), 233–4.

4

ROBERT FOLKENFLIK

Tristram Shandy and eighteenth-century narrative

William Kenrick begins the earliest review of *Tristram Shandy*, published in the *Monthly Review* for December 1759, by locating the work in the tradition of novels, and recognising its extended title – *The Life and Opinions of Tristram Shandy, Gentleman* – as parodying this tradition. 'Of Lives and *Adventures* the public have had enough, and, perhaps, more than enough, long ago', Kenrick writes: 'A consideration that probably induced the droll Mr. Tristram Shandy to entitle the performance before us, his Life and *Opinions*.' Numerous books of fiction with *Life and Adventures* in the title had indeed been published by this time, more if we include such instances as *The Life and Strange Surprizing Adventures of Robinson Crusoe* (1719). Sterne plays on the expected formulas of a new but already familiar genre, and Kenrick finds him, as the review concludes, 'infinitely more ingenious and entertaining than any other of the present race of novelists'.[1]

The title of *Tristram Shandy*, in which a romance given name is undercut by a commonplace, even comic or satirical, surname, had other kinds of precedent in recent fiction. Alongside such examples as *Roderick Random* (1748), *Peregrine Pickle* (1751), and *Ferdinand Count Fathom* (1753), all by Tobias Smollett, *Tristram Shandy* could invite identification as a related kind of novel, though Smollett's *Life and Adventures of Sir Launcelot Greaves* – serialised in monthly magazine instalments and sporting, like Sterne's more leisurely serial, the name of an Arthurian knight – only started to appear in January 1760, when Sterne had already published his opening volumes. Welcoming *Tristram Shandy* in this same month, Smollett's literary periodical, the *Critical Review*, stressed the implicit link with his own fiction. Toby, Trim and Slop were 'excellent imitations of certain characters in a modern truly Cervantic performance', unnamed 'out of regard to the author's delicacy', but undoubtedly *Peregrine Pickle* (CH, 52). In both cases the titles devised by Sterne and Smollett can be taken as oxymorons: rough summaries, in their satirical incongruity, of the mode of writing known as anti-romance or comic romance.[2]

From this perspective of comic romance, Sterne's book extends a creative trajectory running from Cervantes to Fielding, who identified *Joseph Andrews* (1742) as 'Written in Imitation of the *Manner* of CERVANTES, Author of *Don Quixote*', and who famously defined his genre in the novel's preface: 'A comic Romance is a comic Epic-Poem in Prose.'[3] This designation rarely appeared on title pages, though Paul Scarron's *Roman comique* (1651), translated into English as the 'Comical Romance' or 'Comic Romance', was a prototype for some, and Richard Graves's *The Spiritual Quixote* (1773), again with an obvious echo of Cervantes, was characterised on its title page as 'A Comic Romance'.[4] The idea of the comic romance also appeared in influential critical discussions. In the fourth number (31 March 1750) of his periodical the *Rambler*, Samuel Johnson called the most popular contemporary fiction 'the comedy of romance', and in 1783, James Beattie (taking his cue from Fielding, whom he saw as having perfected the form) defined the 'New Comick Romance' in terms of epic.[5] At the same time, the category of 'novel' continued to be associated with fiction of much less substantial kinds, including the farcical or libertine tales that Fielding satirises at several points in *Tom Jones* (which in one chapter mockingly displays a 'young Fellow ... in Bed reading one of Mrs. *Behn*'s Novels; for he had been instructed by a Friend, that he would find no more effectual Method of recommending himself to the Ladies than the improving his Understanding, and filling his Mind with good Literature').[6] In English translations of Scarron, it is the short interpolated tales, not the work overall, that are designated as 'novels', and Johnson's definition of 'Novel' in his *Dictionary* of 1755 ('A small tale, generally of love') evidently refers to modest narratives like these, not to the large, ambitious eighteenth-century fictions that we now describe in this way. The problem does not arise in French and German, which use the term 'roman' indifferently for romance or novel, but the idea that the English novel found some form of stable nomenclature in the middle of the eighteenth century is inaccurate.[7]

Indeed, the five novelists who were widely recognised before the end of the century as the major practitioners of the genre (Defoe, Richardson, Fielding, Smollett, and Sterne) rarely or never used the term 'novel' themselves, either for their own fictions or, as in the case of Sterne, at all. A number of other descriptive categories were used in preference, including 'life' or 'history', and in this respect, Kenrick's immediate identification of *Tristram Shandy* as a novel, like Horace Walpole's more tentative recognition of the work as 'a kind of novel' (*CH* 55), is not fully representative of usage at the time. The varying terminology of Smollett is telling here. In the preface to his first extended fiction, *The Adventures of Roderick Random*, Smollett identified the main tradition behind his writing: Cervantes had forced romance to 'assume the sock' (i.e. become comic), creating a 'method' followed by Le Sage in *Gil Blas* (1715–35), upon which his own practice in turn was loosely 'modelled'. In his dedication to *The Adventures of Ferdinand Count Fathom*, Smollett famously described his form, for the first time, as that of a 'novel', but ten years later he reverted to the language of comic romance when reviewing the anonymous *Peregrinations of Jeremiah Grant* (1763): 'This kind of romance is a diffused comedy unrestrained by the rules of the drama.'[8]

The instability of terminology for long fictions during Sterne's lifetime was one symptom of the experimentalism of prose narrative during the eighteenth century, but Sterne clearly identifies with the tradition of the comic romance. In one of his last letters, dating probably from March 1768, he even writes of 'envy[ing] Scarron', adding (with reference to an unidentified and probably abandoned text): 'I was writing a Romance ... it is most comic' (*Letters* 416). Sterne's only fiction published before *Tristram Shandy*, *A Political Romance* (1759), an odd satire in the mode of Swift's narrative of the three brothers in *A Tale of a Tub*, locates itself as an allegorical romance, but that is part of its comedy. The comic romance, defining itself in opposition to romance proper, is inherently parodic, and in the seventh volume of *Tristram Shandy*, Sterne sends up the *roman de longue haleine* (the long-winded form of romance that prevailed in the mid seventeenth century) by putting the generic he-lover and she-lover, Amandus and Amanda, through their multi-volume paces in a few sentences (*TS* 7.31.627–8). In the choice of his own hero, by contrast, Sterne picks one who seems anything but heroic. He is Tristram, not Sir Tristram, not even the Trismegistus his father desires him to be before the baptism scene (4.8.334). As opposed to the numerous romances of faraway places with same-sounding names, this fiction is located very firmly in Yorkshire – and, as Kenrick notices, Tristram has opinions, not adventures.

One novel with a title that suggests life and events (if we do not take this title as merely redundant), the anonymous *Life and Memoirs of Mr. Ephraim Tristram Bates* (1756), has strong putative connections to *Tristram Shandy*. The hero of this work shares Tristram's name, Toby's occupation, Yorick's fate, and Walter's belief in the efficacy of names. A blend like Sterne's of satire and sentiment, *Ephraim Tristram Bates* was unadmiringly recognised as a novel in the *Monthly Review*, and later identified by Johnson's friend Hester Thrale (also unadmiringly: 'this stupid History') as 'the very Novel from which Sterne took his first Idea'.[9] The eponymous hero, who is usually addressed as Tristram or Tristy, is as obsessed by all things military as Uncle Toby, even building 'a Model, from the Words of the Commentaries, of that famous Bridge *Caesar* threw a-cross the *Rhine*', and he is heard to 'talk often of Doubts, Ride-outs, Ravelins, Javelins, Half-moons, Whole-Moons, Carps, Counter-carps, and the Lord knows what'. In a number of places, this novel uses dashes and asterisks as Sterne does, and the most striking of the visual or typographical similarities comes with the description of the corporal's tomb, which is given a centered, italicised epitaph on a line of its own: '*Alas! poor Bates.*'[10] Sterne knew where to go for the original source, but this adaptation of Hamlet's famous apostrophe as an epitaph certainly might have jogged his memory. *The Life and Memoirs of Ephraim Tristram Bates* is full of quotations of Shakespeare, Milton, Swift, Pope, and the classics (as are other novels of this period), and, over and above its anticipation of the epitaph of Sterne's Yorick, it is nearly as fixated on *Hamlet* as *Tristram Shandy*. All of this said, neither Ephraim Tristram Bates nor the novel that bears his name is very like Sterne's hero or *Tristram Shandy*. Despite the many formal and episodic similarities to Sterne's work, the rhetoric of the novel is largely that of third-person biography, not self-conscious autobiography.

From the technical perspective, Sterne's fiction is full of hypertrophied versions of the novel's conventional routines: the prefatory first-person narration, the interpolated tales, the self-conscious digressions, and other characteristic devices that can be observed from Cervantes to Fielding. Thomas Keymer points out, for example, that the invocation of lines of influence was already a standard feature of the genre by this time, and that minor novelists of the 1750s 'queue[d] up to associate their novels', as Fielding had done and Sterne would do, with Lucian, Rabelais, and Cervantes. Although the status of such invocations as novelistic convention has been disputed by Melvyn New, William Goodall's *Adventures of Capt. Greenland* (1752) begins with satire that proves they were recognised as such: 'Our Readers ... may, very likely, expect our setting forth, according to the accustom'd Manner of many great Authors; with a pompous or sublime Invocation to some, or all, of the numerous Train of the Deities, who are said, or thought, to preside over, and to inspire and assist the whimsical and crack-brain'd Attempts of their many Moonish Histories, Lives, Memoirs, Adventures, and such like, to lend us their Aid, and impregnate our Genius with fertile Inventions.'[11] Goodall's title page announces explicitly that his fiction is 'WRITTEN In Imitation of all those WISE, LEARNED, WITTY and HUMOROUS AUTHORS, who ... Write in the same Stile and Manner' – which means, at a minimum, Fielding, who, we have seen, uses the same 'Written in Imitation' formula in his subtitle for *Joseph Andrews*, and Fielding's own imitators. And yet *Capt. Greenland* also seems, despite its date, to put us in *Shandy* territory, as a 'Moonish' life that calls attention to the whimsicality of the 'crack-brained' – this being one meaning of the word 'Shandy' – hero. Among the many connections that Sterne proposes to the lunar – the source, of course, of lunatics – is Tristram's 'wish', in a novel that famously begins in the optative, that 'I had been born in the Moon' (*TS* 1.5.8).

Wayne Booth says of Goodall's book that 'few read it (there was only one edition)', yet in *The Monastery* (1820), Sir Walter Scott refers to it, and expects readers to catch the reference, nearly seventy years after its publication.[12] A close look at reading habits and circulation library lists shows that a number of works now forgotten were read with interest in and after Sterne's time. Lady Mary Wortley Montagu, for example, read a fair number of the books with self-conscious narrators that Booth names as predecessors of *Tristram Shandy*, including the anonymous *Charlotte Summers* (1749), Sir John Hill's *The Adventures of Mr. Loveill* (1750), and other relevant works that Booth fails to mention, such as Sarah Fielding and Jane Collier's *The Cry* (1754). Lady Bradshaigh was another early reader of *Charlotte Summers*, clearly in response to Samuel Richardson's suggestion, and in *Ferdinand Count Fathom*, Smollett's Captain Minikin offers the hero *The Adventures of Mr. Loveill* and *Young Scarron* among a number of books by 'modern authors that are worth reading'. Finally, the sale catalogue of Sterne's library (cobbled together with other books), whether or not he owned or read the books listed, contains a representative collection of such novels.[13]

An awareness of reigning conventions, and of their growing staleness, shaped the sometimes anxious and defensive experimentalism of novels during these years. Although it would be easy to overemphasise this experimentalism by overlooking the range of earlier English fictions – such as Charles Gildon's *The Post-Boy Robb'd of His Mail* (1692–93) or Jane Barker's *A Patch-Work Screen for the Ladies* (1723) – that stretched received notions about the novel, the decade or so before *Tristram Shandy* saw a conscious burgeoning of fictional forms. Just as Kenrick tires of the novel's conventions, Sarah Fielding and Jane Collier recognise in *The Cry* that readers were tiring of them too, which put the onus on authors to experiment: 'Stories and novels have flowed in such abundance for these last ten years that we would wish, if possible, to strike a little out of a road already so much beaten.' The problem was that 'the real excellence' of a number of these books (by Fielding and Richardson, for example) was difficult 'to equal, much less to surpass'. Like a number of experimental novels, *The Cry* (which its subtitle calls 'A New Dramatic Fable') attempted to recast the author–reader relationship. Fielding and Collier explain their use of 'scenes' instead of chapters as a means of 'avoiding a worn-out practice' and achieving 'variety'. Their title comes from the 'audience' inscribed within the story, a theatrical mob that responds in negative ways to the narrators (figured plural), and especially to the heroine, Portia: 'The Cry, during the time that *Portia* had been declaring her sentiments of friendship, had undergone a various change of countenance. Sometimes their looks indicated an insipid inattention.'

Other authors responded to the dilemma in their own ways. At the chapter ends of Henry Brooke's *The Fool of Quality* (1766–70), the 'Author' and 'Friend' (the latter an inquisitive reader) engage in metafictional colloquies marked off from the narrative text by lines of asterisks. *Charlotte Summers* brims with characters who exist only for the sake of their readerly interjections, made in accordance with their names: Beau Thoughtless, Miss Pert, Arabella Dimple, Dick Dapperwit, Mrs Sit-her-time.[14] Henry Fielding had especially developed the use of the author's address to the reader in his playful and sophisticated introductory chapters to the eighteen books of *Tom Jones*.

One part of the audience came in for enough attention to shape a convention of its own: the critic. *The Cry* begins by addressing 'the candid reader; to the morose critic we know that all address is vain'. Thomas Amory's *The Life of John Buncle* (1756–66), a book with many similarities to Sterne's, is dedicated to 'the Critics'; Edward Kimber, on the other hand, concludes *The Juvenile Adventures of David Ranger* (1757) by taking leave of 'ye tremendous criticks, with whom our times are so replete'. Henry Fielding's developed example was probably decisive in this kind of attention, coming as it did just months before the foundation of the *Monthly Review* in 1749, followed by the *Critical* in 1756 ('written by a Society of Gentlemen'), which effectively institutionalised modern reviewing. In *Tom Jones*, the narrator informs us: 'Reader, I think proper, before we proceed any farther together, to acquaint thee, that I intend to digress, through this whole History, as often as I see Occasion: Of which I am myself a better Judge than any pitiful Critic whatever.'[15] Tristram's promise to clear up a great number of things 'after my life and my opinions shall have been read over ... by all the *world* ... in spight of all the gentlemen reviewers in *Great-Britain*' (*TS* 1.13.40), and to do so *before* critics could attack him or even review him, displays this attitude as inherited. He also begins his second volume with a consideration of the place (at his table) of critics, including the figure of 'Sir Critick' (2.2.97). After the reviews of later volumes turned harsh, he had much to say of critics, hypercritics, and arch-critics, as well as – laying down a challenge that was taken up explicitly by Ralph Griffiths of the *Monthly Review* – 'The REVIEWERS of MY BREECHES' (7.32.632; see *CH* 164).

Fielding's defence of his own procedures asserts his right and intention to digress in opposition to the critics. Digressions were an expected part rhetorically of almost any discourse, and often in novels the narrator apologises for inserting them, or defends their pertinence. Earlier in the century, Jane Barker and Penelope Aubin were entreating their readers, real and fictive, to 'Pardon, Madam, this long Digression' or 'Forgive this Digression', and these gestures continued throughout the period. Henry Fielding was aware enough of the comic effects of digression to have the narrator of *Jonathan Wild* (1743) 'return to my Digression' from a 'Sub-digression'.[16] The quoted passage from *Tom Jones*, however, sets up a different sort of relationship between author and audience, one that was noticed. In *Charlotte Summers*, the narrator, taking 'the worshipful Mr. F——g' as 'Pattern', declares that since Fielding has 'establish'd it as an infallable Doctrine, that an Author ... has an absolute Right to digress when and where he pleases, and to amuse himself and his Readers with any thing that comes uppermost in his Head, whether it has any Connection with the Subject in Hand or not; I here ... put in my Claim to that extensive Priviledge'. William Goodall confesses three years later in *Capt. Greenland*: 'We have thought it, sometimes, highly necessary to follow the Examples of a few of our best modern Authors, by presenting you with now and then a moral Digression.' Like Sterne, whose dedication to the first edition of *Tristram Shandy* would appear in chapter 8 of volume 1 (the dedication to Pitt came in the second edition), and whose preface awaited the third volume, John Kidgell notes that one '*Digression*' of his in *The Card* (1755) 'ought regularly to have *preceded* the whole Work ... by Way of comely Preface and Introduction'.[17]

Although the account of his digressions by the narrator of *Charlotte Summers* has already made them more arbitrary than Fielding's, and rather more like Tristram's ('any thing that comes uppermost in his Head'), and he even writes a 'Chapter on Chapters' before Sterne's,[18] Tristram himself goes a significant step farther than Fielding or his imitators: 'Digressions, incontestably, are the sun-shine;——they are the life, the soul of reading;- - -take them out of this book for instance,- -you might as well take the book along with them' (*TS* 1.22.81). This reverses the relationship of digression and narrative, a switch of their relative importance for which Swift's *A Tale of a Tub* provided an example, but Tristram's positive valuing of his method has the backing of Fielding, not Swift. And, of course, Tristram can fairly claim that his 'work is digressive, and it is progressive too,—and at the same time' (1.22.81).

All attentive readers have long recognised, without being able to prove it (until recently), that Sterne read *Tom Jones*. Tristram's apostrophe to his book following the blank page that invites his reader to portray the Widow Wadman echoes Fielding: 'Thrice happy book! thou wilt have one page, at least, within thy covers, which MALICE will not blacken, and which IGNORANCE cannot misrepresent' (*TS* 6.38.568). In *Tom Jones*, the narrator claims that 'there is no Conduct so fair and disinterested, but that it may be misunderstood by Ignorance, and misrepresented by Malice'; this borrowing comes in a chapter on 'unacknowledged borrowings from other writers', a particular interest of Sterne, who plays wittily throughout *Tristram Shandy* on questions of plagiarism and originality.[19]

A full account of the relationship of *Tom Jones* to *Tristram Shandy* is not possible here, but the importance of Fielding for Sterne either directly or through his influence upon mid eighteenth-century fiction is certain. In addition to similar influences upon Fielding and Sterne (Lucian, Rabelais, Shakespeare, Cervantes, Scarron, Molière, Swift, Marivaux, among others), Tristram shares with the narrator of *Tom Jones*, who has his own rules of writing and will not knuckle under to critics, much that affects his procedures. Even Sterne's choice of starting with Tristram's conception, and spending volumes on events that happen before his birth, sounds like going Fielding one better. The carping narrator of *Mr. Loveill* (1750), with *Tom Jones* in his sights, attacks the 'error' made by 'modern writers of memoirs' in:

> prefixing, with a scrupulous exactness, to the history of the statesman, or the lover, that of the baby, and the school-boy: as if they thought the reader had an equal right to the knowledge of every period and circumstance of the heroe's life, whether any thing to the purpose or not ... 'Tis evident indeed from example, that there is a way of interesting the reader in the very earliest periods of the life of the future heroe of the story; nay, and of making even things preceding those not only accessary, but in some sort essential and necessary to the succeeding history; but it does not appear, that every writer of this kind can be the father of a *foundling*.[20]

The narrator gives no examples, but this line of thought certainly anticipates Sterne's three volumes of content preceding Tristram's birth, while indicting *The History of Tom Jones, A Foundling*.

Wayne Booth influentially argued that the relationship between narrator and reader in *Tom Jones* provides a subplot of friendship, and Tristram too insists upon his growing friendship with the reader, just after asserting that they are 'perfect strangers to each other': 'As you proceed further with me, the slight acquaintance which is now beginning betwixt us, will grow into familiarity; and that, unless one of us is in fault, will terminate in friendship.——— *O diem præclarum!*———then nothing which has touched me will be thought trifling in its nature, or tedious in its telling' (*TS* 1.6.9). Hence, in the next sentence he can refer to his reader as 'my dear friend and companion'. The actual reader may even suspect that Sterne parodies Fielding at this point. Fielding, however, puts his manipulation of the narrative and the developing friendship with the reader to purposes different from those of Sterne. In Fielding, there is no nonsense about an author–reader conversation 'halve[d] ... amicably' (*TS* 2.11.125). Whether we are entering an inn and being offered a bill of fare at the beginning of *Tom Jones*, or taking leave of a stagecoach companion at the conclusion, we are left in no doubt who has done all the talking. Fielding's narrator insists upon his control of the narrative, and builds up the reader's trust in him. 'Control' and 'trust' are not Tristram's watchwords. Fielding promises his reader that 'at the end of the chapter' he may find rest. 'The end of the chapter' for Sterne is more ominous, and on several occasions the phrase is used by Tristram to signify death: one indication that his book and his life are coterminous. Fielding's reader can look forward to the conclusion, but Tristram wants to hold off the end, and the question of whether Sterne actually completed *Tristram Shandy* or planned to resume the work in further volumes is still debated.[21]

Coleridge thought the plot of *Tom Jones* one of the three greatest of all time; in the twentieth century, Dorothy Van Ghent claimed that many individual sentences in *Tom Jones* operate like mini-plots.[22] No one has made similar claims for the plot (if we can call it that) or for the sentences of *Tristram Shandy* – although it has been established that a worked-out chronology of events underpins the novel's chaotic time scheme. The story of 'a COCK and a BULL' told by Tristram (*TS* 9.33.809: the phrase was understood at the time to mean incoherent or disconnected, having 'neither beginning nor end')[23] is filled with sentences containing 'aposiopestick-breaks', to use Tristram's phrase explaining how the hot chestnut down Phutatorius's breech caused his sentence to end prematurely (4.27.383). Tristram's favourite rhetorical figure, aposiopesis, and his most characteristic punctuation, the dash, defeat any sense of plot or even direction at the sentence level. In this connection, it is worth noting that Sterne may have been the one reader of *Tom Jones* who read Fielding's fiction for the essayistic, first-person chapters that introduce the eighteen books, rather than for the plot concerning Tom; the single identified echo of Fielding's masterpiece comes from one of these metafictional chapters, and a similar case arises with *Joseph Andrews*.[24] Yet it is Sterne's own very distinctive narrative voice that makes the range of precursor novels sharing themes and techniques with *Tristram Shandy* seem ultimately very different, and the first-person narrators of other canonical novelists, such as Defoe and Smollett, sound nothing like Tristram. Sterne would seem to have drawn upon autobiography as well as fiction in shaping his mouthpiece, and his work must be seen in the larger context of first-person narrative discourse in the period, including non-fictional forms.

The secular tradition of autobiography was relatively scanty, but at least one book in the tradition has strong links to Sterne's, *An Apology for the Life of Colley Cibber, Comedian* (1740). Sterne alludes to Cibber in a celebrated letter, claiming that he 'wrote not [to] be *fed*, but to be *famous*' (the phrase neatly reverses a quip by Cibber in a pamphlet of 1742, *A Letter from Mr. Cibber to Mr. Pope*), and he probably recommended Cibber's autobiography to Diderot, whose list of books ordered by Sterne seems responsive to Sterne's interests (*Letters* 90, 166). In justifying his autobiography, Cibber charges his own manner of proceeding to his 'hasty Head': 'This Work ... which I hope, they will not expect a Man of my hasty Head shou'd confine to any regular Method: (For I shall make no scruple of leaving my History, when I think a Digression may make it lighter, for my Reader's Digestion.) This Work, I say, shall ... contain the various Impressions of my Mind, (as in *Louis the Fourteenth* his Cabinet you have seen the growing Medals of his Person from Infancy to Old Age).'[25] The linkage of style to temperament, the insistence upon his opposition to regularity, the flagging of his intention to digress, and the emphasis on his own way of thinking all put him in the Shandean camp. Substitute dashes for Cibber's parentheses, and one even finds an approximation of Shandean style; Cibber sounds like a relative of Tristram's who has done well for himself in London.

Cibber's is an 'apology' in the sense of defence. His book is filled with opinions, particularly about himself, that could be taken as proto-Shandean:

> I can no more put off my Follies, than my Skin ... If *Socrates* cou'd take pleasure in playing at *Even* or *Odd* with his Children, or *Agesilaus* divert himself in riding the Hobby-horse with them, am I oblig'd to be as eminent as either of them before I am as frolicksome? If the Emperor *Adrian*, near his death, cou'd play with his very Soul, his *Animula*, &c. and regret that it cou'd be no longer companionable ... sure then these chearful Amusements I am contending for, must have no inconsiderable share in our Happiness ... Give me the Joy I always took in the End of an old Song,
>
>   *My Mind, my Mind is a Kingdom to me!*
>
> If I can please myself with my own Follies, have not I a plentiful Provision for Life? If the World thinks me a Trifler, I don't desire to break in upon their Wisdom ... I live as I write; while my Way amuses me, it's as well as I wish it.[26]

There are numerous points of contact between Cibber and Shandy here. This praise of his own folly shows Cibber as willing as Sterne's narrator to wear the cap and bells of the jester. Like Tristram, he cheerfully exposes his own failings even as he defends his conduct, and his comparison between living and writing, his mind and body, looks forward to Tristram's declaration that 'A Man's body and his mind ... are exactly like a jerkin, and a jerkin's lining;— rumple the one—you rumple the other' (*TS* 3.4.189). Cibber not only insists on doing things his own way, but also takes pleasure in his idiosyncrasies. The passage strikingly invokes the hobby-horse, the fantasy animal that serves as a primary symbol of the relation of imagination to behaviour in *Tristram Shandy*. Although no one would take Cibber for a scholar, there is even an approximation to the 'learned wit' of *Tristram Shandy* in his mention of Hadrian's celebrated address to his own soul and Plutarch's story (which he may have had via Montaigne or the *Tatler*) of the Spartan king *Agesilaus* 'riding the Hobby-horse' to amuse his children. Cibber's misquotation of Sir Edward Dyer's 'My mind to me a kingdom is' points to the increased importance of subjectivity in autobiography, a reminder that Sterne's stream of self-consciousness may owe something to this nascent form in general, and especially to the model of confident autobiographical eccentricity that Cibber provided.

Although Cibber's autobiography has the clearest links to *Tristram Shandy*, other memoirs published before and after his share something of Tristram's terrain. The autobiography of Cibber's disowned, cross-dressing actress daughter, *A Narrative of the Life of Mrs. Charlotte Charke* (1755), is not just theatrical but draws specifically upon the genre of farce – a context that Tristram rejects for his book while inadvertently seeming to confirm it: 'Had this volume been a farce, which, unless every one's life and opinions are to be looked upon as a farce as well as mine, I see no reason to suppose—the last chapter, Sir, had finished the first act of it' (*TS* 5.15.443).

Charke's theatrical sense of life as farce and her associational style make her another forerunner of Sterne, as does her insistence on her 'oddity'. She is 'universally known to be an odd Product of Nature', and her admissions of idiosyncrasy – 'I confess myself to be an odd Mortal' – would not be out of place in Tristram's mouth.[27] Additionally, Charke and Colley Cibber share with Tristram a self-deprecating theatrical humour. They come by their theatricalism through their occupation, as do the characters in such novels of the theatre as *The Comic Romance*, *Young Scarron*, and *David Ranger*. *The Cry* even goes so far as to include a prologue to each part and an epilogue to the book. Sterne's subtler version consists, among other things, of self-conscious scene-changing ('drop the curtain, *Shandy*—I drop it——' (*TS* 5.10.336)), the invocation of dramatic rules in order to subvert them, and the implicit likening of his whole endeavour to Garrick's acting in a colloquy between a nobleman and a critic whose method consists of timing the actor with a stopwatch (*TS* 3.12.213). The theatricality of the private journals of James Boswell, a professed admirer of Sterne, appears most fully in his *London Journal* of 1762–3, but a much earlier autobiography has more particular points of contact.[28] This is John Dunton's eccentric autobiography, *A Voyage around the World* (1691), which rewards comparison with *Tristram Shandy* not only because Dunton may be the earliest to use the formulation 'Life and Opinions' to describe his first-person narrative. His first chapter is entitled 'Of my Rambles before I came into my Mothers Belly, and while I was there', and as his narrative proceeds, he expects those of a similar disposition to 'be pleas'd with my frequent Digressions'. The whole quirkily comic book seemed Shandean enough for an anonymous contemporary of Sterne to publish a highly revised and adapted version in 1762 as *The Life,*

Travels, and Adventures, of Christopher Wagstaff, Gentleman, Grandfather to Tristram Shandy (1762).[29]

Sterne's choice of autobiographical form connects *Tristram Shandy* to individual psychology, and helps mark what is sometimes called the 'inward turn of narrative'.[30] This concern is noticeable in such a mid-century novelistic performance as *The Cry*, its theatricality notwithstanding: 'we beg to inform our readers, that our intention … is not to amuse them with a number of surprising incidents and adventures, but rather to paint the inward mind'. *Tristram Shandy* differs from earlier fictions in that Sterne's first-person narrative, as was recognised (if somewhat inaccurately) from the time of publication, has a theory of mind behind it that relates to Locke on association, though Sterne's theory of mind and language cannot be reduced to Locke's.[31] The shift from 'Life and Adventures' to 'Life and Opinions' implies this inward turn. Thomas Amory's *The Life of John Buncle, Esq; Containing Various Observations and Reflections* anticipates Sterne in its attention to Locke and its claim to present 'a true history of my life and notions'.[32] By 1785, Karl Philipp Moritz could subtitle his *Anton Reiser* (1785–90) '*Ein Psychologischer Roman*' ('a psychological novel').

One possible form of individual psychology is madness, and chronologically speaking, *Tristram Shandy* is flanked by two fictional narratives that devote significant attention to mad characters: Samuel Johnson's *Rasselas* (1759) and Smollett's *Sir Launcelot Greaves*. In *Rasselas*, Johnson's Imlac claims that: 'Perhaps, if we speak with rigorous exactness, no human mind is in its right state'; less philosophically, Smollett's Captain Crowe asserts that 'I think for my part one half of the nation is mad—and the other not very sound.'[33] If we think of Tristram, Walter, and Toby, who would wish to deny the validity of what Imlac and Crowe say, at least in terms of the mid-century novel?

Viktor Shklovsky notoriously claimed that '*Tristram Shandy* is the most typical novel of world literature.'[34] Had he called it the most typical British novel of its time, the remark might still seem outrageous, but it would capture something about *Tristram Shandy* that is usually overlooked. Close attention to eighteenth-century narrative generally and the novel in particular shows the authors in dialogue with their contemporaries, both innovating and responding to the anxieties of influence, in ways that have yet to be taken fully into account.

NOTES

1. CH 46, 47–8. On the implications of this review, see Thomas Keymer, *Sterne, the Moderns, and the Novel* (Oxford: Oxford University Press, 2002), 19–20, 55–6.

2. See Sheridan Baker, '*Humphry Clinker* as Comic Romance', *Papers of the Michigan Academy of Science, Arts, and Letters* 46 (1961), 651–4; also, on the fluctuating meaning of the key generic terms, Dieter Schulz, '"Novel", "Romance", and Popular Fiction in the First Half of the Eighteenth Century', *Studies in Philology* 70 (1973), 77–91.

3. Henry Fielding, *Joseph Andrews*, ed. Martin C. Battestin (Oxford: Clarendon Press, 1967), 4; the previous phrase is from Fielding's title page.

4. First translated in the 1660s, *The Comical Romance* was best known in England through its inclusion in *The Whole Comical Works of Monsr. Scarron* (1700), an edition translated by Thomas Brown, John Savage, and others, and in its seventh edition by 1759. Scarron's early influence in England was complicated by the translation of Antoine Furetière's *Le roman bourgeois*, an unconnected work, as *Scarron's City Romance* (1671).

5. Samuel Johnson, *The Rambler*, eds. W. J. Bate and Albrecht B. Strauss, 3 vols., The Yale Edition of the Works of Samuel Johnson, vols. III–V (New Haven, CT: Yale University Press, 1969), III, 19; James Beattie, 'On Fable and Romance', in his *Dissertations Moral and Critical* (1783), 571.

6. Henry Fielding, *The History of Tom Jones, A Foundling*, eds. Martin C. Battestin and Fredson Bowers (Oxford: Clarendon Press, 1974), 530 (X.ii); see also 722–3 (XIII.ix).

7. For an argument that the novel achieved generic stability around 1750, see Michael McKeon, *The Origins of the English Novel, 1600–1740* (Baltimore, MD: Johns Hopkins University Press, 1987), 19; also the response in Robert Folkenflik, 'Recent Studies in the Restoration and Eighteenth Century', *Studies in English Literature 1500–1900* 27 (1987), 505.

8. Tobias Smollett, *The Adventures of Roderick Random*, ed. Paul-Gabriel Boucé (Oxford: Oxford University Press, 1979), xliv; *The Adventures of Ferdinand Count Fathom*, eds. Jerry C. Beasley and O M Brack (Athens, GA: University of Georgia Press, 1988), 4; *Critical Review* 15 (January 1763), 13.

9. *Monthly Review* 15 (October 1756), 426; *Thraliana: The Diary of Mrs. Hester Lynch Thrale (Later Mrs. Piozzi), 1776–1809*, ed. Katharine C. Balderston, 2nd edn, 2 vols. (Oxford: Clarendon Press, 1951), I, 23–4. On this novel, see Helen Sard Hughes, 'A Precursor of *Tristram Shandy*', *Journal of English and Germanic Philology* 17 (1918), 227–51; also Keymer, *Sterne, the Moderns*, 50–3.

10. *The Life and Memoirs of Mr. Ephraim Tristram Bates* (1756), 17, 18, 238. For Sterne's specifically typographical innovations, see below, ch. 9.

11. See Keymer, *Sterne, the Moderns*, 32, and Melvyn New's counter-argument in *The Eighteenth-Century Novel* 4 (2005), 237; William Goodall, *Adventures of Capt. Greenland*, 4 vols. (1752), I, 1–2.

12. Wayne C. Booth, 'The Self-Conscious Narrator in Comic Fiction before *Tristram Shandy*', *PMLA* 67 (1952), 184; Sir Walter Scott, *The Monastery*, ed. Penny Fielding (Edinburgh: Edinburgh University Press, 2000), 'Answer to the Introductory Epistle', 27.

13. Isobel Grundy, '"Trash, Trumpery, and Idle Time": Lady Mary Wortley Montagu and Fiction', *Eighteenth-Century Fiction* 5 (1993), 293–310; *The Correspondence of Samuel Richardson*, ed. Anna Laetitia Barbauld, 6 vols. (1804), VI, 7 (Lady Bradshaigh to Richardson, 27 March 1750); Smollett, *Ferdinand Count Fathom*, 186; Keymer, *Sterne, the Moderns*, 59–60.

14. Sarah Fielding and Jane Collier, *The Cry*, 3 vols. (1754), I, 8, 15–16, 41; *The History of Charlotte Summers*, 2 vols. (1749), I, 24, 71–2; II, 221. Patricia Spacks, *Novel Beginnings: Experiments in Eighteenth-Century English Fiction* (New Haven, NJ: Yale University Press, 2006) pays particular attention to *The Cry* and other novels by women.
15. Fielding and Collier, *The Cry*, I, 1; Thomas Amory, *The Life of John Buncle*, 4 vols. (1756–66), I, [iii]; Edward Kimber, *The Juvenile Adventures of David Ranger*, 2 vols. (1757), II, 286; Fielding, *Tom Jones*, 37 (I.ii).
16. Jane Barker, *A Patch-work Screen for the Ladies* (1723), 54; Penelope Aubin, *Charlotta Du Pont* (1723), 14; Henry Fielding, *Miscellanies, Volume III*, eds. Bertrand A. Goldgar and Hugh Amory (Oxford: Clarendon Press, 1997), 125 (III. xi).
17. *Charlotte Summers*, I, 28–9; Goodall, *Capt. Greenland*, I, 3; John Kidgell, *The Card*, 2 vols. (1755), I, 15.
18. *Charlotte Summers*, I, 34; cf. *TS* 4.10.336–8.
19. Fielding, *Tom Jones*, 620 (XII.i); Ian Campbell Ross, 'Did Sterne Read *Tom Jones?*', *Shandean* 13 (2003), 109–11. The most cleverly recursive example of Sterne's silent borrowing is his use of metaphors from Robert Burton's discussion of plagiarism in *The Anatomy of Melancholy* (*TS* 5.1.408).
20. Sir John Hill, *The Adventures of Mr. Loveill*, 2 vols. (1750), I, 2–3.
21. On Fielding's narrator, see Wayne C. Booth, *The Rhetoric of Fiction*, 2nd edn (Chicago, IL: University of Chicago Press, 1983), 215–18. For a range of views on the ending of *Tristram Shandy*, see Wayne Booth, 'Did Sterne Complete *Tristram Shandy?*', *Modern Philology* 48 (1951), 172–83; Marcia Allentuck, 'In Defense of an Unfinished *Tristram Shandy*: Laurence Sterne and the *Non Finito*', in *The Winged Skull: Papers from the Laurence Sterne Bicentenary Conference*, eds. Arthur H. Cash and John M. Stedmond (London: Methuen, 1971), 145–55; Keymer, *Sterne, the Moderns*, 143–9; *Tristram Shandy*, ed. Robert Folkenflik (New York, NY: Modern Library, 2004), Introduction, xix–xxii.
22. Samuel Taylor Coleridge, *Table Talk*, ed. Carl Woodring, 2 vols. (Princeton, NJ: Princeton University Press, 1990), I, 295; Dorothy Van Ghent, *The English Novel: Form and Function* (New York, NY: Harper Torchbook, 1961), 80.
23. Thomas à Kempis (attrib.), *The Christian's Exercise* (1714), 273, quoted in *OED2*, s.v. Cock-and-bull.
24. See above, n. 19; also, on the echo of *Joseph Andrews* (89–90 (II.i)) in the same volume of *Tristram Shandy* (6.1.491), Thomas Keymer, 'Readers and Stagecoaches in Fielding and Sterne', *Notes and Queries* 41 (1994), 209–11.
25. Colley Cibber, *An Apology for the Life of Colley Cibber*, ed. B. R. S. Fone (Ann Arbor, MI: University of Michigan Press, 1968), 7. Melvyn New plausibly reads the relationship between Sterne and Cibber as satiric in 'The Dunce Revisited: Colley Cibber and Tristram Shandy', *South Atlantic Quarterly* 72 (1973), 547–59.
26. Cibber, *Apology*, 15–16.
27. Charlotte Charke, *A Narrative of the Life of Mrs. Charlotte Charke* (1755), 86, 271. For Charke and farce, see Robert Folkenflik, 'Gender, Genre, and Theatricality in the Autobiography of Charlotte Charke', in *Representations of the Self from the Renaissance to Romanticism*, eds. Patrick Coleman, Jayne Lewis, and Jill Kowalik (Cambridge: Cambridge University Press, 2000), 97–116.
28. For Boswell's theatricality, see Robert Folkenflik, 'Genre and the Boswellian Imagination', *Studies on Voltaire and the Eighteenth Century* 192 (1980), 1287–95.

29. John Dunton, *A Voyage around the World*, 3 vols. (1691), III, 19; I, 27; III, 4.
30. Erich Kahler argues that Tristram's 'life … *is* his opinions, both his own and his family's', in *The Inward Turn of Narrative*, trans. Richard and Clara Winston (Princeton, NJ: Princeton University Press, 1973), 182.
31. Fielding and Collier, *The Cry*, I, 11. The pseudonymous Jeremiah Kunastrokius calls Sterne's work 'an assemblage of ideas, according to Locke', in *Explanatory Remarks upon the Life and Opinions of Tristram Shandy* (1760), 11; see also *Tristram Shandy*, ed. Folkenflik, xxviii.
32. Amory, *John Buncle*, I, 5; see Keymer, *Sterne, the Moderns*, 63–4.
33. Samuel Johnson, *Rasselas and Other Tales*, ed. Gwin J. Kolb (New Haven, CT: Yale University Press, 1990), 150; Tobias Smollett, *The Life and Adventures of Sir Launcelot Greaves*, eds. Robert Folkenflik and Barbara Laning Fitzpatrick (Athens, GA: University of Georgia Press, 2002), 50.
34. Viktor Shklovsky, 'A Parodying Novel: Sterne's *Tristram Shandy*' (1929), trans. W. George Isaak, in *Laurence Sterne: A Collection of Critical Essays*, ed. John Traugott (Englewood Cliffs, NJ: Prentice Hall, 1968), 89.

5

TIM PARNELL

The Sermons of Mr. Yorick: the commonplace and the rhetoric of the heart

Celebrating the remarkable metamorphosis of an obscure country cleric into a metropolitan literary lion, the young James Boswell's 'A Poetical Epistle to Doctor Sterne, Parson Yorick, and Tristram Shandy' fetes Sterne not only as the creator of *Tristram Shandy*, but also as the author of modish sermons:

> Next from the press there issues forth
> A sage divine fresh from the north;
> On Sterne's discourses we grew mad,
> Sermons! where are they to be had?
> Then with the fashionable Guards
> The Psalms supply the place of Cards
> A Strange enthusiastic rage
> For sacred text now seis'd the age   (CH 83)

That Sterne had talent as a sermonist is clear from his reputation as a popular and moving preacher in his own parishes, the frequency with which he preached from the pulpit of York minster, and the fact that he was called upon to do so at prestigious occasions such as the enthronement of Archbishop Herring in 1743. It was literary celebrity, however, that gave his sermons the kind of cachet they needed to succeed in a notoriously over-stocked market. Outstripping the bestselling *Tristram Shandy* in terms of lifetime editions, the first two volumes of *The Sermons of Mr. Yorick* (1760) were carefully marketed to make the most of the fashionable buzz generated by the novel. Two further volumes followed in 1766; three more were post-humously published in 1769.

In *Tristram Shandy*, Sterne skilfully builds a key scene around the reading of *The Abuses of Conscience*, a sermon that he had preached and published in York almost a decade earlier, and concludes the episode with a suggestion that reveals a considered plan. If 'the character of parson *Yorick*, and this sample of his sermons is liked,' says Tristram, 'there are now in the possession of the *Shandy* Family, as many as will make a handsome volume,

64

at the world's service' (*TS* 2.17.167). Confidently, or perhaps optimistically, preparing the ground before he left York for London at the beginning of March 1760, Sterne arranged for an advertisement to be printed in the *York Courant*, in which it was announced that Tristram Shandy would soon be publishing the 'DRAMATICK SERMONS OF Mr. YORICK'. Although the adjective was eventually dropped, a sense of the dramatic qualities Sterne valued can be gleaned from his response to the preaching of the abbé Denis-Xavier Clément in Paris: 'Père Clement ... delights me much ... his matter solid, and to the purpose; his manner, more than theatrical ... he has infinite variety, and keeps up the attention by it wonderfully; his pulpit ... [is] a stage, and the variety of his tones would make you imagine there were no less than five or six actors on it together' (*Letters* 154–5). Whatever Sterne may have had in mind when he named Tristram as publisher, it was the leading London booksellers, R. and J. Dodsley, who bought the copyright and, at a time when £20 often secured the outright purchase of a novelist's manuscript, paid him the princely sum of 400 guineas for the privilege.[1]

When Yorick's discourses appeared at the end of May, readers whose palates may have been jaded by the glut of printed sermons were tempted by means of a prestigious list of subscribers and a frontispiece engraving of Joshua Reynolds's recently completed portrait of the author. Balancing the glamour of celebrity and fashion with more conventional piety, the text was printed with two title pages, one (in its usual place) proclaiming the authorship of *Tristram Shandy*'s parson Yorick, the other (placed somewhat apologetically after the preface and the twenty-four-page subscription list) prosaically attributing the sermons to 'Laurence Sterne, A. M. Prebendary of York, and Vicar of Sutton on the Forest, and Stillington near York'.

Aware that the effort to catch some readers might alienate others, Sterne began his preface expressing the hope that 'the most serious reader' would not take offence at a strategy meant simply to 'serve the bookseller's purpose' (*Sermons* 1). Passing the buck to the publisher betrays, perhaps, a sense of embarrassment that commercial acumen had ensured that his purse and his readers' souls would prosper together, but sales of these and subsequent volumes suggest that the ploy paid off. In a climate of opinion already coloured by the shocking discovery that the author of the much talked-about bawdy novel was a clergyman, however, some 'serious' readers did take offence. With characteristic hyperbole, the *Monthly Review* found the 'manner' of publication to be 'the greatest outrage against Sense and Decency, that has been offered since the first establishment of Christianity'. Are 'the solemn dictates of religion', asked the reviewer, 'fit to be conveyed from the mouths of Buffoons and ludicrous Romancers? Would any man believe that a

Preacher was in earnest, who would mount the pulpit in a *Harlequin's coat?*' (*CH* 77). Responding less to the sermons themselves than to an authorial persona that combined (as Boswell perceptively grasped) the roles of the Reverend Sterne, Parson Yorick and Tristram Shandy, Thomas Gray was similarly disturbed by the perceived presence of a self-conscious comedian 'often tottering on the verge of laughter, & ready to throw his perriwig in the face of his audience' (*CH* 89).

Partly because Sterne's modern commentators have not typically found the fiction to be informed by religiously sanctioned certainties, the demurs of these early readers have sometimes been taken as proof that the sermons are in some way Shandean or touched by a liberating whiff of unorthodoxy.[2] Readers looking for Shandean humour in the sermons will, though, be disappointed. Following the practice of Bishop Joseph Hall among others, a number of Sterne's sermons begin with rhetorically provocative opening statements, but as Melvyn New notes, 'there is what might be called an opening jest in only six of the forty-five surviving sermons [and] in no sermon is there anything that can legitimately be called humor after the second paragraph' (*Sermons Notes* vii–viii). Moreover, it was not doctrinal unorthodoxy that troubled some of Sterne's earliest readers, but rather a sense of the fundamental incompatibility of the roles of divine and 'ludicrous Romancer'. The *Monthly Review*, in spite of its strictures on the manner of publication and a predisposition against Anglican sermons arising from the nonconformist affiliations of its editors, actually found Sterne's discourses abounding with 'moral and religious precepts, clearly and forcibly expressed', and their matter so 'unexceptionable' as to recommend them 'as models for many of his brethren to copy from' (*CH* 78). With none of its rival's qualms about Sterne's willingness to offer the world both comic fiction and sermons, the *Critical Review* positively welcomed the 'son of Comus descending from the chair of mirth and frolick, to inspire sentiments of piety, and read lectures in morality' (*CH* 76).

When Sterne's sermons did occasionally provoke objections on doctrinal grounds, they did so not because of heterodoxies peculiar to the Yorkshire vicar, but because of a Christian society's broader debates about the emphases of orthodox Anglican theology. Thus the poet and evangelical Protestant William Cowper found Sterne 'a great master of the pathetic' (*CH* 173), but objected that the rhetorical strategies of the sermons were not sufficiently calculated to address the essentially corrupt nature of man. For Cowper, as for Methodists and many dissenting Protestants, the Church of England's teachings on human nature implied a level of autonomy that left too little room for the role of faith and the operations of divine grace. Because of their emphasis on practical morality rather than doctrine,

Anglicans – including such eminent divines as Archbishop Tillotson as well as Sterne – were regularly accused by their opponents of writing sermons that were little more than moral essays. But, as we shall see, their ethical system was consistently grounded in religious doctrine. While the disputants often saw it as a conflict between true and false believers, retrospect suggests that these debates between conservative and more liberal Protestants took place within a shared context of belief.

Interestingly, Cowper's response to *The Sermons of Mr. Yorick* re-enacts the central theological debate of the mid to late seventeenth century. Defining themselves by their opposition not only to Roman Catholics, deists, and materialists, but also Protestant 'enthusiasts' (those, including puritans, who clearly separated reason and faith and privileged faith before works), the so-called latitudinarian divines of the Restoration redirected Anglican thought in a way that involved the reassessment of key aspects of the Reformation legacy.[3] Cowper's sense that 'the evil of a corrupt nature is too deeply rooted in us all' to be overcome by anything but 'faith in Christ' (*CH* 173) belongs to a Calvinist tradition that the most influential latitudinarian divines – Benjamin Whichcote, John Wilkins, Tillotson, Simon Patrick, Isaac Barrow, and Edward Stillingfleet – were concerned to revise. Where Calvin insisted on the depravity of human nature and the salvation through grace of God's elect, the latitudinarians stressed the divine residue in the human constitution, and argued that Christ's redemption was open to all. Where Calvin's understanding of fallen man left no room for human agency on the path to salvation, the latitudinarians' more optimistic account of human nature emphasised the role of reason in co-operating with God to achieve a religious life compatible with earthly felicity. Beginning in opposition to the dominant and broadly Calvinist Reformation tradition, the success of latitudinarianism was such that its revisionist Arminian teachings came to typify mainstream Anglican thought in the eighteenth century.

Although a retrospective knowledge of the history of ideas suggests that the latitudinarian effort to steer a course between Protestant fundamentalists and deists ultimately contributed to the process by which ethics and religion were eventually separated, this was an unforeseen consequence of a pragmatic endeavour, based in the theological middle ground, to defend the Anglican faith.[4] Contrary to the allegations of their critics, latitudinarians did not preach that human beings were innately good, or that morality could be divorced from religion. Thus, in the sermon headed 'Inquiry after happiness', Sterne argues 'that there can be no real happiness without religion and virtue, and the assistance of GOD's grace and Holy Spirit to direct our lives in the true pursuit of it' (*Sermons* 1.6). In a later sermon that tellingly deploys the arguments of a Restoration polemic, *The Spirit of Enthusiasm Exorcised*

(1680), against the 'enthusiasm' of the Methodists (*Sermons* Notes 386–98), Sterne is equally clear about fallen human nature. 'We come not into the world equipt with virtues, as we do with talents', he argues. Such virtues as continency, patience, and humility are not innate, but are 'insensibly wrought in us by the endeavours of our own wills and concurrent influences of a gracious agent'. Moreover, will and grace have to do battle with 'the stream of our affections and appetites', which 'naturally carry us the other way' (*Sermons* 38.361–2).

Characteristically, part of the argument and some of the phrasing here derive from another sermonist. In this instance, Sterne borrows from Edward Young the Elder's 'A sermon concerning nature and grace' (1699), but the particular source is less significant than the fact of Sterne's broader indebtedness to his predecessors. As a minor cleric composing sermons long after most of the theological arguments of the Restoration had been won by major divines such as Tillotson, Sterne belonged to a more humble clerical body whose job it was to be a conduit for established Anglican teachings. Accordingly, Sterne's homilies are unexceptionably orthodox and, in keeping with the original function of most of them (as sermons delivered in his rural parishes), largely derivative.

The extent to which the sermons articulate the central concerns of the latitudinarian tradition is suggested in the *Critical Review*'s response to the first two volumes in 1760: 'The reverend Mr. Sterne aims at mending the heart, without paying any great regard to the instruction of the head; inculcating every moral virtue by precepts, deduced from reason and the sacred oracles' (*CH* 76). Locating its few and simple truths in God-given reason and the teachings of Scripture, Anglican practical divinity eschewed theological debate, and sought instead to encourage virtue that would have a direct manifestation in good works. Accordingly, Sterne suggests that his sermons 'turn chiefly upon philanthropy, and those kindred virtues to it, upon which hang all the law and the prophets' (*Sermons* 2). For all the insistence on what Locke called the reasonableness of Christianity, Anglican sermons regularly appealed to feeling rather than intellect when it came to endorsing their teachings. Thus Sterne's linking of the matter of the sermons to their apparently spontaneous mode of composition – they proceeded, according to the preface, 'more from the heart than the head' (*Sermons* 2) – is a conventional one. The Anglican self-definition as 'the Religion of the Heart'[5] was a corollary of the calculated decision to limit rational debate about the mysterious aspects of belief.

While the orthodoxy of Sterne's homilies had never been questioned in a systematic way, lingering doubts were largely put to rest by the first scholarly edition of the sermons in 1996. Researching Sterne's sources more thoroughly than any of his predecessors, and building on newly inflected accounts of the integrity of the latitudinarian tradition, Melvyn New as editor makes an impressively informed and cogent case for the place of *The Sermons of Mr. Yorick* in the Anglican mainstream. If sometimes grudgingly, most commentators now accept New's argument that the Sterne of the sermons is an orthodox Church-of-England man, and 'not a jester in the pulpit, nor ... a secularist or Shaftesburian' (*Sermons Notes* 17). Yet New's larger thesis that the religious concerns of the sermons also inform the fiction has proved much more contentious. Indeed, the question of the degree to which the fiction and the sermons share common ground has become one of the key issues in modern Sterne studies. Sharing some of the doubts expressed by eighteenth-century readers about the compatibility of ribald and anarchic fiction with Anglican piety, some critics have found further grounds for suspicion in the biographical evidence of Sterne's occasional dilatoriness as a clergyman, his sexual infidelities, and his willingness to keep company with known sceptics like John Hall-Stevenson, John Wilkes, and the circle who gathered round the Baron d'Holbach in Paris. Given his need to make his way in the church, the argument goes, it is unsurprising that Sterne's sermons are orthodox, but, such orthodoxy in no way *proves* belief.[6]

To what extent, then, is it legitimate to see in the sermons a meaningful context for the fiction? Faced with objections to *Tristram Shandy*'s bawdy comedy, Sterne was quick to affiliate his own practice with that of other priest-satirists such as Rabelais, Burton, and Swift. Frustrated with the strictures of the reviewers, he insisted that *Tristram Shandy* was 'a moral work, more read than understood' (*Sermons* 12.255). In the case of *A Sentimental Journey*, there is evidence that Sterne thought the work would redeem his tarnished reputation, and the claim that it was written 'to teach us to love the world and our fellow creatures better than we do' (*Letters* 401) suggests a common purpose with sermons that 'turn chiefly upon philanthropy'. If, however, we compare Sterne's fiction to, say, Defoe's, Richardson's, and Fielding's, we are less likely to be immediately struck by a sense of an informing Christian world view. Where Defoe's *Robinson Crusoe* (1719) seeks to 'justify and honour the Wisdom of Providence',[7] Richardson's novels painstakingly chart the trials of their Christian protagonists, and Fielding overtly champions the latitudinarian teachings of Benjamin Hoadly and Isaac Barrow, *Tristram Shandy* and *A Sentimental Journey* can seem too playfully sceptical to endorse belief of any kind.

Certainly, Sterne has none of Richardson's mission to reform a genre that typically tended, as the title page of *Pamela* (1740) has it, to '*inflame* the Minds [it] should *instruct*'. Yet, while they are not primarily didactic in intent, Sterne's idiosyncratic contributions to the development of the emerging novel are informed by Anglican thought in a number of significant ways. As is clear from explicitly political sermons such as 'National mercies considered', 'Thirtieth of January', and 'The ingratitude of Israel', religious identity in the period was coloured as much by the politics of Protestant Britishness as it was by theology. In *Tristram Shandy* in particular, such a politics manifests itself negatively in the form of pervasive anti-Catholicism and, more positively, in the idealised treatment of Captain Toby Shandy and Corporal Trim. Indeed, it might be further argued that the hobby-horsical eccentricities of the Shandy family are able to thrive precisely because of the nurturing freedoms of a Protestant 'land of liberty' (*Sermons* 27.267). Where the tyrannical constraints of Catholic France resulted in a national character of bland homogeneity, Britain, the argument went, produced quirky but lovable humorists. More centrally, *Tristram Shandy*'s satire on perceived abuses in the arts and sciences is linked to the novel's fundamental concern with the limits of human reason. Joining a tradition of Christian anti-intellectualism that includes such favourite writers as Erasmus, Montaigne, and Swift, *Tristram Shandy*'s very form enacts an acceptance of the folly of various human efforts to master and control the 'riddles and mysteries' (*TS* 4.17.350) of God's universe. If such fideism is not unique to latitudinarian Protestantism, it is nonetheless consistent with its suspicion of over-zealous rationalism and its often uneasy handling of the boundaries between reason and faith.[8]

At a more local level, the concerns of individual sermons are echoed on a number of occasions in *Tristram Shandy* and *A Sentimental Journey*. Commenting on the beauty and sublimity of Job 14:1–2 ('Man *that* is born of a woman, *is* of few days, and full of trouble. He cometh forth like a flower, and is cut down: he fleeth also as a shadow, and continueth not'), the sermon headed 'Job's account of the shortness and troubles of life, considered' argues that 'one might challenge the writings of the most celebrated orators of antiquity, to produce a specimen of eloquence, so noble and thoroughly affecting' (*Sermons* 10.91). Behind the contrasting responses of Walter and Trim to the death of Bobby Shandy lies just such an opposition between empty rhetoric and the inspired simplicity of Scripture. Drawing on '*Cato*, and *Seneca*, and *Epictetus*', Walter proceeds 'from period to period, by metaphor and allusion', while Trim 'without wit or antithesis, or point, or turn' goes 'strait forwards as nature could lead him, to the heart' (*TS* 5.6.428–9). Tellingly, Sterne has Trim echo some of Job's words when he recalls the Order for the Burial of the Dead from the Book of Common Prayer: 'are we not like a flower of the field ... is not all flesh grass?' (*TS* 5.9.435). Having published 'Job's account' eighteen months before the third instalment of *Tristram Shandy*, Sterne might well have expected his readers to be alert to such parallels. The common ground between the ethical concerns of *A Sentimental Journey* and a number of homilies from the third and fourth volumes of sermons (see *SJ/BJ* xvi–xvii) suggests that Sterne may have had similar expectations of readers of his last work.

In *Tristram Shandy*, making extensive use of the language of a sermon as well as its argumentative thrust, Sterne cleverly weaves material from the opening of 'Trust in God' into a characteristic exchange between Walter and Toby:

> WHEN I reflect, brother *Toby*, upon MAN; and take a view of that dark side of him which represents his life as open to so many causes of trouble—when I consider … how oft we eat the bread of affliction, and that we are born to it, as to the portion of our inheritance … 'tis wonderful by what hidden resources the mind is enabled to stand it out, and bear itself up. (*TS* 4.7.332)

Drawing Walter's words more or less verbatim from the sermon, Sterne uses the fictional context of *Tristram Shandy* to dialogise aspects of the original monologue. Thus Walter happily embraces the position characterised in the sermon as over-reliant on self-love, while Toby piously responds with the homily's central message. Cutting 'the knot', as Walter protests, 'instead of untying it', Toby reminds his brother that we endure adversity 'by the assistance of Almighty God', and 'are upheld by the grace and assistance of the best of Beings' (4.7.332). Not for the first time, Walter is defeated by Toby's recourse to '*Grangousier*'s solution' (3.41.284): the simple but unanswerable claim that the causes that so intrigue the speculative thinker are best explained by the will of God.

Finding the 'author of *Tristram Shandy* discernible in every page' of the third and fourth volumes of *The Sermons of Mr. Yorick*, the *Critical Review* pointed among other things to 'the same art in moving the tender affections of nature' (*CH* 171). For the reviewer, as for many early readers, it was Sterne's mastery of pathos, and his concern to 'inculcate that great *Magna Charta* of mankind, humanity and benevolence',[9] that distinguished him as both a sermonist and writer of fiction. Replete with sentimental tableaux, and regularly deploying pathos for didactic ends, the sermons provide one of the most important contexts for understanding the much-debated sentimentalism of the fiction. With its emphasis on philanthropy and affective religion, Anglican theology played an important role in the complex of ideas informing the mid eighteenth century's preoccupation with sentiment and sensibility.

In keeping with the emphases of latitudinarian theology, a number of Sterne's sermons focus on good nature and fellow feeling. Where a sermon such as 'On enthusiasm' stresses the negative effects of the fall of man, 'Vindication of human nature' finds the image of God in 'all that is generous and friendly in the heart of man' (*Sermons* 7.66), and argues that 'the desire of society, and ... spontaneous love towards those of his kind' is one of the 'first and leading propensities of [man's] nature' (7.69). Similarly, in 'Philanthropy recommended', Sterne maintains that self-love is generally balanced by 'a certain generosity and tenderness of nature which disposes us for compassion' (3.23). Dramatising the thoughts of the good Samaritan, the sermon presents him as the type of the man of feeling: 'I shall comfort him at least in his last hour—and, if I can do nothing else,—I shall soften his misfortunes by dropping a tear of pity over them' (3.28). Significantly, the sermon also attempts to counter materialist accounts of the sources of compassion. Sudden as the Samaritan's 'emotion' was, Sterne argues, 'you are not to imagine that it was mechanical, but that there was a settled principle of humanity and goodness which operated within him' (3.27). Here, as elsewhere in the sermons concerned with 'social virtue' (7.66), the ethical issues explored in *Tristram Shandy* in such episodes as the 'Story of Le Fever', and throughout *A Sentimental Journey*, are clearly adumbrated.

Where modern readers are apt to be suspicious of emotional rhetoric, it was justified for Sterne and his contemporaries by a qualified equation of truth with feeling. Sentimental in some respects, the affective rhetoric of Anglican sermons was not predicated on naïve optimism about human nature. Indeed, justification for employing what Sterne calls 'a story painted to the heart' (*TS* 3.20.233) came in part from a sense of the imperfection of fallen man. Arguing that 'lessons of wisdom have never such power over us, as when they are wrought into the heart, through the ground-work of a story which engages the passions', one sermon asks: 'Is the heart so in love with deceit, that ... we must cheat it with a fable, in order to come at truth?' (*Sermons* 20.186).

More developed and more complex in their effects than the pathetic fables of the sermons, the sentimental episodes of the fiction belong to the same recognisable milieu. Thus, the 'Story of Le Fever' engages its readers' emotions in order to add weight to its recommendation of philanthropy. Suspiciously sentimental to some modern tastes, the story nonetheless follows the sermons' relatively hard-nosed assessment of human nature. Learning of Le Fever's plight, Toby is at first divided between benevolent and self-interestedly hobby-horsical impulses. As pity for Le Fever begins to deflect the old soldier from his obsession, Sterne takes care to show the hard-won defeat of the hobby-horse by compassion that, on this occasion at least, leads to practical actions.

Tellingly, in the famous rhetorically heightened conclusion to the Le Fever episode, Sterne draws on material from a sermon by John Norris, 'The importance of a religious life considered from the happy conclusion of it'.

Here Norris evokes the finality of death to commend a life of virtue, painting a scene that Sterne clearly found suggestive:

> When I shall lie faint and languishing upon my Dying Bed, with my Friends all sad about me, and my Blood and Spirits waxing cold and slow within; when I begin to reckon my Life not by the Striking of the Clock, but by the throbbings of my Pulse, every stroak of which beats a *Surrender* to the Pale Conqueror, in this great *Ebb* of Nature, when the Stream of Life runs low, and the [Eccles. 12:6] Wheel at the *Cistern* can hardly turn round its Circle, it will be then no Pleasure or Comfort to ... reflect upon the great Estate that I have got ...[10]

Picking up Norris's rendering of the verse from Ecclesiastes at the beginning of the chapter, Sterne concludes with a clear echo of the sermon's language in the description of the 'blood and spirits' of Le Fever 'waxing slow and cold within him'. More interestingly, Sterne also develops the resonant image of the pulse-throbbing surrender to death, and dramatises the lieutenant's final moments with a typographically embellished enactment of Norris's words: 'Nature instantly ebb'd again,——the film returned to its place,—— the pulse fluttered——stopp'd——went on——throb'd——stopp'd again—— moved——stopp'd——shall I go on?——No' (*TS* 6.10.512–13).

As with the numerous reworkings of borrowed material that lie behind the sermons and the fiction, Sterne's use of Norris here tells us much about his processes of composition. Evidently, the commonplace books that served him as he wrote homilies were also extensively used as he composed the fiction of his final years. Although none of these books have survived, their trace is apparent in both the sermons and fiction in the deftness with which he combines material on a given topic from a variety of disparate sources. Sterne would have learned the habit of recording key passages in a systematic way while training to be a divine at Cambridge. Undergraduates were encouraged to learn the conventions of composition from a canon of model sermonists, and to draw on them to construct commonplace books that would serve as resources from which discourses on any number of conventional subjects could be derived. Armed with modern notions of authorship and intellectual property, readers have sometimes been scandalised by the degree to which Sterne's sermons rely on the language and arguments of his predecessors, but this is to misunderstand the role of minor clergymen, who, as we have seen, were expected to pass on received wisdom, and encouraged to make free use of the words of eminent divines.

That said, if straightforward charges of plagiarism are irrelevant to the sermons, the culling and recycling of material from Tillotson, Hall, Norris, and others does raise problems of which Sterne was clearly aware. Conscious that unacknowledged borrowings in discourses delivered orally to parishioners have a different status in print, the preface to the first instalment of *The Sermons of Mr. Yorick* offers a rather anxious apology to cover the possibility that Sterne may have inadvertently 'made free with' the words of others (*Sermons* 2). In the different context of the fiction, he is less coy. Playfully alluding to an issue that was probably something of an in-joke among clerics, Tristram quotes the comments recorded by Yorick on the first leaf of a sermon: '*For this sermon I shall be hanged,—for I have stolen the greatest part of it. Doctor* Paidagunes *found me out.* ☞ *Set a thief to catch a thief.* ——' (*TS* 6.11.514). In the 'Rabelaisian Fragment', the crossing of the boundary between legitimate use of a model and outright robbery is treated with comic relish. Needing to finish a sermon in a hurry and having reached an impasse, Homenas wonders why a man may not 'lawfully call in for Help, in this, as well as any other human Emergency'. Grabbing a handy volume of Samuel Clarke's sermons, he begins 'to clapp me in ... Five whole Pages, nine round Paragraphs, and a Dozen and a half of good Thoughts all of a Row' (*RF* 1089). In Sterne's case, for all his extensive borrowings, it is rare for him simply to 'clapp in' undigested material. Typically, he rephrases or in some way reworks his sources. Nonetheless, his compositional methods sit uncomfortably with the regular claims that the sermons are products of the heart rather than the head.

Discussing Sterne's probable approach to composition, New argues that such claims need to be understood in a special sense: 'Preaching from "the heart" is, for Sterne, the preaching of received religion, the Word inscribed within the Anglican establishment' (*Sermons Notes* 11). Insofar as Sterne felt that the message was more important than the messenger, there is something in this view. Yet this generous reading of the trope is belied by what was clearly a workmanlike process, in which sermons were made (as Tristram puts it in a playful borrowing from Burton's *Anatomy of Melancholy*) 'as apothecaries make new mixtures, by pouring only out of one vessel into another' (*TS* 5.1.408). When, in a letter accompanying a gift of his books to Eliza Draper, Sterne half dismisses *Tristram Shandy* as a product of his head, and elevates the sermons as having come 'all hot from the heart' (*Letters* 298), he is clearly not presenting himself as a humble vehicle for the Word. Rather, he is attempting to persuade Mrs Draper that his true self is best reflected in the honest and spontaneous pieties of the sermons. More disinterested, but similarly conventional, is Yorick's defence of his use of a sermon as a pipe lighter on the grounds that 'it came from my head instead of my heart' (*TS* 4.26.376–7). While the trope itself is an Anglican commonplace, and the necessary counterpart of preaching aimed 'point blank to the heart' (4.26.377), it remains difficult to find integrity in this verbal sleight of hand.

Sterne's use of commonplace books as repositories of recyclable material also has much larger interpretative ramifications in terms of the significance we assign to a given borrowing. Because his sources are often so recondite, or so woven into the fabric of his prose, they cannot be treated as if they were allusions that Sterne expected his readers to uncover and interpret. A case in point is the material from Hall's *Quo Vadis?* that is seamlessly integrated into the preface to *A Sentimental Journey* (*SJ/BJ* 16–17; see also 249–50). Unnoticed for two hundred years, the borrowing appears to be a straightforward appropriation of some of Hall's thoughts, with no hint of the resonances associated with deliberate allusion. Given Sterne's practice here and elsewhere, we need to ask how much of a particular borrowing's original context can legitimately be brought to bear in the process of interpretation. The ending of the Le Fever episode may well result from Sterne's creative use of a recorded commonplace, but it is highly unlikely that he expected his readers to be aware that he was reworking Norris. Even with knowledge of the source, it might be argued that Tristram's comic discourse transforms the original to the point where its meaning is no longer stable. Indeed, the same broad point about the necessarily different meanings generated by different contexts might also be applied on those occasions when Sterne makes use of material from the sermons in the fiction. How, for example, are we to take the message of 'Trust in God' when the soft-hearted and simple uncle Toby becomes its strongest advocate, or of 'Job's account' when Trim becomes the vehicle for sublime utterance? A resourceful literary *bricoleur*, Sterne seems to have used passages gathered in his commonplace books with the kind of flexibility that characterises Yorick's use of the drummer's letter in *A Sentimental Journey* (*SJ/BJ* 63–4). That he did so warns us to be cautious in our readings of some of the fiction's most frequently discussed passages.

Ruminating on his father's response to his unfortunate misnaming, Tristram is led, by way of an illustrative anecdote about his response to mistakenly burning a fair sheet of manuscript, to a generalisation about the order of things: 'But mark, madam, we live amongst riddles and mysteries— the most obvious things, which come in our way, have dark sides, which the quickest sight cannot penetrate into; and even the clearest and most exalted understandings amongst us find ourselves puzzled and at a loss in almost every cranny of nature's works' (*TS* 4.17.350). Versions of the passage appear in two of the sermons ('Felix's behaviour towards Paul, examined' and 'The ways of providence justified to man'), and it is clear that Sterne was familiar with both the ultimate source in Locke's *Essay Concerning Human Understanding* and a reworking of it in Norris's 'A discourse concerning the folly of covetousness' (*Sermons Notes* 218–20). In Sterne's sermons, as in his sources, we have eloquent articulations of Christian scepticism about the limits of reason, but it is questionable whether comparable profundity attaches to the passage as it appears in *Tristram Shandy*. While the riddles and mysteries remain those that explain nature's capacity to relieve distress by unexpected means, the distresses in question are now comically trivial ones. Similarly, while it is nature's knack of satisfying human needs that again leads Tristram to refer to 'a world beset on all sides with mysteries and riddles' (*TS* 9.22.776) in the final volume, the context – bawdy jokes about women's interest in the content of men's 'panniers', and nature's bungling creation of married men – makes it inappropriate to invoke Sterne's ultimate sources. One suspects that Sterne, looking for some general observations about 'Nature', found his phrasing by referring to the relevant section of one of his commonplace books.

A similarly inventive and transforming use of sources is evident in the borrowings from Norris's sixth discourse on the Beatitudes, which appear in 'Our conversation in heaven' and *A Sentimental Journey*. Following Norris, Sterne's sermon argues that the 'gross and polluted spirit' carrying appetites to heaven 'for which there could be found no suitable objects' would not be happy 'could the happiest mansion in heaven be supposed to be allotted' to it (*Sermons* 29.280). The emphasis here, as in Norris, is on the need to escape the senses in order to fit the self for heaven, but when Sterne reworks the material in Yorick's assessment of Smelfungus and Mundungus, the meaning is rather different. Now 'heaven itself ... would want objects to give' these travellers, because they are constitutionally splenetic, unable to make 'generous' connections with others, and lacking in 'faculties for this work; and was the happiest mansion in heaven to be allotted to [them], they would be so far from being happy, that [their] souls ... would do penance there to all eternity' (*SJ/BJ* 38). Where the sermon finds no place in heaven for those in pursuit of 'an impure desire' or 'consumed in intemperance' (*Sermons* 29.281), *A Sentimental Journey*, concerned to defend the threads of 'love and desire' entangled in nature's 'web of kindness' (*SJ/BJ* 124), excludes those who cannot enjoy what life offers.[11] Happily recycling material for different ends, Sterne clearly did not expect his readers to reinterpret Yorick's words in light of Norris's sermon.

Sensing a disjunction between the Sterne of the pulpit and the Sterne of the fiction, some commentators have looked for signs of unorthodoxy in the sermons themselves. Yet, as Wilkes's possibly partial comment on Sterne's preaching inadvertently reveals, the sermons have an inscrutability born of their very orthodoxy: 'Tristram pleads his cause well, tho' he does not believe one word of it.'[12] *The Sermons of Mr. Yorick* are not, and were never intended to be, articulations of personal belief or theology, but rather statements of commonplace Anglican thought. Such thought, as we have seen, is also manifest in *Tristram Shandy* and *A Sentimental Journey*. There remains, however, enough ambiguity about the ways in which the concerns of the sermons and the fiction meet to leave open the question of whether Sterne's 'true' self is best represented by the pious Doctor Sterne, the more heteroclite Parson Yorick, or the playful, irreverent, and sceptical Tristram Shandy. When Nietzsche found Sterne the 'great master of *ambiguity*', he was in part projecting his own values onto the eighteenth-century clergyman, but in assessing the relationship between the sermons and the fiction, it is indeed hard, as Gray found, to be sure whether Yorick is in jest or earnest. Here, as in a number of the key interpretative issues surrounding the fiction, the 'reader who demands to know what Sterne really thinks of a thing, whether he is making a serious or a laughing face, must be given up for lost'.[13]

NOTES

1. This is the figure given by Sterne to his banker (*Letters* 190). For payments made by booksellers in the period, see James Raven, *British Fiction 1750–1770* (Newark, NJ: University of Delaware Press, 1987), 23–4.
2. For the argument that some of the negative responses to the sermons suggest their unorthodoxy, see Paul Goring, 'Thomas Weales's *The Christian Orator Delineated* (1778) and the Early Reception of Sterne's Sermons', *Shandean* 13 (2002), 87–97.
3. For a lucid and illuminating account of latitudinarian theology and its origins, see Isabel Rivers, *Reason, Grace, and Sentiment: A Study of the Language of Religion and Ethics in England, Volume I: Whichcote to Wesley* (Cambridge: Cambridge University Press, 1991), ch. 2.
4. The ways in which secular, sentimental ethics built on the implications of Anglican thought are explored in Isabel Rivers, *Reason, Grace, and Sentiment, Volume II: Shaftesbury to Hume* (Cambridge: Cambridge University Press, 2000).
5. Thomas Herring, *Seven Sermons on Public Occasions* (1763), 37, quoted in *Sermons Notes* 43, n. 39.
6. For a sceptical treatment of the relationship between the sermons and Sterne's private beliefs, see Ian Campbell Ross, *Laurence Sterne: A Life* (Oxford: Oxford University Press, 2000), 227–45.
7. Daniel Defoe, *Robinson Crusoe*, eds. Thomas Keymer and James Kelly (Oxford: Oxford University Press, 2007), 1.
8. For an insightful treatment of Sterne's place in the tradition of Christian fideism, see Donald Wehrs, 'Sterne, Cervantes, Montaigne: Fideistic Skepticism and the Rhetoric of Desire', *Comparative Literature Studies* 25 (1988), 127–55. For the relationship between reason and faith in Anglican discourse, see Gerard Reedy, SJ, *The Bible and Reason: Anglicans and Scripture in Late Seventeenth-Century England* (Philadelphia, PA: University of Pennsylvania Press, 1985).
9. Richard Griffith, *The Triumvirate* (1764), xiv.
10. John Norris, *Practical Discourses upon Several Divine Subjects* (1691), 165–6. For fuller discussion of the significance of Sterne's use of Norris here, see Tim

Parnell, 'A Story Painted to the Heart? *Tristram Shandy* and Sentimentalism Reconsidered', *Shandean* 9 (1997), 128–30.

11. For a different reading of Sterne's use of Norris, see *SJ/BJ* 273–5.

12. From a letter to Suard of 25 March 1764, quoted in Joel Gold, 'Tristram Shandy at the Ambassador's Chapel', *Philological Quarterly* 48 (1969), 423.

13. Friedrich Nietzsche, *Human, All Too Human: A Book for Free Spirits*, trans. R. J. Hollingdale, intr. Erich Heller (Cambridge: Cambridge University Press, 1986), 238–9.

6

THOMAS KEYMER

A Sentimental Journey and the failure of feeling

It was *Tristram Shandy* that propelled Sterne to fame, and his reputation centres today on the virtuoso combination of erudite, transgressive wit and playfully disrupted textuality for which 'Shandean' remains our shorthand term. In the decades following his death, however, Sterne was celebrated above all for *A Sentimental Journey through France and Italy*, and in Britain, Europe, and North America, editions of this later, shorter work outnumbered reprints of *Tristram Shandy* well into the nineteenth century. Overarching trends and local contingencies combined to shape this episode in the history of taste. In the first category was an increasingly dominant culture of politeness and sensibility in which Sterne's Rabelaisian side was deplored while his focus on sympathy and benevolence gained prestige; in the second, Sterne's death just weeks after publishing *A Sentimental Journey*, which irresistibly dramatised the pathos of the work, and the damage done to *Tristram Shandy* by John Ferriar's allegations of plagiarism in the 1790s, which left the *Journey* relatively unscathed.

Cultural change and individual initiative can both be seen at work in *The Beauties of Sterne* (1782), an enterprising compilation by the young William Holland, later a fashionable publisher of satirical prints, which exploited the recent collapse of perpetual copyright by reprinting affecting extracts from the novels, 'selected', Holland's subtitle declares, 'for the heart of sensibility'. More than any other, it was this mawkish volume that fixed Sterne's reputation as the genius of the sensibility vogue. *A Sentimental Journey* sets the tone of the volume and gets disproportionate prominence in its pages, which Holland introduces by disparaging the obscenity of *Tristram Shandy* and instead celebrating the emotive power of Sterne's most delicate scenes – scenes that might even, as concentrated here, 'be too closely connected for the *feeling* reader, and ... wound the bosom of *sensibility* too deeply'.[1] *The Beauties of Sterne* was in its twelfth edition by 1793 (now minus the name of its editor, who had shifted from sentimental into radical chic, and was in prison for seditious libel[2]), and it is possible that during this period more readers came to know Sterne through Holland's highly selective filter than through direct access to the original texts, in all their multiple aspects and jostling tones.

Of course, many of the hallmarks of literary sentimentalism are already on display in *Tristram Shandy*: vignettes of felt benevolence and emotionally fragmented syntax; wordless recognitions of sympathetic mutuality and consolatory exchanges of tears; a pathology of nervous response and disorder, debilitating in the face of grief; above all, an understanding of virtue, and of personal identity and human society, that places the capacity for exquisite feeling at the very centre. Numerous passages in *Tristram Shandy* were suitable enough, with judicious editing, for repackaging by Holland, and it would be easy now to draw up and illustrate a full repertoire of sentimental conventions and routines in Sterne's works without even opening *A Sentimental Journey*. Good examples occur as early as the first instalment of *Tristram Shandy*, such as 'the lesson of universal good-will' that Toby teaches by sparing the life of a house-fly, so setting the ten-year-old Tristram's 'whole frame into one vibration of most pleasurable sensation' (*TS* 2.12.131): here one need only forget Toby's incongruous enthusiasm for battlefield slaughter, and his unyielding opposition to peace treaties, to find the perfect sentimental moment, an enraptured celebration of philanthropic ethics that is physiologically affirmed. The most telling instances of *Tristram Shandy*'s flirtation with the emerging rhetoric of sentimental fiction come in later volumes, especially the ninth, written when Sterne was already projecting *A Sentimental Journey* and anxious to prepare his readers for its style and content. Toby's tender act is deftly recalled in the 'poor negro girl ... flapping away flies—not killing them' of volume 9, and (as Donald Wehrs argues below, in ch. 12) the chapter devoted to her predicament, like other sentimental treatments of slavery in the period, enlists the language of feeling in the cause of reform: 'she had suffered persecution, Trim, and had learnt mercy' (*TS* 9.6.747). Later in volume 9 comes what in retrospect is plainly a trailer for the new work to come, a digression introducing the decorously deranged figure of Maria of Moulins, who returns near the culmination of *A Sentimental Journey*.

In this context, we can see the predominance and intensity of similar episodes in *A Sentimental Journey* as the completion of a long-running process, not an abrupt *volte face*. *Tristram Shandy* was always, in its ostentatiously disorganised structure and serialising mode of publication, an open and fluid work, able to reinvent itself as it went along, assuming new characteristics from trends emerging or developing in the culture at large. By returning at irregular intervals to the reading public, responsive to its latest enthusiasms or shifting concerns, Sterne could adjust whatever overarching plan he had for *Tristram Shandy* in light of changing tastes, and so ensure that the work continued to be 'the Fashion', as he exulted of the opening instalment (*Letters* 102). This achievement was not always easily won, however. With characteristic self-consciousness, Sterne inscribes within the 1765 instalment of *Tristram Shandy* a panicky sense of its own declining marketability – 'thou hast ten cart-loads of thy fifth and sixth volumes still—still unsold' (*TS* 8.6.663) – and a recently discovered letter of the same year displays his recognition that serial works must always confront the law of diminishing returns: 'You say truely', he tells his former publisher James Dodsley, 'that continuations of Works seldom keep up their sale'.[3] In the end, Sterne's solution to the problem, and perhaps also to his own sense of creative impasse, was no longer to persevere in recasting the emphasis of *Tristram Shandy* from its satirical-Scriblerian origins towards its sentimental-novelistic close, but instead to start afresh with a new work, albeit one explicitly connected to *Tristram Shandy*. As he told a correspondent while writing the ninth volume in 1766, 'I shall publish but one this year, and the next I shall begin a new work of four volumes, which when finish'd, I shall continue Tristram with fresh spirit' (*Letters* 284). In the event, Sterne never returned to *Tristram Shandy*, nor produced more than two volumes of *A Sentimental Journey*, though both works can be interpreted as reaching a perverse kind of conclusion.

The two stages of this process – the increasing sentimentalism of *Tristram Shandy* and Sterne's eventual decision to launch a fresh vehicle – can be traced in the new but already powerful reviewing periodicals of the day, which as early as 1762 were urging him to adapt to audience demand and play to his rhetorical strengths. Responding to volumes 5 and 6, the *Critical Review* dismissed 'his extravagant rhapsodies, his abrupt transitions, his flux of matter' as mere sub-Rabelaisian gimmickry, and singled out for praise instead the 'beautifully pathetic' Le Fever episode and the representation of Toby and Trim 'in such a point of view as must endear them to every reader of sensibility' (*CH* 139–40). Likewise, the *Monthly Review* cited the Le Fever chapters in volume 6 as evidence that Sterne's 'excellence lay not so much in the humorous as in the pathetic' (*CH* 141). At this point, the appeal to change tack is only implicit. But by 1765, after volumes 7 and 8 of *Tristram Shandy* had appeared, the influential editor of the *Monthly Review*, Ralph Griffiths, was openly advising Sterne that the public had now tired of the work, which should not be resumed. Yet Sterne had also shown himself 'a master in the science of *human feelings*, and the art of describing them', and should now 'strike out a new plan', with this as his exclusive concern:

Paint Nature in her loveliest dress—her native simplicity. Draw natural scenes, and interesting situations … excite our passions to *laudable* purposes—awake our affections, engage our hearts—arouze, transport, refine, improve us. Let morality, let the cultivation of virtue be your aim—let wit, humour, elegance and pathos be the means; and the grateful applause of mankind will be your reward.   (CH 167–8)

There could be no better summary than this of the new style of fiction that was now flowing from the press in titles such as Frances Brooke's *Lady Julia Mandeville* (1763), Henry Brooke's *The Fool of Quality* (1765–70), and Sarah Scott's *Sir George Ellison* (1766): decorous in representation and delicate in tone, arousing the feelings and enlisting the sympathies in the cause of philanthropic virtue.

When *A Sentimental Journey* at last appeared, Ralph Griffiths welcomed it as a work of just this kind, and was quick to claim the credit for reforming Sterne's muse: 'Now, Reader, did we not tell thee, in a former Review … that the highest excellence of this genuine, this legitimate son of humour, lies not in his humorous but in his pathetic vein?' (*CH* 200). But the altered mode of *A Sentimental Journey* was more than some merely pragmatic response to market forces or book-trade advice, or so it would seem from several letters sent by Sterne during the year of composition. Repeatedly, albeit sometimes in evident anticipation of disbelief, he protests the overwhelming sincerity of his sentimental turn. His first priority may have been to ensure a healthy return, and in February 1767 he exuberantly predicts that the work 'will bring me a thousand guineas (au moins)—twil be an Original—in large Quarto—the Subscription half a Guinea' (*Letters* 300). On starting to write, however, Sterne also starts (like his notably parsimonious hero in the work) to harmonise the rigour of his accountancy with the softer tones of a painfully responsive heart. In September 1767 he tells one reader, with preening self-approval: 'my Sentimental Journey will, I dare say, convince you that my feelings are from the heart, and that that heart is not of the worst of molds— praised be God for my sensibility!' (395–6). In November he informs another (in words he would closely paraphrase in the text itself) that his work in progress 'suits the frame of mind I have been in for some time past—I told you my design in it was to teach us to love the world and our fellow creatures better than we do—so it runs most upon those gentler passions and affections, which aid so much to it' (*Letters* 401; see *SJ/BJ*, 111). Later the same month he thanks an unknown peer

> for your letter of enquiry about Yorick—he has worn out both his spirits and body with the Sentimental Journey—'tis true that an author must feel himself, or his reader will not—but I have torn my whole frame into pieces by my feelings— … I have long been a sentimental being—whatever your Lordship may think to the contrary. —The world has imagined, because I wrote Tristram Shandy, that I was

myself more Shandean than I really ever was—'tis a good-natured world we live in, and we are often painted in divers colours according to the ideas each one frames in his head.—

(*Letters* 402–3)

Clearly enough, the colours that Sterne – ever committed to protean identity and the mobile self – now wished to show the world were those not of Tristram but of Yorick. Characterised by a chaste and moral sensibility, *A Sentimental Journey* would at last negate his dubious reputation as a dealer in bawdry and farce. Much the same emphasis, though with additional hints, is on show in Sterne's reported characterisation of *A Sentimental Journey* as his 'Work of Redemption' (*Letters* 399), a phrase that wittily accommodates the range of things in need of redeeming as he wrote: his sins and his Christian soul, of course, but also his scandalous reputation, and his persistent debts.

'Sentimental' is now almost invariably a pejorative usage. But by talking in these terms (of feeling as a sign of the virtuous heart, and as a tool for inculcating philanthropy), Sterne indicates the very respectable status of sensibility in eighteenth-century thought. Cultural historians often point to a tradition of 'moral sense' philosophy that looks back to the Earl of Shaftesbury early in the century, and finds its classic expression, as Sterne was writing, in products of the Scottish Enlightenment such as Adam Smith's *The Theory of Moral Sentiments* (1759). The key texts differ subtly and sometimes profoundly, and their intricacies resist conflation; but the common thread of feeling runs through them all. In Shaftesbury, a recurrent theme is the existence in human nature of a 'natural moral sense', accessible more by intuition and emotion than by pure reason, predisposed to recognise and favour virtue while recoiling from vice, and leaning towards sociability and benevolence as a matter of impulse. Personal fulfilment arises from the cultivation of this state, for '*to have the natural affections, such as are founded in ... a sympathy with the kind or species, is to have the chief means and power of self-enjoyment*'; and this happiness is nowhere more fully felt than in 'the exercises of benignity and goodness, where, together with the most delightful affection of the soul, there is joined a pleasing assent and approbation of the mind'.[4]

With Hume a generation later, the elevation of sympathy and the rootedness of virtue in feeling are carried further. 'Morality ... is more properly felt than judg'd of', Hume memorably contends, while sympathy in the largest sense becomes 'the chief source of moral distinctions'.[5] It is as though, in the absence of transcendent objective certainties, moral ideas can be accessed and guaranteed instead 'by an immediate feeling and finer internal sense'. Accompanying this emphasis on a naturally intuitive sentiment of morality is Hume's insistence that, as well as being innate (there are 'a thousand ... marks of a general benevolence in human nature'), sympathy is the most attractive and productive human virtue: 'No qualities are more intitled to the general good-will and approbation of mankind', he declares in *An Enquiry Concerning the Principles of Morals* (1751), 'than beneficence and human-ity ... or whatever proceeds from a tender sympathy with others'. In this later work there develops an increased emphasis on the delicacy of sympathetic feeling, as well as on its beneficial – indeed constitutive – role in human society. When Hume expatiates on the intertwined merits and pleasures of benevolence, moreover, we hear not only the valorisation of sensibility that would become standard in classic novels of sentiment such as Henry Mackenzie's *The Man of Feeling* (1771), but also the same rhetoric. 'The tear naturally starts in our eye on the apprehension of a warm sentiment of this nature', Hume writes: 'our breast heaves, our heart is agitated, and every humane tender principle of our frame is set in motion, and gives us the purest and most satisfactory enjoyment'.[6]

Adam Smith is more guarded, especially in later editions of *The Theory of Moral Sentiments*, but here too the capacity to enter sympathetically into the position and feelings – especially the sorrows – of others is basic to the forma-tion of moral attitudes. Smith anticipates the language of sentimental fiction as much as Hume, and in an early passage he considers the moral resonances of the kind of scenario that would arise with Sterne's Maria, in which victims of misfortune relive, yet also relieve, their distresses by communicating with a sympathetic witness: 'They take pleasure ... and, it is evident, are sensibly relieved by it; because the sweetness of his sympathy more than compensates the bitterness of that sorrow, which, in order to excite this sympathy, they had thus enlivened and renewed.' Yet there also lurks in Smith a fear that the emotional participation underlying this ideal model of sympathetic exchange might easily evaporate. A later passage represents sympathy as much less powerful and productive, and sets 'the languid emotions' of the sympathising witness in troubling contrast with the victim's choking passions. 'We may even inwardly reproach ourselves with our own want of sensibility', Smith writes, 'and perhaps, on that account, work ourselves up into an artificial sympathy, which ... is always the slightest and most transitory imaginable'. For all the moral importance and practical efficacy of sympathy, it will sometimes only work through contrivance as opposed to spontaneous impulse, 'and generally, as soon as we have left the room, vanishes, and is gone for ever'. Convinced of the importance of fellow feeling, yet fearful for its survival, Smith often sounds anxious rather than celebratory in his account of sympathy, and instead of blandly endorsing its power, he tends to regret its feeble and fugitive character. It is because of our ordinarily 'dull sensibility to the distresses of others' that he devotes so much attention to the mechanisms that might render it more active, and in this context he even allots a role to narrative fiction. In view of his misgivings about stoicism, it may sound like faint praise when he identifies three recent novelists (Richardson, Marivaux, and Riccoboni) as 'much better instructors than Zeno, Chrysippus, or Epictetus'.[7] But it is worth noting that further attention to the capacity of novels to develop 'the tender emotions' is paid in the lectures on belles lettres that Smith delivered in the 1760s, now known only from notes.[8]

The eighteenth-century attempt to stabilise notions of virtue, morality, and justice with reference to innate feeling is sometimes seen as a response to, or expression of, religious scepticism. Yet the discourse of sentiment and sympathy that finds its most sophisticated expression in Hume and Smith is also to be found in religious works, and it would misrepresent the fluidity of theological and philosophical traditions in the period to separate them too sharply. The traditions intertwine from the outset, as when Shaftesbury draws on Benjamin Whichcote (a prominent divine whose sermons Shaftesbury edited, calling him 'the Preacher of Good-Nature'), and thereafter free-thinking philosophers could find common ground with Anglican bishops in attributing an essential philanthropy to the human spirit: 'our Divines maintain against *Hobbs*', as the deist Matthew Tindal put it in 1730, that man is 'a social Creature, who naturally loves his own Species, and is full of Pity, Tenderness, and Benevolence'.[9] In numerous sermons, as well as in secular texts, we meet the central assumptions of sentimentalism: the definition of virtue in terms of 'universal benevolence', a formulation frequently used by sermon-writers to describe sympathetic fellow-feeling and the philanthropic attitude it was held to promote; the anti-Hobbesian contention that such impulses are innate, inherently the possession of a species predisposed to mutual affection and benign sociability; and the anti-stoical contention that the tender passions should be nurtured rather than repressed, and that they generate not only pleasurable self-approval but also altruism and active virtue.

Both traditions inform Sterne's own sermons, which are of particular interest for their way of moving between celebratory and sceptical accounts of sympathy. The opening (1760) volumes of *The Sermons of Mr. Yorick* repeatedly applaud the irrepressible flow of human compassion and the benign consequences of feeling – 'Ask the man who has a tear of tenderness always ready to shed over the unfortunate' (*Sermons* 5.48) – while taking care to stress the spiritual origin of benevolent impulse. The most sustained example is Sermon 3, 'Philanthropy recommended', which turns the Good Samaritan of Luke 10: 25–37 into a modern man of feeling: a figure who demonstrates 'a certain generosity and tenderness of nature which disposes us for compassion, abstracted from all considerations of self. So that without any observable act of the will, we suffer with the unfortunate, and feel a weight upon our spirits we know not why ...' (*Sermons* 3.23). Yet Sterne always stops short of finding the operation of sympathy inevitable or universal, and even at this most euphoric moment in the *Sermons* he remains troubled – note the expressive interruptive dashes – by the Hobbesian alternative:

> So that when one considers this friendly part of our nature without looking farther, one would think it impossible for man to look upon misery, without finding himself in some measure attached to the interest of him who suffers it.—I say, one would think it impossible—for there are some tempers—how shall I describe them?—formed either of such impenetrable matter, or wrought up by habitual selfishness to such an utter insensibility of what becomes of the fortunes of their fellow-creatures, as if they were not partakers of the same nature, or had no lot or connection at all with the species.   (*Sermons* 5.23)

Elsewhere, this insensibility develops from isolated aberration into an alarming vision of collective anaesthesia, and the final sermon of 1760 concludes by contemplating a grim alternative picture of shared human nature, in which 'we bear the misfortunes of others with excellent tranquility' (15.148). This mock-stoical notion spoke forcefully enough to Sterne for him to repeat it elsewhere ('we bear the Sufferings of other people with great Philosophy' (*Letters* 118)), and it may be significant that this kind of resistance to the more comfortable assumptions of sentimentalism grows in prominence in later instalments of the *Sermons*. In the volumes of 1766, published as Sterne began to contemplate *A Sentimental Journey* (though some of the contents may have been first drafted decades earlier), we find a passage attuned to Smith's anxiety that sensibility could dwindle into shallow self-indulgence, with no moral outcome at all: 'we are apt to interest ourselves no otherwise, than merely as the incidents themselves strike our passions, without carrying the lesson further:——in a word—we realize nothing:——we sigh——we wipe away the tear,—and there ends the story of misery, and the moral with it' (*Sermons* 22.207).

As well as voicing Sterne's own concerns about the complacency associated with the culture of sensibility, passages of this kind interestingly anticipate a backlash against sentimental fiction that grew in force and eloquence in the final quarter of the eighteenth century. As time wore on, the attack on sensibility developed along different lines from different political positions, including, for example, the specifically feminist critique of Mary Wollstonecraft in the 1790s, and became entangled in complex ways with debates about the French revolution. But perhaps the most telling argument against sentimental fiction, and certainly the one most relevant to Sterne, emanated from conservative, often evangelical, writers who questioned the reliability of mere feeling, as opposed to the disciplines of conscience and duty, as a source of moral action, and who saw in fictional representations of misfortune and injustice a distraction from, not a spur to, practical philanthropic effort. Some years after his retirement as a novelist, Henry Mackenzie surveyed the emerging subgenres of fiction and singled out for criticism 'that species called the *Sentimental*' as directly subverting its own most basic claim: the claim that, by engaging readers' sympathies with misfortune, it could not only represent but also activate 'the most exalted benevolence'. For Mackenzie, feeling had become an end in itself, narcissistically attentive to nothing more than its own exquisite style. Deploring the inertia of 'refined sentimentalists ... who open their minds to impression which never have any effect upon their conduct', Mackenzie attributes to sentimental fiction a dangerous 'separation of conscience from feeling', at the former's expense.[10] Even in its foremost examples, the sentimental novel cultivates nothing better than self-congratulation, and disengages the will from forms of practical action that only less modish virtues – religious principle, ethical commitment – have the power to impel.

The attack on sensibility had its lighter side, seen at its simplest in a graphic satire of 1788 by Thomas Rowlandson, entitled 'The Man of Feeling', which punctures the idea of feeling as anything better than exploitative self-gratification by placing at its centre a slavering parson who greedily feels the breast of a peasant girl. The image (which Rowlandson reinvented in later versions, alongside a scene of frenzied copulation entitled 'Sympathy') is often mentioned by historians of sensibility.[11] But it acquires particular interest here from the identity of its publisher, William Holland, who had now moved on from his strictures against the obscenity of *Tristram Shandy* in *The Beauties of Sterne* to become one of London's leading publishers of obscene prints. Sterne is not directly implicated in 'The Man of Feeling', where the laugh falls most obviously on Mackenzie. But both targets coalesce in *The Man of Failing*, an anonymous novel of 1789 that recognisably implicates Sterne,[12] and *A Sentimental Journey* was rarely far from view in the arguments levelled against the whole genre of sentimental fiction after his death.

Many of these arguments exploited the gap between Sterne's allegedly callous conduct in life and his philanthropic effusions on the page. He 'had too much sentiment to have any feeling', sneered Horace Walpole; 'a dead ass was more important to him than a living mother' (*CH* 305). Often, however, this kind of judgment was more than merely a response to scandal and rumour concerning Sterne's emotional cruelty to his female relations. For Elizabeth Carter, to whom a correspondent made the mistake of quoting *A Sentimental Journey* soon after publication, the real objection was that Sterne had proposed an innovative morality based on nothing more substantial than instinct and posture. To make 'benevolence ... a substitute for virtue', Carter caustically observed, was no less than to 'confound all differences of right and wrong. Merely to be struck by a sudden impulse of compassion at the view of an object of distress, is no more benevolence than it is a fit of the gout', she went on: 'Real benevolence would never suffer a husband and a father to neglect and injure those whom the ties of nature, the order of Providence, and the general sense of mankind have entitled to his first regards' (CH 203).

The weightiest versions of this critique emanated from reformers who, by virtue of their strenuous humanitarian campaigning against slavery and other abuses, seem well qualified to evaluate the philanthropic claims of sentimental fiction. A distinguished example is Hannah More, whose poem 'Sensibility' (drafted 1775, published 1782) is sometimes read as uncritically celebrating 'the feeling heart' and 'Sympathy Divine' as agents of practical benevolence. Even in More's original version, however, key passages are highly sceptical of sentimental ethics, lamenting the subordination of traditional notions of justice, faith, and virtue to mere feeling, and finding in the picturesque misfortunes of sentimental writing a decoy that leaves real injustice ignored, or at best acknowledges it 'cheaply with a tear'. Better one charitable act, More adds, 'Than all the periods Feeling e'er can turn, | Than all thy soothing pages, polish'd Sterne'.[13] More's later revision of this passage to read 'perverted Sterne' typifies her hardening attitude to 'the modish page' of sentimental literature, which displaces 'the sterner virtues' and solicits tears for merely fictional distresses, 'While real mis'ry unreliev'd retires'.[14]

Elsewhere, More deplores the self-indulgent torpor of sentimental readers at a time when dutiful Christians 'of less natural sympathy ... have been quietly furnishing a regular provision for miseries';[15] and in both early and late versions, the impulse of 'Sensibility' is clearly to reassert traditional piety, as opposed to the caprice of feeling, as the only reliable source of benevolent action. More is echoed in this by her fellow abolitionist William Wilberforce, who in the 1790s was trenchantly upbraiding readers of novels who make 'imaginary exertions in behalf of ideal misery, and yet shrink from the labours of active benevolence'. For Wilberforce, there was no connection at all between the chimeras of sentimental fiction and fixed philanthropic commitment: 'never was delicate sensibility proved to be more distinct from plain practical benevolence, than in the writings of the author to whom I allude', he adds in a long footnote on Sterne.[16]

One possible response to all these objections, of course, is that Yorick's failure to move from exquisite sympathy to practical action may have been exactly Sterne's point, and that he was no less aware than Mackenzie or More of the dangers of making sentiment the linchpin of a moral system. By focusing on passages such as Yorick's lament for the ass (which has a satirical pedigree in Cervantes, and eventually collapses in smutty innuendo and bathos), Sterne's most strenuous early critics make what now seems the basic methodological error of assuming that whatever a narrator says is authorially endorsed, and of failing to recognise Sterne's periodic adoption of the Yorick persona – or personae, for Yorick's identity is differently constructed in *Tristram Shandy*, and again in the *Sermons* – for the ludic performance it was. Could it be that in finding the hero of *A Sentimental Journey* shallow and self-regarding, always superficially touched by distress but never practically moved by it, Sterne's critics were merely drawing out implications that he had knowingly embedded in his text, with ironies at Yorick's expense?

That this interpretative option is worth pursuing is suggested not only by Sterne's reservations in particular sermons about the power and efficacy of sympathy, but also by surviving letters of 1767, which, though written just days apart from the straightforwardly sentimental letters quoted earlier in this chapter, continue to speak in tones more Shandean than sentimental. Nowhere does Sterne classify *A Sentimental Journey* as simply a satire, a category he had earlier invoked to call the tour through France in volume 7 of *Tristram Shandy* 'a laughing good temperd Satyr against Traveling' (*Letters* 231). But he does suggest that tears and feeling are not the only available response, nor even necessarily his own: *A Sentimental Journey*, he tells the otherwise unidentified Hannah, 'shall make you cry as much as ever it made me laugh—or I'll give up the Business of sentimental writing—& write to the Body' (*Letters* 401). Here sensibility sounds more like a rhetorical challenge than anything else: a set of procedures carefully fashioned to elicit from readers an affective response, and an activity or occupation to which Sterne's commitment is by no means permanent. Moreover, this particular example can be consumed in different ways by different categories of reader, much as *Tristram Shandy*, to quote perhaps Sterne's most famous letter of this period, had offered '*more handles than one*', including a handle of sensibility, for readers to seize as dictated by their individual tastes (*Letters* 411). A similar idea is in play when Sterne describes the *Journey* to his publisher Thomas Becket as a work 'likely to take in all Kinds of Readers' (*Letters* 393). It will take in all, not necessarily in the sense of perpetrating a hoax on all (though this meaning was current at the time), but in the sense of catering or providing for all in an open or ambiguous text – an exploratory, delicately balanced work that could be read as celebrating the refinement of sensibility or as mocking its shortcomings and excesses.

Perhaps the best reading of *A Sentimental Journey* is one that keeps its grasp on both these interpretative handles, for on close inspection the novel fails, or refuses, to sustain any clear distinction between sentimental sincerity and Shandean satire. At one level, the painstaking account that Yorick gives of the flux of feeling is a heartfelt (as well as technically groundbreaking) attempt to register on the page the complexities of inward experience, including the impulses of sympathy and benevolence, and written in the face, Sterne clearly intimates, of impending death. Yet Yorick's effusions of sentiment border too often on sickly concupiscence; his words and deeds are too often undermined by ironic innuendo; he is too self-absorbed, too fickle in his attentions, too much enraptured by the aesthetics of distress not to seem, at times, an object of implicit mockery. As John Mullan has shown, part of the interest of *The Beauties of Sterne* lies in the sheer difficulty its editor has in resolving even Sterne's most celebrated sentimental set pieces, with their characteristic accompanying nuances and hints, to a category of uncomplicated sensibility.[17] Again and again, Holland finds himself having to crop aggressively in order to keep unwelcome ironies at bay, a revealing case being the first of the two famous vignettes concerning Maria of Moulins. At one level, Tristram's response to Maria's becoming woe is a classic instance of tender fellow feeling, an experience so intense that it leaves him barely able to walk; at another, it ironically identifies his sentimental voyeurism – which makes Maria look pointedly 'at her goat——and then at me——and then at her goat again' (*TS* 9.24.783) – as lecherously exploitative, almost in the style of Rowlandson's groping parson. Most disruptive of all is the insouciant final line of the episode, in which, with the words 'What an excellent inn at Moulins!' (9.24.784), Tristram passes abruptly from Maria's plight to other pleasures, his daily fix of feeling now obtained. For the *Monthly Review*, this was 'an ill-tim'd stroke of levity; like a ludicrous epilogue ... unnaturally tagged to the end of a deep tragedy, only, as it were, to efface every elevated, generous or tender sentiment' (*CH* 182). In *The Beauties of Sterne*, Holland feels compelled to delete the closing exclamation.

A Sentimental Journey builds towards an extended reprise of the Maria episode, but far from paring back disruptive elements of this kind, Sterne only intensifies them, deftly contriving the survival of the very qualities – the Shandean qualities of bawdry and satire – that reviewers had urged him to abandon as he turned to pathos. Here sentiment and satire coexist and compete in shifting proportions, allowing readers to read the text according to either rubric. But as Yorick's distinctive vein of sympathy develops its track record (withholding cash from beggars and urchins while pruriently feeling shopgirls' pulses and pleasurably inserting his crown into chambermaids' purses[18]), it becomes increasingly hard to view his sensibility in terms of selfless philanthropic engagement, as opposed to self-gratification. There is no better illustration than the second Maria episode, shot through as it is with subversive hints that render ludicrous the object of Yorick's sympathy while implicitly mocking his response as drooling affectation. In the culmination of the passage, a suggestively eroticised exchange of bodily fluids gives way to a conclusion in which sentimental sympathy dwindles, to the exclusion of its object, into smug or even callous egotism. Steeping his handkerchief in his own tears, 'and then in hers—and then in mine—and then I wip'd hers again—and as I did it, I felt such undescribable emotions within me', Yorick ecstatically combines the sentimental pleasures of casual sympathy and smug self-approval: 'I am positive I have a soul; nor can all the books with which materialists have pester'd the world ever convince me of the contrary' (*SJ/BJ* 151). At the close of the scene, just as what really matters to Tristram is his dinner in Moulins, Maria becomes no more than the means to an end for Yorick, left high and dry on the bank of her river while he achieves euphoric self-validation. For at least one of Sterne's early readers, the deepest irony lurking in the text at such moments is that Yorick is absolutely wrong about himself: even as he looks to his effusive feelings as proof of his immortal soul, they demonstrate him to be just what materialist philosophers would argue, 'a mere Machine wrought upon by internal and External Application'.[19]

No less damaging to the standard claims of sentimentalism is another of Yorick's most celebrated exercises in sentimental objectification, in the chapter headed 'The Captive'. As scholars have long known, this passage is, like the episode of the 'poor negro girl' in *Tristram Shandy*, Sterne's response to an appeal made to him by Ignatius Sancho, a former slave now living in freedom in London, to write about Caribbean slavery.[20] 'Think in me', Sancho had written, 'you behold the uplifted hands of Millions of my moorish brethren—Grief (you pathetically observe) is eloquent—figure to yourselves their attitudes—hear their supplicatory address—humanity must comply' (*Letters* 283). Although the connection with Sancho's appeal is often made, however, scholars rarely note the strangely indirect nature of Sterne's response – a response quite unlike, for example, the otherwise similar case of *Candide* (1759), in which Voltaire was prompted to insert a harrowing last-minute chapter about slavery in modern Surinam: 'This is what we suffer for your eating sugar in Europe', as an early translator rendered Voltaire's slave's complaint.[21] Even in *Tristram Shandy*, the story of the African girl is interrupted and postponed until 'some dismal winter's evening, when your honour is in the humour' (*TS* 9.6.747), and in *A Sentimental Journey*, far from directly representing Caribbean slavery or urging philanthropic action, Yorick soon abandons the effort as unsuitable to his purpose, and as personally unpleasing. In both cases, Sterne's point is not that his characters talk about slavery, but rather that – one might draw a line here to Austen's ironies in *Mansfield Park* – as soon as they start, they stop.

As the passage develops, the result is conspicuously at odds with any sentimental assumption that novels might work to stimulate an engaged and active philanthropy. Rather than have his sentimental tourist really worry about Sancho's 'moorish brethren', or try to involve readers with their plight, Sterne subtly identifies the subject as beyond Yorick's sympathetic reach. It is only the threat of personal imprisonment that makes Yorick even remember 'the miseries of confinement', and the exercise rapidly collapses in picturesque abstraction:

> I was going to begin with the millions of my fellow creatures born to no inheritance but slavery; but finding, however affecting the picture was, that I could not bring it near me, and that the multitude of sad groups in it did but distract me—
>
> —I took a single captive, and having first shut him up in his dungeon, I then look'd through the twilight of his grated door to take his picture.   (SJ/BJ 97)

Negligent of slavery as a real-world problem requiring philanthropic action, Yorick approaches the imaginary 'portrait' on which he then embarks with a connoisseurly relish that displays nothing so much as the inadequacy, evasiveness, and self-indulgence of sentimental response. Unable to imagine Sancho's brethren as his own, and unconcerned with the human cost of his readers' taste for sugar, he weeps only for a victim who resembles himself, and whose predicament implicates only the convenient bugbear of foreign absolutism.

Of course, the seriousness with which this episode was later rendered on the canvas by artists of the stature of Joseph Wright of Derby (who illustrated 'The Captive' more than once, and produced the haunting related painting on the cover of this volume) bears witness to its availability for purely sentimental consumption. The images displayed as a result on the walls of the Royal Academy and countless print shops, however, were not at all what Sancho had in mind, and even as representations of an individual captive, they screened out all Sterne's hints that his narrator's vision was little more than an exercise in precautionary self-pity. As with the Maria episode, the devil is in the detail of Sterne's prose at this point, and on close scrutiny far too much is in excess of, or directly at odds with, sentimental reading for such a reading to seem wholly secure. Sterne was offering his audience a text in which sentimental tastes were at one level amply catered for, but at another level mocked as shallow and self-deluding, and subjected to implicit critique. From this perspective, if *A Sentimental Journey* is indeed a novel with a lesson, the lesson may be an unsettling one: that we bear the misfortunes of others with excellent tranquillity.

NOTES

1. *The Beauties of Sterne*, ed. William Holland, 5th edn (1782), vi. Holland's editorship of this much discussed volume has not previously been noted, but he signs his dedication in this edition. For the 1774 copyright case of *Donaldson versus Becket* (Sterne's publisher, though this dispute concerned the poet Thomson), and the flood of anthologies that followed, see William St Clair, *The Reading Nation in the Romantic Period* (Cambridge: Cambridge University Press, 2004), 107–21, 539–47.

2. On Holland's scandalous career and his year-long imprisonment of 1793, see Vic Gatrell, *City of Laughter: Sex and Satire in Eighteenth-Century London* (London: Atlantic, 2006), 493–4, 601; Holland was convicted of selling Tom Paine's *Letter Addressed to the Addressers*, though the underlying prosecution motive seems to have been that he 'carried on a business full as pernicious as that of disseminating seditious publications – namely the publishing and exposing to sale prints of the most indecent kind'.

3. Melvyn New, 'A New Sterne Letter and an Old Mystery Closer to Solution', *Shandean* 17 (2006), 82.

4. Anthony Ashley Cooper, Third Earl of Shaftesbury, *Characteristics*, ed. Laurence E. Klein (Cambridge: Cambridge University Press, 1999), 180, 200, 203.

5. David Hume, *A Treatise of Human Nature*, ed. L. A. Selby-Bigge, rev. P. H. Nidditch (Oxford: Clarendon Press, 1978), 470, 618.

6. David Hume, *Enquiries Concerning Human Understanding and Concerning the Principles of Morals*, ed. L. A. Selby-Bigge, rev. P. H. Nidditch (Oxford: Clarendon Press, 1975), 170, 300, 178, 257.

7. Adam Smith, *The Theory of Moral Sentiments*, eds. D. D. Raphael and A. L. Mcfie (Oxford: Oxford University Press, 1983), 15, 47, 143.

8. Adam Smith, *Lectures on Rhetoric and Belles Lettres*, ed. J. C. Bryce (Oxford: Oxford University Press, 1983), 111.

9. Shaftesbury's preface to Benjamin Whichcote, *Select Sermons* (1698), A8, quoted by Isabel Rivers, *Reason, Grace, and Sentiment: A Study of the Language of Religion and Ethics in England, 1660–1780*, 2 vols. (Cambridge: Cambridge University Press, 1991–2000), I, 77; Matthew Tindal, *Christianity as Old as the Creation*, 8° edn (1730), 48.

10. Henry Mackenzie, *Lounger* 20 (18 June 1785), in *Novel and Romance, 1700–1800: A Documentary Record*, ed. Ioan Williams (London: Routledge, 1970), 329–30.

11. Gatrell reproduces the first version of 'The Man of Feeling' alongside 'Sympathy' (*City of Laughter*, 445–6); for the 1811 version, in which the man of feeling becomes a salivating academic, see Thomas Keymer, 'Sentimental Fiction: Ethics, Social Critique, and Philanthropy', in *The Cambridge History of English Literature, 1660–1780*, ed. John Richetti (Cambridge: Cambridge University Press, 2005), 600.

12. See Peter Garside, James Raven, *et al.*, *The English Novel 1770–1829: A Bibliographical Survey*, 2 vols. (Oxford: Oxford University Press, 2000), I, 461.

13. Hannah More, 'Sensibility', in *'Sacred Dramas'* (1782), 276, 281, 284, 285.

14. Hannah More, 'Sensibility', in *'Poems'* (1816), intro. Caroline Franklin (London: Routledge, 1996), 182, 179, 180.

15. Hannah More, *Strictures on Female Education*, 2 vols. (1799), II, 111.
16. William Wilberforce, *A Practical View of the Prevailing Religious System of Professed Christians* (1797), 283, 284n.
17. See John Mullan, *Sentiment and Sociability: The Language of Feeling in the Eighteenth Century* (Oxford: Clarendon Press, 1988), 155.
18. 'I never gave a girl a crown in my life which gave me half the pleasure' (*SJ/BJ* 88). The Florida editors gloss this passage nicely, with reference to the earlier edition by Gardner Stout. 'Nothing suggests Stout's chaste editorial mind better than his question at this point: "Is there, perhaps, a sexual innuendo here based on the meaning of 'purse'?"' (*SJ/BJ* 321).
19. Paul Franssen, '"Great Lessons of Political Instruction": The Earl of Clonmell Reads Sterne', *Shandean* 2 (1990), 165. For Sterne's complicated response to the 'thinking matter' debate and La Mettrie's *L'Homme machine*, see Thomas Keymer, 'Materialism, Mechanism, and the Novel', in *Literary Milieux: Essays in Text and Context Presented to Howard Erskine-Hill*, eds. David Womersley and Richard McCabe (Newark, NJ: University of Delaware Press, 2008), 307–33.
20. The best account is by Markman Ellis, *The Politics of Sensibility: Race, Gender, and Commerce in the Sentimental Novel* (Cambridge: Cambridge University Press, 1996), 49–86; see also, for Sancho's perspective, Brycchan Carey, *British Abolitionism and the Rhetoric of Sensibility* (Basingstoke: Palgrave Macmillan, 2005), 57–63.
21. *Candid; or, All for the Best* (1759), 75; for the origin of ch. 19 in Voltaire's reading of Helvétius after completing his manuscript, see *Candide and Related Texts*, trans. and ed. David Wootton (Indianapolis, IN: Hackett, 2000), 43n.

7

CAROL WATTS

Sterne's 'politicks', Ireland, and evil speaking

In a collection donated to Cambridge University Library by Henry Bradshaw, a nineteenth-century scholar-librarian with interests in eighteenth-century Ireland, there is a scrapbook he called his 'Sterne volume'.[1] Sterne's most recent biographer, Ian Campbell Ross, notes the existence of this volume – a compilation of 132 texts of political and satirical material, most printed, some written by hand, dating from the 1720s and 1730s – as possible evidence of Sterne's continuing interest in Ireland.[2] Its survival is intriguing to anyone interested in Shandean whodunits, since it holds out the seductive fantasy of working out what Sterne's identification with the country of his birth might have been. While his Irish provenance was unknown to many of his contemporaries, it was occasionally acknowledged. Accused of ridiculing Irish friends, Sterne had remonstrated: 'Besides, I am myself of their own country:—My father was a considerable time on duty with his regiment in Ireland; and my mother gave me to the world when she was there, on duty with him.'[3] In what ways Sterne's imputed mockery of Irishness may have been already predicated on a condition of *self*-mockery is something to consider.

A formative period of Sterne's life was spent in barracks in Ireland, intermittently 'home' in the peripatetic wandering of an army family posted to counter the Jacobite threat; this included a year in Westmeath with his wealthy 'kind-relation' Brigadier-General Robert Stearne, whose experiences at Namur found their way into *Tristram Shandy*.[4] His mother's family hailed from Clonmel, in County Tipperary. Sterne's relation to these beginnings (he was sent to school and austerity with his uncles in Yorkshire at the age of ten, never to return) remains a matter for speculation. While his place in a tradition of Irish humour and fictional experiment including Flann O'Brien, Beckett, and Joyce (who claimed him as a 'fellow country-man'[5]) is undoubtedly assured, it is harder to weigh the nature of the exilic energies that positioned him 'askew in metropolitan society', as Terry Eagleton puts it.[6]

If Sterne was one of several 'good-natured Gaels' (the term, again, is Eagleton's) who generated the very terms of English sociable culture at the mid eighteenth century, he nonetheless playfully fashioned his assault on metropolitan imperial gravity from 'four *English* miles diameter' of a Yorkshire parish (*TS* 1.7.10). In this light, his location of *Tristram Shandy* in the English peripheries suggests a displacement of – or solidarity with – a more extreme state of colonial isolation from the centres of prestige and power. Yet Sterne's was at once a celebrity conferred by the metropolis, that 'nerve center – and blind spot – of a patched-together empire', as Katie Trumpener describes it;[7] this was a 'patching' that had shaped his barracks childhood in devastating ways, and would later make *Tristram Shandy*, at the height of an imperial war, 'the book of the hour' (*Letters* 103). For Eagleton, Sterne's work traverses two options open to the eighteenth-century Irish expatriate, marked by the contradictions of exclusion and assimilation: satire and sentimentalism. Where Swift's status as an outsider produces in his satire a 'pathological drive to deface', and contrastingly Steele and Goldsmith employ sentiment to ease their way to recognition within the cultural mainstream, Sterne's writing ambivalently blends both modes, swimming with, yet always more idiosyncratically extreme than, the metropolitan tide.[8] This unsettling – Shandean – movement, with its relation to the speculative place of Ireland in Sterne's wider 'politicks',[9] is the object of the present chapter.

'This was made by a Footman'

One scrap of writing among Henry Bradshaw's Irish ephemera explains why he saw the scrapbook as his own 'Sterne' volume. J. C. T. Oates, a later Cambridge librarian and author of *Shandyism and Sentiment* (1968), docketed this item as follows in 1965: 'the annotation to no. 52 is thought to be by Laurence Sterne [and most certainly is by him]'. No. 52 is a handwritten satirical ballad, anonymous and undated. This 'Ballispellan balad' relates the plight of the servants and poor at the fashionable Ballyspellan spa, near Kilkenny, where the wealthy go to take the waters:

> Let every one say what they will
> I mean of Ballispellan
> It is a barren hungry hill
> Or I am a ruge [rogue] or a villain
> Their morning slops
> And evening hops
> Are not worth while to tell on
> While we y^t serve
> Are like to starve
> At this fam'd Ballispellan

While the rich can benefit from the medicinal properties of the Ballyspellan waters, the ballad suggests, the condition of the poor there is abject:

> We pick our Bones
> As bear as stones
> Which I'm asham'd to tell on
> And lye like hogs
> Among the dogs
> At this damn'd Ballispellan

The complainant imagines 'old Kate' blocking the water supply at the end of the season, a direct action that might prompt those arriving to take lodgings at the spa to make 'new laws'. Near the foot of the poem is a short comment in another hand (Sterne's), which notes of the text: 'This was made by a Footman.'

Assessing the meaning of this ballad, and of Sterne's annotation, is an interesting exercise. The language of the poem picks up on familiar representations of the Irish poor, articulated in such texts as Swift's *Short View of the State of Ireland* (1727–8), in which tenants live 'in Filth and Nastiness... without a Shoe or Stocking to their Feet; or a House so convenient as an *English* Hog-sty, to receive them'.[10] The late 1720s were marked in Ireland by a 'three terrible years' dearth of corn', as Swift wrote to Pope in 1729, and the miseries of this time, when Ireland was 'strewed with beggars', were polemically observed by Swift and Thomas Sheridan, among others.[11] The acute sense of scarcity emerging in the ballad – those in servitude picking their bones clean, an image that also suggests being worked to the bone, and perhaps even hints of the rhetoric of cannibalism associated with the Irish poor during times of famine[12] – may well have related to this moment, from which other items in the scrapbook certainly date, at a time when Sterne himself was in Yorkshire, en route to Cambridge.

In literary terms, the connection with Swift and his associates is clear. In 1728, Sheridan had written a poem on the subject of 'Ballyspellin', playing with the number of rhymes he could find for the word. His poem celebrates the cures to be had at the baths, and also evokes the sexual intrigues often associated with spa towns in literature of the period:

> Good Chear, sweet Air, much Joy, no Care,
> Your Sight, your Taste, your Smelling,
> Your Ears, your Touch, transporteth much
> Each Day at *Ballyspellin*.
>
> Within this Ground we all sleep sound,
> No noisy Dogs a yelling;

> Except you wake, for *Caelia's* Sake,
> All Night at *Ballyspellin*.[13]

Sheridan's poem had been countered by Swift, who outdid him with more rhymes, 'employed ... in abusing his ballad, and Ballyspelling too', much to Sheridan's reported irritation.[14] In this 'Answer', Swift takes a more pungent satirical line:

> Now, as I live,
> I would not give
> A Stiver or a Skellin
> To towse and kiss
> The finest Miss
> That leaks at Ballyspellin.
> Who'er will raise
> Such Lyes as these
> Deserves a good Cud-gelling
> Who falsely boasts
> Of Belles and Toasts
> At dirty Ballyspellin

Just as the forcing of rhymes appears not to ring true, suggests Swift's 'Answer', so the celebration of the Ballyspellan cure amounts to 'senseless praise', to 'dull Intregues | 'Twixt Jades and Teagues'.[15] There is nothing recuperable about Ballyspellan in Swift's version, which imagines a parade of human lousiness that no amount of literary ornament can elevate.

Sterne's annotation of the manuscript 'Ballispellan balad' – 'This was made by a Footman' – is a statement that can be read as the most literal and yet rhetorical of gestures. It may be a simple statement of truth. It may also be a way of giving a servant his due, though there is a potential doubleness here, like that dramatised in *A Sentimental Journey* when Yorick negotiates his relationship to La Fleur. There, Yorick's underlining of the second-hand nature of his servant's clothes allows him to bask in his generosity to a subordinate, while confirming his difference from him, thus allaying anxieties about potential mistaken identity between master and servant. There is some reason to think about the figure of the footman particularly in these terms, as one focus of a widespread concern about social misprisions and corresponding kinds of status uncertainty. Swift himself had ridiculed such uncertainties in his *Humble Petition of the Footmen in and about the City of Dublin* (1732), which, ventriloquising the collective voice of 'true genuine *Irish Footmen*', complains indignantly about counterfeits who pass for the real thing, hoping to 'procure Favour' with ladies:

They can be proved to be no better than common *Toupees*; as a judicious Eye may soon discover, by their *awkward, clumsy, ungenteel* Gait, and Behaviour; by their Unskilfulness in Dress, even with the Advantage of wearing our Habits; by their ill-favoured Countenances; with an Air of *Impudence* and *Dullness* peculiar to the rest of their Brethren: Who have not yet arrived at that transcendent Pitch of Assurance.[16]

Swift's ironies work in a number of directions here, at once displacing and invoking the fear that 'counterfeits' may pass for their betters, while also satirising the *'strutting, staring, swearing and swaggering'*[17] that signal social aspiration among the servant classes.

My point here is not the literal one that Sterne aimed to avoid confusion with the author of the crude stanzas of the 'Ballispellan balad', which are clearly other than his own. But rather that, in such a gesture ('This was made by a Footman'), there is a potential moment of disavowal provoked by the matter of Ireland and servitude, which can also be traced elsewhere in his work, sometimes as a tang of discomfort, occasionally as denial, even anger. If Sterne later moved in fashionable circles of the kind whose members frequented watering holes like Ballyspellan, he may also have felt positioned less securely. There is a continuity of disturbance in his writing about status, about the cost and potential counterfeiture of achieving what Swift ironises as 'that transcendent Pitch of Assurance', which may explain his later intense investment in literary fame.

In the pages that follow, disturbances of this kind are tracked through the 'politicks' of Sterne's journalism in the 1740s to the legacy they leave in his later writing. If Sterne's satirical method had been honed in local cockfights in the York press, another form of political language emerges in reaction to such anxieties of status in the climate of the 1760s. My account is coloured in part by questions that now form discussions of 'hate speech', asking what it means to identify with, and disavow, forms of social repudiation of which one may feel oneself to be a secret object. Does the connection with Ireland feed that ambivalent quality in Sterne's writing, in which the blend of satire and sentiment remains, in a serious and productive sense, undecidable? If so, in what ways is it generative of one horizon of the political in mid-century culture, where new kinds of equality might begin to be glimpsed?

Dependency and local 'politicks'

A familiar account of Laurence Sterne's life as a writer would regard his transition from local satire to the sudden celebrity of the first volumes of *Tristram Shandy* in 1759, at the age of forty-six, as something of a relief. No longer would he be dogged by familial and financial dependency, expected to work as a hack in the pages of York newspapers on behalf of his powerful uncle Jaques, Archdeacon of York, on whom his preferments relied. Caught in his early career in the intricacies of Minster manoeuvrings, or exposed in the raw cut and thrust of political infighting, Sterne had little choice but to accept what he later called the 'dirty work' of promoting his uncle's party line (*Letters* 4). Reading accounts of his entanglements up to and including *A Political Romance*, in which his polemical and satirical forays had an unerring tendency to backfire, it is difficult to avoid the truth (as the narrator of *Tristram Shandy* wryly concludes, playing on 'composition' in the now redundant sense of composing or resolving differences) 'that the life of a writer ... was not so much a state of *composition*, as a state of *warfare*' (*TS* 5.16.447). In 1759, Sterne's uncle died. The moment of his 'turning author' was a declaration of a form of independence: 'truly I am tired of employing my brains for other people's advantage' (*Letters* 84).

Sterne's inheritance among the various notables of his family, who numbered landowners in Yorkshire and Ireland as well as assorted bishops and soldiers, was a sometimes painful sense of dependency, an emotional and financial debt. The insecurity of his early years as he passed from military camp to camp – his father, a lowly ensign who never found promotion, was seen to have married beneath his status, and squandered the financial means he had – was more than material. There were mortal costs: in siblings who never survived, and in his father's death in Jamaica in 1731, by which time Sterne was already a dependent of wealthy relatives in Yorkshire. His Cambridge education was enabled through the generosity of a cousin, and at Jesus College (where his great-grandfather had once been Master, and established scholarships for poorer boys, from which he would benefit), he was first enrolled as a sizar, which 'confirmed his inferior status, for Cambridge sizars earned extra money by such humble tasks as waiting at table, while taking their own meals in the buttery to avoid the excessive costs of eating in hall'.[18] There was a fine line between security and servitude, and maintenance of the former might seem in certain circumstances to imply the latter. Debt, understood in the broadest terms, could make one cross that line definitively, as we can see in a large number of sentimental narratives from the mid century. If one of the plot scenarios associated with this social drama was a vigorous upward mobility (the way in which Richardson's Pamela might find her virtue rewarded, or footmen, like Sterne's renowned publisher Robert Dodsley, could in reality establish a life in genteel society), the reverse was the degradation of losing a foothold, or finding oneself 'driven out naked into the World', as Sterne described the hazards of his own youth, forced to 'shift' to survive (*Letters* 34).

Sterne's entry into the world of the Church thrust him into one of the most political arenas in public life. The way in which local patronage and party allegiances informed the distribution and number of 'livings' (parishes or other benefices awarded to a clergyman) was well known. As popular poetry from the period suggests, the figure of the vicar as a pluralist (a holder of multiple livings) was not always trusted, engaged as he was for personal financial gain and the interests of others; the character of Yorick in *Tristram Shandy*, who dies after being repeatedly beaten down by ecclesiastical blows, is a symbolic rendition of the other side of the story. On his uncle's behalf, Sterne turned journalist, defending Walpole's Whig ministry in its dying throes, seeing off local Tory interests, and also developing that breed of *ad hominem* invective and public lampoon that went by the name of political debate in the newspapers. If it is difficult to tell how far Sterne's views tallied with his uncle's (at times they appear very close), what is interesting is the nature of the 'opportunistic currency' of his journalism, as Pat Rogers describes it,[19] and the way it seemed to rebound on him.

Sterne's involvement in the York elections of 1741 and 1742 was first detailed by Lewis Perry Curtis in *The Politicks of Laurence Sterne*, an account later augmented by Kenneth Monkman (though Monkman's attribution to Sterne of further journalism from the mid 1740s has been disputed).[20] The drama is animated in Ross's biography, which charts the vagaries of point and counterpoint in the *York Courant* and *York Gazetteer*, and the changing fortunes of political camps with the final demise of the Walpole ministry in 1742. A moment of disturbance arises in the periphery of Sterne's activities in 1741, involving a successful campaign against the Tory candidate, George Fox. Fox was a wealthy man from an Anglo-Irish family, and a former Wiltshire member of parliament, his wife a Yorkshire heiress; though born and raised in England, he had extensive estates in Ireland, which some believed would divide his loyalty to local commercial interests at a time when the Yorkshire woollen industry was being undercut by Irish wool smuggled to France. This was a point made by Sterne in the *Courant*, and in order to prosecute it against an 'Irishman' who was thereby deemed a foreigner, he entered into an anonymous exchange with Fox's own polemicist, one 'J.S.'

Both Curtis and Ross follow the progress of this exchange, with the ripples that spread from it in York and London. Sterne's attempt to 'out' his anonymous adversary was curiously based on a misnaming, for both Jaques and his nephew mistakenly thought they had 'J.S.' in their sights as one James Scott, a vicar of Leeds. Sterne's political odium reached Swiftian extremes, and in the *Courant* for 10 November 1741, he compared 'J.S.' to a 'certain nasty Animal in Egypt' who 'covers his Retreat with the Fumes of his own

Filth and Excrement'. These imputations brought Scott out into the open in indignation. Sterne was now himself uncomfortably exposed in a falsehood, and blundered on, questioning in print the probity of the printer of the *Courant*, Caesar Ward. The affair finally blew itself out. In the following year, Fox was returned as M.P. for York on the death of the incumbent, and Sterne, extraordinarily, made a public apology to Ward in the *Courant* for 27 July 1742. Opening with the words 'I find by some late Preferments, that it may not be improper to change Sides', he signed himself 'your Penitent Friend and Servant'.

This curious gesture confirmed one local view of Sterne as someone who would see which way the wind blew in his own self-interest, and its candour about the *volte-face* implied by changing circumstances is disarming. According to Monkman, Sterne wrote a further letter to the *York Gazetteer*, published on 2 November 1742, which may illuminate his self-disclosure further. His subject was the nature of political language itself, prompted by the fact of 'Party-Writers of late Years having been so notoriously Scurrilous and Abusive, so aud[a]ciously intemperate in Personal Reproaches and Invectives, not only beyond the Rules of Decency but *Morality*'. As he considered:

> If there be Morality in Writing, as there Certainly is, as well as in any other Art, how different is this manner of Writing from it? The Great Law of Morality is, to treat Others, as They wou'd have Others treat them; and which of them wou'd like to be treated with the same Freedom in his Person and Character, as They in their Writing treat Others ...?

Sterne's disgust at his own part in such 'dirty work' may have caused him to retreat, as is generally assumed. But what is fascinating is the particular confessional structure of this reflection, and the discomfort that accompanies it, which might reveal the disgust in another light. Even jokes involve debt, writes the narrator of *Tristram Shandy*, pursuing the comparison between a jester and mortgager: 'one raises a sum and one a laugh at your expence', but payment of interest 'still runs on in both cases ... till, at length, in some evil hour,----pop comes the creditor upon each, and by demanding principal upon the spot, together with full interest to the very day, makes them both feel the full extent of their obligations' (*TS* 1.12.30). Sterne evidently felt the need to make amends for his scurrilous raising of 'expence', which had begun as a game of anonymous penmanship and had quickly become a question of reputation. What seemed uncomfortable was the personal exposure, the rebounding of invective on himself, despite his efforts. It is interesting that the true object of his journalistic repudiation, the 'Irishman' George Fox, is displaced from this scene; how far such problems of identification and naming were part of Sterne's discomfiture is intriguing to consider. Writing a letter to the *Courant*, a paper aligned with his opponents, may have felt like a means to wipe the slate clean, and a wise one (it was, after all, Caesar Ward's widow, Ann, who would print the first volumes of *Tristram Shandy* in 1759). Yet Sterne seems to have experienced in these two years the sting of employing a political discourse whose very volatility could return its injury in kind, discovering that lives and livings, including his own, could be put in 'jeopardy by words' (*TS* 2.2.101). This realisation continues to inform his writing long after the dust had settled on the elections of 1741–2.

The consequences of evil-speaking

In his Preface to *A Tale of a Tub*, Swift discusses the impotence of a general satire in which the target is not specifically honed: "'Tis but a *Ball* bandied to and fro, and every Man carries a *Racket* about Him to strike it from himself among the rest of the Company.'[21] As Ian Higgins argues, Swift's mockery of ineffective broad-brush satire always contains a kernel of personalised invective that generates its own energies, along with a subtle sense of the strategies needed to avoid payback, whether literary or legal in kind.[22] As Swift himself explains, 'in describing the Virtues and Vices of Mankind, it is convenient, upon every Article, to have some eminent Person in our Eye, from whence we copy our Description'.[23] The transition from the rhetoric of political writing to the world of the novel was, in Sterne's case, accompanied by a declaration to his publisher that his satire was to become more 'general' (*Letters* 81), though the early volumes of *Tristram Shandy* were trailed by rumours of the likely targets of his wit. His allegory of local ecclesiastical manoeuvrings, *A Political Romance* (which took Swift's *Tale* as its form) had earlier that year been burned at the insistence of Church authorities, which Sterne appeared to take in his stride, and an incendiary reputation may indeed have given his subsequent project a boost. If such a rhetoric had its tactics and rules, however, there were other kinds of obligation generated by injurious language that proved more difficult to control; other kinds of '*Racket*', in the acoustic sense of Swift's word, which reverberated long after memory of the event had died down.

'It is not things themselves, but opinions concerning things, which disturb men', announces the epigraph from Epictetus on the original title page of *Tristram Shandy*. The 'disturbance' of 1741–2 produced an attempt to think about the nature of a political writing that would – in the absence of a Christian morality in which you do as you would be done by – at least set out the ground rules for partisanship. Sterne's letter to the *Gazetteer* describes the nature of party-political allegiance in terms still familiar in politics today: the logic of backing your candidate though you may believe him to be wrong, and of attacking your opposite number, however persuaded you may be of his case. It is as if Sterne is attempting to minimise the fallout – moral and political – of his own now visible expediencies, forced as he is to live in contradiction with himself. Quite what might be the nature of the disturbance here is suggested by a text that considers such a condition of self-inconsistency: Sterne's rewriting of Tillotson's sermon of 1694, 'Of Evil-speaking', first published in 1760 in the opening volumes of *The Sermons of Mr. Yorick*.

Sterne's version of Tillotson adapts the original as was common among eighteenth-century sermonisers. Tillotson's lesson was taken from Paul's letter to Titus, in which, after underlining the teaching of obedience ('Put them in mind to be subject to principalities and powers, to obey magistrates, to be ready to every good work'), Paul expresses a prohibition: 'To speak evil of no man' (Titus 3:1–2). Tillotson is concerned here to test the extent of this prohibition, and he outlines a series of forms of slander that have 'almost become the general entertainment of all Companies ... the *Sawce* of Conversation'. Satire is one such diversion. 'The Wit of Man doth more naturally vent it self in *Satyr* and Censure, than in Praise and *Panegyrick*', he declares:

> in the way of *Invective*, the Invention of Man is a plentiful and never failing Spring: And this kind of Wit is not more easy than it is acceptable: It is greedily entertain'd and greatly applauded, and every Man is glad to hear others abused, not considering how soon it may come to his own turn to lie down and make sport for others.[24]

Such slander, he suggests, is at its most vicious among '*Zealots* of all *Parties*' who 'have got a *scurvy Trick* of lying for the Truth'; among those of religious differences (Tillotson has the standard adversary, Catholicism, in his sights) it can take on a 'Salvage and murderous disposition', and 'they will flie at one anothers Reputation, and tear it in pieces'. As for those who are the blameless objects of such slander, 'it is an Injury beyond Imagination, and beyond all possible Reparation'.[25]

Responding to Tillotson's litany of slander, Sterne's sermon imagines states of injury through carefully sketched vignettes of feeling. 'How often does the reputation of a helpless creature bleed by a report—which the party, who is at pains to propagate it, beholds with so much pity and fellow-feeling,—that she is heartily sorry for it,——hopes in God it is not true', Sterne asks:

> if these smoother weapons cut so sore,—what shall we say of open and unblush-ing scandal—subjected to no caution,—tied down to no restraints?—If the one,

like an arrow shot in the dark does nevertheless so much secret mischief,—this like the pestilence, which rageth at noon day, sweeps all before it, levelling without distinction the good and the bad ...——they fall,—so rent and torn in this tender part of them, so unmercifully butchered, as sometimes never to recover either the wounds,—or the anguish of heart,—which they have occasioned.—

(Sermons 11.108–9)

While Sterne follows the sense of the Tillotson sermon, his particular empha-sis is on the nature of a lived contradiction, in which people are not consistent with themselves. His text is James 1:26: 'If any man among you seem to be religious, and bridleth not his tongue, but deceiveth his own heart, this man's religion is vain.' The effects of such an internal splitting, of the fundamental nature of hypocrisy, are evident in the passage above. The pleasures derived from the circulation of damaging rumour, when words uttered seem on the surface to attest compassion, are one end of a violent continuum in which language can, at another extreme, shred and butcher its victim.

Yet if Sterne's lesson takes on the full force of the tongue's potential for poison, it also follows Tillotson in considering the limits of such a prohibition. The injunction 'to speak evil of no man' is not an absolute, the Archbishop suggests.[26] Evil-speaking has a function, as a critical curb that reins in excesses of behaviour where conscience fails. As Sterne argues:

after all our exhortations against it,—'tis not to be feared, but that there will be evil-speaking enough left in the world to chastise the guilty,—and we may safely trust them to an ill-natured world, that there will be no failure of justice upon this score. ——The passions of men are pretty severe executioners, and to them let us leave this ungrateful task,——and rather ourselves endeavour to cultivate that more friendly one, recommended by the apostle,—of letting all bitterness, and wrath, and clamour, and evil-speaking, be put away from us ...

(Sermons 11.111–12)

As if not quite convinced by this gesture, in a world that has to admit such contradictions, Sterne also suggests another remedy, which is to turn away like Uncle Toby from the dangerous zone of language altogether. What is evidently required is a means of managing such 'evil-speaking', understood for all its 'clamour' as a necessary corrective – and as a route to justice.

Tempora mutantur: the language of mid-century 'politicks'

Injury marks the potentially pathological terrain of Sterne's 'politicks': the 'thread running through all his work that twitches in response to the scanda-lising of a vulnerable reputation', as Jonathan Lamb observes.[27] Dependency, loss of autonomy, a kind of shame: these informed an uncertainty of status in which his Irish roots had a part to play, and to which fame could seem an antidote. Most notoriously, the arrival of Sterne's mother and sister from Ireland with inflated notions of his income produced sensational rumours of his selfishness that lasted well into the nineteenth century. In the deeply partisan years of the mid century, when the Jacobite rebellion may have reignited his political journalism in York once more, toleration seemed a luxury; and it did not extend for Sterne into familial territories either.

A symbolic victimhood haunts Sterne's forays into the language of religious and political difference, dramatised in the tribulations of Yorick and Toby in *Tristram Shandy*, and projected onto other systemic forms of persecution, as in the comic force of Catholic excommunication: 'For my own part, I could not have a heart to curse my dog so' (*TS* 3.11.207). Just as Toby blithely whistles the song 'Lillabullero', apparently oblivious to its cruel attack on the Gaelic-inflected accents of Catholic Ireland (this song originated among Irish Protestants as an anti-papist ballad, and was popular in the Williamite army, of which Toby is a veteran), language comes freighted with sometimes unintelligible prejudice, unspoken histories, detonating and wounding where it may. In this light, the jokes and miscommunications of Sterne's comic novel – 'How could you, Madam, be so inattentive in reading the last chapter? I told you in it, *That my mother was not a papist*' (*TS* 1.22.64) – take on more complex resonances. The fierce, sometimes satirical, repudiation of Catholic Ireland that was part of his religious and familial inheritance arguably kept more than 'papists' at bay: the interpellations of an Irishness rather closer to the bone, replete with associations of poverty and colonial exclusion.

Around 1759, the year of *Tristram Shandy*'s first emergence, political discourse appears to shift its ground. During the Seven Years' War (1756–63), a global conflict fought with France for territories and markets in North America, West Africa and India, partisanship in British domestic politics took on new discursive shapes. The language of the patriot, exemplified by the rhetoric of William Pitt, the war's architect, to whom the first and last instalments of *Tristram Shandy* are dedicated, held itself above party-political vitriol; this language could avail itself not only of the rhetoric of patrician retreat ('the dream language of political exile', as Jonathan Lamb describes it illuminatingly[28]), but also of an individuated style capable of riding the expediencies of the moment. At the same time, the language of sympathy was brought to bear on more universalising concerns, underwriting the 'civilising' expansion of British power with humanitarian equivalences that neatly circumvented the question of justice for those under its dominion.[29]

Those with a stake in the political exchange of public culture radically increased in number at this time. A slightly later commentary on 'evil-speaking', preached as a sermon in Cambridge soon after Sterne's death, shows that new concerns were on the agenda (stimulated in part by the agitations of Sterne's sometime friend, the radical John Wilkes). In this text of 1771, John Gordon deplores the destabilising effects of conquest and prosperity on the social order, and singles out the role of newspapers in producing 'sullen, discontented, insolent, untractable citizen[s]' while also generating claims to political expression within 'every common mechanic'. 'But who ever heard of the Government of *all*?', Gordon asks:

> The height of liberty, which we have long enjoyed, has given a boundless scope to all our thoughts, words, and actions: in which free range it is almost impossible not to strike against something or other, that will offend us: when immediately, like wayward children too much indulged, we are out of humor at discovering that any thing should dare interrupt us.[30]

It is not only the 'boundless scope' of liberty – and consequent waywardness – that chimes here with Sterne's narratives from the 1760s. Within this vision of 'intractable citizens', determined to seize their right to 'evil-speaking', we might also include the voice of the narrator from *Tristram Shandy*: 'not but the planet is well enough, provided a man could be born in it to a great title or to a great estate; or could any how contrive to be called up to publick charges, and employments of dignity or power;—but that is not my case;- - - - and therefore every man will speak of the fair as his own market has gone in it;—for which cause I affirm it over again to be one of the vilest worlds that ever was made' (*TS* 1.5.8). If there is disturbance in Gordon's sermon of 1771, it highlights another order of threat: that of a generalised critical consciousness among lower social ranks, that could prompt them, like the footman of the ballad, to speak of their own 'case'. A threat of equality, perhaps, in which the generalised nature of evil-speaking becomes a means of thinking about the wider reach of political life and its exclusions, and about the challenge to traditional forms of authority, which now threatened insurrectionary tumults across the empire.

There is undoubtedly a paradox in this simultaneous conjuring of equality and repudiation, exchange and exclusion, one that might be read as a transitional moment in a political culture responding to the radical transformations occasioned by imperial expansion. The unsettling movement between satire and sentiment inhabited by Sterne is a sign of its negotiation. Injurious speech causes disorientation, 'putting its addressee out of control', writes Judith Butler: 'Exposed at the moment of such a shattering is precisely the volatility of one's "place" within the community of speakers; one can be "put in one's place" by such speech, but such a place may be no place.'[31] Eighteenth-century public culture in Britain was marked by the assaults and provocations of such linguistic violence, which continued to take the most xenophobic and personally devastating of forms.

Yet Sterne's experience of political writing – and his exilic energies – suggest this volatility could rebound on the speaker in generative ways. A story of dependency and uncertainty of status gives way to a constitution of identity in language that is altogether more ironically alive to its provisionality in the world, and to the subtle calibrations of social debt, flung much further afield than the four miles diameter of a Yorkshire parish. The experience of the cost of belonging, the weight of exclusion (of which Sterne's family may have found themselves both instrument and object), becomes in a curious sense an insight into a form of mid-century political modernity, and into the scandalous possibility of formal equality implied by this modernity. What would it mean to think of the story of the Good Samaritan in such a context, Sterne's sermons ask: a foreigner who in the circumstances – *'national dislike'*, *'mutual ill offices'*, religious differences (*Sermons* 3.26) – should enjoy his adversary's plight and pass by on the other side? What would it mean to think of the outsider as oneself? What would it mean to consider the case of a ballad 'made by a Footman'? Or, as one puff, possibly engineered by Sterne himself, reflected wryly in 1760, what unsettling 'comfort' could it be that *Tristram Shandy* – a work threatening to 'blow up all that is sacred in our moral, religious, and political system' – 'hath been born in *Ireland*, the realm of salacity; and that *Old England* is not guilty of the Birth of so fell a monster'?[32]

NOTES

1. The shelfmark for the volume collected by Henry Bradshaw and donated in 1886 is HIB 3.730.1. I would like to thank Brian Jenkins at Cambridge University Library for his assistance.
2. Ian Campbell Ross, *Laurence Sterne: A Life* (Oxford: Oxford University Press, 2001), 445, n. 64. Ross assumes that the scrapbook was kept by Sterne, though there seems to be no direct evidence for this.
3. *Letters* 250. This passage comes from Sterne's only letter acknowledging his Irish background, written to William Combe on 11 June 1765, and is subject to some uncertainty, since Combe forged other letters. Curtis takes it to be genuine, as (more guardedly) do Melvyn New and Peter de Voogd in the forthcoming Florida edition of Sterne's letters.
4. See Ross, *Laurence Sterne: A Life*, 28, 436 n. 27.
5. Eugene Jolas, 'My Friend James Joyce', in *James Joyce: Two Decades of Criticism*, ed. Seon Givens (New York, NY: Vanguard, 1948), 12.
6. Terry Eagleton, 'The Good-Natured Gael', in his *Crazy John and the Bishop and Other Essays on Irish Culture* (Cork: Cork University Press, 1998), 84.
7. Katie Trumpener, *Bardic Nationalism: The Romantic Novel and the British Empire* (Princeton, NJ: Princeton University Press, 1997), 15.

8. Eagleton, 'Good-Natured Gael', 124–5.

9. My spelling of 'politicks' echoes Lewis Perry Curtis's study of Sterne's early journalism, *The Politicks of Laurence Sterne* (London: Oxford University Press, 1929), where 'politicks' connotes an intense but also unstable partisanship.

10. *The Prose Works of Jonathan Swift*, eds. Herbert Davis *et al.*, 14 vols. (Oxford: Blackwell, 1939–74), XII, 10.

11. Jonathan Swift to Alexander Pope, 11 August 1729, quoted in Davis's introduction, *Prose Works of Swift*, XII, xix.

12. See Claude Rawson, *God, Gulliver, and Genocide: Barbarism and the European Imagination, 1492–1945* (Oxford: Oxford University Press, 2001), 79–91.

13. Thomas Sheridan, 'Ballyspellin', in *The Poems of Jonathan Swift*, ed. Harold Williams, 2nd edn, 3 vols. (Oxford: Clarendon Press, 1958), II, 439 (lines 57–64).

14. Jonathan Swift to John Worrall, 28 September 1728, quoted by Williams, *Poems of Swift*, II, 437; for the larger context, see Harold Love, 'Satirical Wells from Bath to Ballyspellan', in *Swift's Travels: Eighteenth-Century Satire and Its Legacy*, eds. Nicholas Hudson and Aaron Santesso (Cambridge: Cambridge University Press, 2008), 55–73.

15. Jonathan Swift, 'An Answer to the Ballyspellin Ballad', in *Poems of Swift*, II, 442 (lines 73–84); II, 441 (lines 28–9).

16. *Prose Works of Swift*, XII, 235.

17. *Prose Works of Swift*, XII, 236.

18. Ross, *Laurence Sterne: A Life*, 40.

19. Pat Rogers, 'Sterne and Journalism', in *The Winged Skull: Papers from the Laurence Sterne Bicentenary Conference*, eds. Arthur H. Cash and John M. Stedmond (London: Methuen, 1971), 141.

20. Kenneth Monkman, 'More of Sterne's *Politicks* 1741–2', *Shandean* 1 (1989), 53–108; 'Sterne and the '45 (1743–8)', *Shandean* 2 (1990), 45–136; 'Sterne's Farewell to Politics', *Shandean* 3 (1991), 98–125. For the case against, see Melvyn New, 'Attribution and Sponsorship: The Delicate Case of Sterne', *Eighteenth-Century Fiction* 8.4 (1996), 525–8.

21. Jonathan Swift, *A Tale of a Tub*, eds. A. C. Guthkelch and D. Nichol Smith, 2nd edn (Oxford: Oxford University Press, 1958), 52.

22. Ian Higgins, *Jonathan Swift* (Plymouth: Northcote House, 2004), 24–6.

23. *Prose Works of Swift*, III, 10–11.

24. John Tillotson, *Of Evil-speaking: A Sermon*, 4th edn (1707), 6.

25. Tillotson, *Of Evil-speaking*, 6, 8.

26. Tillotson, *Of Evil-speaking*, 3.

27. Jonathan Lamb, 'Sterne and Irregular Oratory', in *The Cambridge Companion to the Eighteenth-Century Novel*, ed. John Richetti (Cambridge: Cambridge University Press, 1996), 163–4.

28. Lamb, 'Sterne and Irregular Oratory', 164.

29. See Carol Watts, *The Cultural Work of Empire: The Seven Years' War and the Imagining of the Shandean State* (Edinburgh: Edinburgh University Press, 2007) for an account of this period in relation to Sterne's writing.

30. John Gordon, *The Causes and Consequences of Evil Speaking Against Government* (Cambridge, 1771), 13, 8, 12.

31. Judith Butler, *Excitable Speech: A Politics of the Performative* (London: Routledge, 1997), 4.

32. *The Clockmakers Outcry against the Author of the Life and Opinions of Tristram Shandy* (1760), 10, 44; the case for Sterne's involvement is outlined by Anne Bandry in 'Imitations of *Tristram Shandy*', in *Critical Essays on Laurence Sterne*, ed. Melvyn New (New York, NY: G. K. Hall, 1998), 43–4.

8

ELIZABETH W. HARRIES

Words, sex, and gender in Sterne's novels

'Matter copulative and introductory'

Like many novels, *Tristram Shandy* is about three things: 'Birth, and copulation, and death', as T. S. Eliot sums up the matter in 'Sweeney Agonistes'.[1] It begins with a bedroom scene (however oblique), focuses on Tristram's difficult birth, and is haunted by death, from Parson Yorick's in the first volume, through Tristram's flight from 'DEATH himself' in the seventh (*TS* 7.1.576), to the death of Corporal Trim's brother in the last. (Many other characters die, from Tristram's older brother Bobby to Uncle Toby's friend Le Fever; death scenes recur throughout the text.) But, more than most novels, *Tristram Shandy* is concerned, some might say obsessed, with 'matter copulative' (8.8.665). Almost any paragraph can make us think of sex, genitalia, male and female organs. We quickly become aware that noses, whiskers, buttonholes, hobby-horses, crevices in the wall, slits in petticoats, old cock'd hats, green petticoats, and even 'things' have more than one meaning – and that Sterne *wants* us to be aware of them all.

Tristram Shandy begins with a joke that structures the whole novel. In the opening chapter, Tristram complains about his parents' inattention as they were busy conceiving him: 'I wish either my father or my mother, or indeed both of them, as they were in duty both equally bound to it, had minded what they were about when they begot me' (*TS* 1.1.1). Tristram's mother, who has come to associate the two duties that Walter Shandy performs in his regular way on the first Sunday of every month, suddenly asks her husband if he has remembered to wind up the clock. This 'unseasonable question' interrupts their sexual 'conversation',[2] and leads to the first of many disasters in Tristram's life, the scattering of his 'animal spirits' (1.2.2). It is no surprise that the tall Shandy clock, with all its sexual connections, looms in the background of both the illustrations that William Hogarth, the famous British painter and contemporary of Sterne, contributed to the second edition of the novel (see below, Fig. 5, p. 144).

The opening scene reflects, as in a funhouse mirror, the 'conversations' that take place between Tristram's parents, or between the Shandy brothers, or between Toby and his friend and servant Trim, or between Tristram and his many readers. These conversations are always halting, always tending toward monologue, always marked by the inadequacies of words and the expressiveness of gesture or gaze. The opening joke is also the first reference to Locke's theories about the association of ideas, the Pavlovian correlation of things that have no natural link, or, as Locke puts it, 'this wrong Connexion in our Minds of *Ideas* in themselves, loose and independent one of another' – a consistent source of funny, sometimes fruitful, misunderstanding in the novel. But the joke also depends on Sterne's play with double meanings and verbal ambiguities, or what Locke elsewhere calls 'the Imperfection of Words'.[3] As Tristram says of Uncle Toby: ''Twas not by ideas,——by heaven! his life was put in jeopardy by words' (*TS* 2.2.101).

Sterne loves to emphasise the possible sexual connotations of the words that he and his characters use – or do not use. In one passage, he suggests several ways to end a sentence in which Toby attempts to explain why Mrs Shandy wants the midwife, not Dr Slop, to be present at Tristram's birth:

> ——"My sister, mayhap, quoth my uncle *Toby*, does not choose to let a man come so near her ****" Make this dash,——'tis an Aposiopesis.—Take the dash away, and write Backside,—'tis Bawdy.—Scratch Backside out, and put *Cover'd-way* in,—'tis a Metaphor;—and, I dare say, as fortification ran so much in my uncle *Toby*'s head, that if he had been left to have added one word to the sentence,—that word was it. (*TS* 2.6.116)

Sterne expects that his readers, by this time thoroughly sensitised to bawdy suggestions, will interpret the asterisks as 'arse'. But if Uncle Toby has not finished his sentence, a possibility the text leaves open, how else could he have ended it? The substitutions show the way vocabulary works in the novel. Readers should be alert to the many registers of language, rhetorical to bawdy to metaphorical; they must read asterisks, dashes, and blank spaces, as well as the many connotations of the words themselves. Toby's military vocabulary ('Cover'd-way', for example) can be just as sexual as blunter language. As he suggests in this passage, Sterne uses all these registers in his constant efforts to stimulate our prurient minds. In the paragraph before this one, Tristram exclaims: 'How do the slight touches of the chisel, the pencil, the pen, the fiddle-stick, *et caetera*,—give the true swell, which gives the true pleasure!' (2.6.115–16). If we fail to read 'touches' and 'the true swell' and 'the true pleasure' as erotic (probably also 'chisel', 'pencil' and 'pen', and certainly 'fiddle-stick' as well: see 9.18–19.788–9), we are missing half the sentence – and half the novel.

We see the same tactic at work in the 'visitation dinner', a gathering of learned divines where Walter Shandy hopes to find that it is permissible to change his Tristram's 'scurvy' name after the christening has taken place. One chapter in the scene opens with the forceful exclamation 'ZOUNDS!' (an old, abbreviated euphemism for 'By God's wounds'), followed by what may be the longest dash in the novel and then a discussion of the exclamation and its possible causes (*TS* 4.27.377). We eventually learn that Phutatorius's 'ZOUNDS!' is a response not to the learned debate in progress but rather to the 'perpendicular' descent of a hot chestnut into an 'aperture' in his breeches: 'the true cause of his exclamation lay at least a yard below,' as Tristram explains, punning on 'yard' as slang in the period for 'penis' (4.27.379). As so often in the novel, the onlookers interpret this event in the sphere of the argument; their mistake, as Sterne once said in another context, is to 'look too high—tis ever the fate of low minds' (*Letters* 122). Like Freud, Sterne is interested in feats of displacement upward, our tendency to screen off the sexual by talking about the nose instead of the penis, learned debate rather than male physical agony.

Sterne returns to this theme in volume 8:

> "It is with Love as with Cuckoldom"—the suffering party is at least the *third*, but generally the last in the house who knows any thing about the matter: this comes, as all the world knows, from having half a dozen words for one thing; and so long, as what in this vessel of the human frame, is *Love*—may be *Hatred*, in that——*Sentiment* half a yard higher——and *Nonsense*———no Madam,—not there——I mean at the part I am now pointing to with my forefinger——how can we help ourselves?
>
> (*TS* 8.4.659)

Where is 'Madam', one of Tristram's many fictive readers, looking? Lower? Where is Tristram pointing? 'Half a yard higher'? Madam's prurient interest indicates that women are if anything less delicate than the Shandy men, more ready to confront the sexual, as we see too in the Widow Wadman's blushing desire to 'see the very place' where Uncle Toby received his wound at Namur (9.20.772), fixing her mind on Toby's groin while Toby thinks only of his map. 'Madam' is constantly mocked and chided for her sexual curiosity. In Tristram's imagination, women go more or less directly to the 'place'; men displace and defer the sexual in the endless play of language.

Language for Sterne, then, is not just a source of human confusion and misunderstanding. It is the 'North west passage' (*TS* 5.42.484) to the half-suppressed (or, as Freud would say, sublimated) world of sexuality in its most physical and primitive forms: bodily protuberances and concave surfaces, touch and friction, intercourse and masturbation.[4] Words like 'copulation' and 'conversation' oscillate between their rhetorical and their sexual meanings, never staying put for long. And if the promised chapters on 'whiskers' and 'button-holes' are long delayed, even deferred for ever, Sterne finds many other charged and ambiguous words to take their places. He never forgets, and never allows us to forget, what human bodies look like (in basic and crude outline, at least) and how they can interact. His language always reminds us.

'Nothing was well hung'

Sometimes readers have reacted to Sterne's linguistic play as if it were a male adolescent aberration, the verbal equivalent of coarse sexual graffiti on bathroom walls. As post-Victorians, and even as post-Freudians, we are unaccustomed to seeing graphic representations of sexual organs in open and public places, and we are unaccustomed to reading constant references to them in supposedly proper texts. As an unknown early reader exclaimed, posing as a leading Methodist minister in a spurious pamphlet entitled *A Letter from the Rev. George Whitefield, M. A. to the Rev. Laurence Sterne, M. A.* (1760), 'Oh, *Sterne*! thou art scabby, and such is the leprosy of thy mind that it is not to be cured like the leprosy of the body, by dipping nine times in the river Jordan' (*CH* 100). Or, as one of my students once said, trying to explain why she had enjoyed my class in eighteenth-century fiction, 'Where else could I get credit for reading so many dirty novels?'

Sterne's fixed, repetitive attention to sexed bodies and to crudely represented body parts, however, reflects what may seem at first to be the fixed gender economy of *Tristram Shandy*. As many critics have pointed out, the women in the novel are shadowy, if disturbing, presences, rarely taking centre stage and often portrayed as watching events through a keyhole or as eavesdropping on important conversations. Tristram's birth goes on for volumes, but readers never see the room where the birth is taking place. Rather we stay in the back parlour where the Shandy brothers, Corporal Trim, and Dr Slop are talking and cursing and waiting for the birth, while Mrs Shandy labours on, offstage, with only the midwife and her maid in attendance. After the birth, we see Walter Shandy prostrate across his bed, mourning the injury that Slop's forceps have done to Tristram's nose, rather than Mrs Shandy on her own bed of pain. And the Widow Wadman remains more of a threat than a delight to the Shandy men. The scene where we actually see her kicking off the corking pins that close up her night-shift (*TS* 8.9.667–8), a scene of sexual decision and even joyful anticipation, leads to eleven years of preoccupation (with the wars in Flanders) and indecision on Toby's part. Tristram's world is a world where women, their hopes, and their opinions are relegated to the margins.

Sterne often returns to what have been called these 'anachronistic' gender patterns, a frequent 'segregation of women from men' throughout the novel that reflects the assumptions and practices of an earlier age.[5] Tristram refers to the Widow Wadman as a 'daughter of Eve' (TS 8.8.664), connecting her with sexual temptation and Biblical transgression – and, of course, naming her as different and dangerous. One of Walter's typical misogynist 'demonstrations' makes the connection explicit:

> not only, 'That the devil was in women, and that the whole of the affair was lust;' but that every evil and disorder in the world of what kind or nature soever, from the first fall of Adam, down to my Uncle Toby's (inclusive) was owing one way or other to the same unruly appetite. (TS 9.32.805)

Parson Yorick hastens to 'temper' this tirade, and certainly the novel as a whole takes a more moderate or modern view of women than Walter's. But all of the Shandy men persist in echoing traditional, misogynistic notions.

And Tristram, of course, is one of the Shandy men. Even when the Provençal woman Nanette recalls him from the dance of death at the end of volume 7, he wishes the slit in her petticoat away, retreating (like his Uncle Toby) from possible sexual engagement. Under her coaxing, he finally joins the dance of joy:

> *Viva la joia!* was in her lips—*Viva la joia!* was in her eyes ... Just disposer of our joys and sorrows, cried I, why could not a man sit down in the lap of content here—and dance, and sing, and say his prayers, and go to heaven with this nut brown maid? capriciously did she bend her head on one side, and dance up insiduous——Then 'tis time to dance off, quoth I ... (TS 7.43.651)

Though he joins the dance, however, Tristram still finds Nanette's movements both 'capricious' and 'insiduous'.[6] He sees women both as temptresses *and* as innocent 'nut brown maids'. He also claims that in the Shandy family 'the females had no character at all' (1.21.73), echoing the much-quoted opening lines of Alexander Pope's *Epistle to a Lady* (1735). The exception is his great-aunt Dinah – but she is an exception only because of her 'unruly appetite' and sexual transgression, running off with the coachman. Though women are usually in the wings, they are often dismissed, deplored, or even excoriated by the male figures who continue to talk endlessly centre stage.

As one feminist critic has put it, 'the narrative spotlight comes to rest most often and most continually upon men alone, talking. In its very form, *Tristram Shandy* shows how the eroticised verbal functions in the bonding between men.'[7] In other words, the pervasive language of sexual innuendo and double meaning in the novel helps to create the world of 'men alone, talking'. Many novels of the eighteenth century, whether by men or by women, from *Moll Flanders* (1722) to *Clarissa* (1747–8) to *Evelina* (1778), focus on the characteristic personal dilemmas faced by women and their subjective reactions to social pressures. Sterne, on the other hand, creates a world centered on men and their reactions to the fundamental dilemmas of being male. This may have well been a response to other novels that were popular at the time.[8] But Sterne's novel is also a comic and anxious – comically anxious, anxiously comic – meditation on the perils of gender and the gender divide.

Sterne would not have used the word 'gender' in this way, of course. He used it either as a grammatical term or as a substitute for the biological sex of a person. In *A Sentimental Journey*, for example, Yorick talks about his snap judgments of people that depend on 'the mood I am in, and the case—and I may add the gender too, of the person I am to govern' (*SJ/BJ* 41), playing with the double meanings of his grammatical terms. Tristram suggests that his father is just as absorbed in Bruscambille's 'prologue upon long noses' as the reader would have been in his first mistress: 'To those who do not yet know of which gender *Bruscambille* is,——inasmuch as a prologue upon long noses might easily be done by either,——'twill be no objection against the simile' (*TS* 3.35.266). He uses the word 'gender' here just as Lady Mary Wortley Montagu does in a letter quoted in the current edition of the *Oxford English Dictionary*: 'Of the fair Sex ... my only Consolation for being of that Gender has been the assurance it gave me of never being marry'd to any one amongst them.'[9] Our current use of the word, far from being 'a euphemism for the sex of a human being', as *OED2* surprisingly claims, reflects the recent cultural explorations of the various meanings of biological sex in different societies, and particularly of the rigidly defined, binary, and biased distinction between the sexes that has persisted in the West for centuries.[10]

Walter Shandy's angry tirades against all women as dangerous and corrupt, as well as Lady Mary's disdain for her own sex, reflect an outdated version of this distinction. But in the mid eighteenth century, when Sterne was writing his novels, the deep differences between the sexes were still a given. Women were thought to be closer to nature and the body, less capable of rational thought, suited only for the household and domestic concerns. Only men could profit from higher education and play a role in public life. Various women writers, from Mary Astell and Anne Finch at the beginning of the century to Mary Wollstonecraft at the end, questioned these assumptions, but their protests had little effect on either received opinions or the continuing organisation of social roles.

While *Tristram Shandy* tends to shore up traditional definitions of the 'female', however, the novel repeatedly questions traditional definitions of the 'male'. In fact, we could read it as an extended exploration of the trials and tribulations of wounded masculinity, a condition manifested in Tristram himself and echoed in other members of the Shandy family. All the disasters of Tristram's first five years – his interrupted conception; his birth, with the damage to his nose; his bungled christening; his accident with the sash-window that circumcises him (or worse)[11] – call his full masculinity and his origins into question. Like Toby throughout the Widow Wadman episodes, and like the Shandy bull in the last chapter of the novel, he has to endure 'suspicions' about his 'character' or reputation as a potent male (*TS* 9.33.808). In the family as a whole, as Tristram himself says, 'nothing was well hung', neither sash-windows nor male members (5.17.449). Throughout the novel, his repeated returns to 'noses' and other suggestive substitutions for the penis (or the symbolic phallus, as the Freudian theorist Lacan would say) are part of his obsessive quest both to hide and to reveal his uncertainties, uncertainties that Sterne is eager to exploit and explore. As Helene Moglen puts it, 'Sterne participates, with Lacan and Freud, in the displacement of anxiety that he is able to describe with real acuteness'.[12] For example, Tristram ruefully recounts an incident with his 'dear Jenny', calling it:

> the most oppressive of its kind which could befall me as a man, proud, as he ought to be, of his manhood——
> 'Tis enough, said'st thou [Jenny], coming close up to me, as I stood with my garters in my hand, reflecting upon what had *not* pass'd—— (*TS* 7.29.624)

In describing this moment of sexual humiliation, Tristram initially equates being a 'man' with having pride in his 'manhood', his sexual potency and prowess. But he then goes on to suggest that Jenny's sexual generosity has salved his psychic wound, that he has not been completely undone by his 'oppressive' failure. This pattern of male sexual inadequacy and partial – though only partial – recuperation recurs throughout *Tristram Shandy*. In *A Sentimental Journey*, Yorick's equivocal encounter with the fair *fille de chambre* in chapters headed 'The Temptation' and 'The Conquest' (*SJ/BJ* 121–4) hints at the same difficulties.

Tristram's doubts about his masculinity are also part of a much larger pattern. Walter is always eager to deny that women play any part in the reproductive process, reaching back again to ancient, anachronistic theories of the 'homunculus' as developing from the sperm alone, and of the womb as merely the vessel for its growth. Perhaps because of the age-old difficulty in proving fatherhood (at least until the discovery of DNA and genetic testing), perhaps because he may not actually be the father of Tristram (who is born only eight months after the night that begins the novel), Walter would like to claim everything parental for men, from the moment of conception on.

Women, on this theory, are scarcely necessary. From Walter's point of view, women upset the sovereign male patriarchal applecart: they are sexually aggressive and sly, they have no interest in following his arcane theoretical arguments, and they always ask questions at just the wrong time.

And Walter would certainly like to believe that sex is not necessary, either. At one point early in the novel, his brother Toby expresses his delight in having nephews:

> for you do increase my pleasure very much, in begetting children for the *Shandy* Family at your time of life. ——But, by that, Sir, quoth Dr. *Slop*, Mr. *Shandy* increases his own. ——Not a jot, quoth my father. (*TS* 2.12.133)

Intercourse is just one of those 'little family concernments' that Walter likes to get out of the way once a month, like winding the clock, and then 'be no more plagu'd and pester'd with them the rest of the month' (1.4.6). He regularly expresses his contempt for things of the body by using the word 'ass' as an abbreviation for 'passions':

> It pleased my father well; it was not only a laconick way of expressing—— but of libelling, at the same time, the desires and appetites of the lower part of us; so that for many years of my father's life, 'twas his constant mode of expression—he never used the word *passions* once—but *ass* always instead of them—— (*TS* 8.31.716)

His fear of the feminine and fear of the flesh have fused to become one overriding fear, a fear of and even contempt for his own sexuality.

To put this another way, Walter Shandy's life consistently belies his own rigid ideas about the masculine and the feminine. Though he subscribes to antiquated doctrines of patriarchal power, he is completely unable to exercise that power in his own household; nothing in his son Tristram's life or in his relationship with his wife turns out the way he has planned. He cannot write his treatise on education, the *Tristrapaedia*, quickly enough to influence Tristram's upbringing, and becomes absorbed in the task to the point of self-defeat: Tristram 'was all that time totally neglected and abandoned to my mother' (5.16.448), even though Walter believes that the mother is essentially no relation to her child and should play little or no part in his development. Though he denies his own sexual desires, he is sometimes reluctantly forced to acknowledge them. Though he tries to blame his wife for her female concupiscence, he eventually sees that she is, if anything, even less interested in sex than he is; her 'chill' eye and her 'temperate current of blood' (9.1.736) show no trace of desire – suggesting that he himself is responsible for the sexual contact, rare though it is, that they do have. His abstract and extreme ideas about everything, from education to sex, are always undercut.

Walter Shandy and Uncle Toby, and most obviously Tristram, certainly are always centre stage and always talking. Women are indeed on the sidelines. But the novel as a whole remains a strange mixture of misogyny and male anxieties about the body, castration, and impotence. (Or perhaps extreme misogyny is always self-contradictory in this way, engendering its own opposite.[13]) As several critics have pointed out, Trim and Toby have formed a fraternal alliance that is often described in terms of sexual desire: 'Never did lover post down to a belov'd mistress with more heat and expectation, than my uncle Toby did', as Tristram puts it when Toby hurries to his bowling green for a war-gaming assignation with Trim (*TS* 2.5.113). Even Trim's elaborate flourish with his stick, often merrily described as 'the line of freedom' and reproduced on the cover of all volumes of the Florida edition, is actually part of his attempt to persuade Toby not to marry the Widow Wadman, and thus to escape 'confinement for life' (9.4.742–3). Walter is the most thoroughly anti-feminist, but all the male characters characteristically attempt to avoid, negate, or even take over the female and the maternal, concentrating instead on their own paternal and fraternal relationships, or on their varied but absorbing hobby-horses. In its focus on the dramas of wounded masculinity and suspect paternity, the novel stages a twisted family romance that Freud might not have recognised, but that still is pervasive in our culture.

'Getting out of the body'

Critics began worrying about the way Sterne represents sexuality and gender more than a quarter of a century ago. Previous articles about sexual innuendo in Sterne, notably by A. R. Towers, Robert Alter, and Frank Brady, had treated Sterne's erotic language as part of a rollicking male conversation with a male reader; all focus on what they call Sterne's 'sexual comedy'.[14] Early attempts by Ruth Marie Faurot and Leigh A. Ehlers to rehabilitate Mrs Shandy, making her a figure of comfort and healing in the novel, were ingenious but unconvincing.[15] Several critics in the late 1980s and early 1990s argued that Sterne's novels are in fact thoroughly sexist, denigrating women in traditional ways and deploying the typical misogynist tactics that have permeated Western literature throughout its history.[16]

Since then, a number of critics have rejected these assumptions, claiming that the misogyny in the novel is primarily Walter Shandy's, sometimes Tristram's, but never Sterne's. For example, Juliet McMaster, in her witty article 'Walter Shandy, Sterne, and Gender', concludes that '*Tristram Shandy* is *about* misogyny, and against it'. Paula Loscocco arrives at much the same conclusion by a different route, arguing that '*Tristram Shandy* insists intransigently on the *fact* of the antifeminist *error*'.[17] It is certainly possible to distinguish between Walter Shandy's diatribes against women and attitudes like Parson Yorick's, Uncle Toby's, or Tristram's. But is it possible to disentangle Sterne's ideas about women from Tristram's?

In a puzzling moment in volume 6, Tristram inserts a strange parenthesis in his meditations on Uncle Toby's amours. He has been detailing the damage done to Toby's life by the Treaty of Utrecht (the treaty that made it impossible for him to carry on with his all-absorbing imitation of the war in Flanders on the bowling green), and then goes on:

> Of the few legitimate sons of *Adam*, whose breasts never felt what the sting of love was,—(maintaining first, all mysogynists to be bastards)—the greatest heroes of ancient and modern story have carried off amongst them, nine parts in ten of the honour ... (*TS* 6.30.551)

Tristram is arguing that military heroes are most likely to be untouched by 'the sting of love', presumably because they, like Toby in his mock-military campaigns, 'had all of them something else to do'. (Typically, Tristram seems to consider this to be a good thing.) But why does he place them among 'the few legitimate sons of Adam'? And why does he pause to maintain 'first, all mysogynists to be bastards'? Is this a moment when Tristram is given a serious opinion that Sterne endorses? Is he suggesting that men without recognised, legitimate fathers are more likely to fear and despise women? Or is he simply, casually, calling them names? Tristram himself has just referred in the previous chapter to Toby's 'unmistrusting ignorance of the plies and foldings of the heart of woman' (6.29.550), playing as usual on traditional notions about female serpentine wiliness.

We might also consider what Tristram says late in the novel: 'I love the Pythagoreans (much more than ever I dare tell my dear Jenny) for their ... "*getting out of the body, in order to think well*"' (*TS* 7.13.593). Tristram knows, of course, that this is impossible, as we see in his earlier comments about the soul and the body being indivisible, like the jerkin and the jerkin's lining (3.4.189). Yet he seems to hope against hope, like his father, that he can leave the body behind. His 'dear Jenny' becomes yet again the one who is more attached to it, more deeply connected to the flesh, as women have traditionally been said to be. Sterne may be exposing Tristram's deep-seated sexism, or he may be participating in it. In *A Sentimental Journey*, he certainly suggests that minds and bodies vibrate together, that Yorick's tremulous encounters with various women throughout his journey lead to greater understanding (as well as to a series of *double entendres*). During his tearful meeting with the mad Maria, for example, Yorick suddenly exclaims: 'I am positive I have a soul' (*SJ/BJ* 151). In this last, slightly later novel, Sterne paints the relations between the sexes in a somewhat fuller and more sympathetic way.

In *Tristram Shandy*, Sterne takes pains to show us that Walter's anachronistic sexism is both funny and untenable. He also, with much more affection, shows us the darker sides of Toby's willed ignorance of women, and of Tristram's alternately combative and flirtatious relationship with his female reader, 'Madam', and with his occasional addressee, his 'dear, dear *Jenny*' (*TS* 1.18.56). But Sterne is also thoroughly enmeshed in the world and the language of his day. He cannot resist – and seems not to want to resist, either consciously or unconsciously – the fertile puns and metaphors that play on patterns of sexist thought that have come down through centuries. In *Othello*, Shakespeare could not undo or escape the contrasts between black and white that inform early modern discourse; Sterne, in much the same way, inherited a language that depends on contrasts between male and female, concave and convex, fullness and lack. And he tends to exploit those aspects of his language to the fullest. He has not forged a sovereign, unbiased position that rises above the traditional tangled relations between men and women, between men and other men; nor do I think he could have done. Perhaps the world (and I) have fancied Sterne more misogynist than he ever was; perhaps, on the other hand, we have not completely understood the impulses (and impasses) in the novel that reflect the thinking of his time. I now believe that we have to accept the contradictions in his thought, even when we might wish them otherwise. In short, I think the novel is sexist, and I think it is not.[18]

Near the end of the brief essay about sexism in Sterne's novels that I wrote in the 1980s, I asked questions about *Tristram Shandy* that I could not answer then, and that still have not been completely answered: 'What is the relationship between the novel's sexist bias and its self-conscious, fragmented, digressive narration? How are we to understand – and teach – a text that, while undermining conventional expectations about narrative and language, at the same time shores up many prejudices and cultural myths about gender?'[19] Now I would phrase those questions more carefully, and in a more nuanced way. I no longer believe that the novel has an unambiguous 'sexist bias'; I think that it both shores up *and questions* cultural myths about gender. It is also probably naïve to think that a novel that is unconventional in one way is going to be so in all other ways. But the question, even in a revised form, still gets at an important problem in our understanding of the novel. What is the relationship between Sterne's constant returns to the myths and miseries of gender and his equally constant games with narrative form?

Some critics have argued that the fear of impotence that haunts *Tristram Shandy* – from Walter's anxieties about paternity in the first volume to

Tristram's melancholy about 'what had *not* passed' (*TS* 7.29.624) to the questions about Uncle Toby and the Shandy bull in the last chapters – mirrors, or perhaps engenders, the fear of finishing, the digressions and swerves, that structure the novel. As Calvin Thomas says, 'writing, plotting, narration, the effort to unify, to fix meaning, are all caught up in sexual division and meaning's flight, impotence, unmastery, unavoidable castration'.[20] If a perfect plot depends on the male sexual pattern of excitation, climax, and release, as psychoanalytic critics often claim, *Tristram Shandy* certainly fails to follow that pattern, and is anti-climactic and anti-plot all at once.

But perhaps we should listen more carefully to one of Tristram's own observations: his often-quoted claim that 'writing, when properly managed, (as you may be sure I think mine is) is but a different name for conversation' (*TS* 2.11.125). His book resembles nothing so much as the meandering conversation of a summer's afternoon, doubling back on itself, contradicting itself, ending up years before it began. Like the sexual 'conversations' of the novel, the conversations between the Shandy brothers and between Tristram and his readers are often interrupted, never conclusive. And we as readers gradually learn to be patient with, even delight in, this inconclusiveness. Sterne asks us to suspend our irritable reaching after truth and fact and plot, our need to place him as proto-feminist or misogynist. We need to add a word to the list this chapter begins with: 'Birth, and copulation, and death – and conversation.'

NOTES

1. T. S. Eliot, *Collected Poems, 1909–1962* (London: Faber, 1963), 131.
2. In eighteenth-century usage, 'conversation' meant both 'interchange of thoughts and words; familiar dialogue or talk' and 'sexual intercourse or intimacy' (now usually a legal sense). 'Copulative' and 'copulation' referred both to connections between things, usually grammatical, and to 'the union of the sexes in the act of generation' (now usually a zoological sense). See *OED2*, s.v. Conversation, 7 and 3a; Copulation, 2.
3. John Locke, *An Essay Concerning Human Understanding*, ed. Peter H. Nidditch (Oxford: Clarendon Press, 1975), 397 (ii.33.§9); see also, on the imperfection of words, 475–90 (ii.9.§1–23).
4. For a stimulating discussion of Sterne's language in Freudian and Lacanian terms, see Ruth Perry, 'Words for Sex: The Verbal-Sexual Continuum in *Tristram Shandy*', *Studies in the Novel* 20 (1988), 27–42.
5. Carol Kay, *Political Constructions: Defoe, Richardson, and Sterne in Relation to Hobbes, Hume, and Burke* (Ithaca, NY: Cornell University Press, 1988), 232.
6. 'Insiduous' may perhaps be a mistake for 'insidious', as the Florida editors suggest (*TS Notes* 497), or perhaps a pre-Carroll, pre-Joyce portmanteau word that

combines 'insidious' and 'insinuate' (a verb Milton uses for the serpent in *Paradise Lost*, iv.348).

7. Perry, 'Words for Sex', 39.

8. As Thomas Keymer remarks, Tristram as narrator 'evokes, exaggerates, and subverts the techniques of modern fiction' (*Sterne, the Moderns, and the Novel* (Oxford: Oxford University Press, 2002), 8). Far from being indifferent to the novels of his time, Sterne may have deliberately set out to compete with and perhaps overturn them.

9. *The Complete Letters of Lady Mary Wortley Montagu*, ed. Robert Halsband, 3 vols. (Oxford: Clarendon Press, 1966), II, 33 (to Barbara Calthorpe, 7 December 1723). Quoting this letter (s.v. Gender, 3a), *OED2* follows an erroneous early edition of Montagu's correspondence by dating it to 1709.

10. See *OED2*, s.v. Gender, 3b. Much ink has been spilled in recent years over the distinction between sex and gender: does the conception of 'gender' ultimately return us to the same rigid dichotomies that biological 'sex' has always presented? In this essay I will provisionally stay with the sex/gender distinction as offering a way out of narrow biological impasses, but I recommend the following books for difficult but rewarding work on the subject: Judith Butler, *Gender Trouble: Feminism and the Subversion of Identity*, 2nd edn (New York, NY: Routledge, 1999); Butler, *Undoing Gender* (New York, NY: Routledge, 2004); Toril Moi, *What is a Woman? and Other Essays* (Oxford: Oxford University Press, 1999).

11. Cf. a wonderful comment by A. R. Towers: 'One is struck here by the way Sterne seems to anticipate the modern anthropologists and psychoanalysts who regard circumcision as a ritualistic substitute for the graver deprivation' ('Sterne's Cock and Bull Story', *ELH* 24 (1957), 16).

12. Helene Moglen, *The Trauma of Gender: A Feminist Theory of the English Novel* (Berkeley, CA: University of California Press, 2001), 171 n. 11.

13. As Calvin Thomas puts it, 'misogyny is an effect of castration anxiety, and the disavowal of castration, the assumption of "mastery," thereby necessitates the disavowal of the feminine and the maternal, the mastery of language, sexuality, temporality, "woman," "meaning," and death' ('*Tristram Shandy*'s Consent to Incompleteness: Discourse, Disavowal, Disruption', in *Critical Essays on Laurence Sterne*, ed. Melvyn New (New York, NY: G. K. Hall, 1998), 225). Here Thomas makes larger Lacanian claims about language and 'meaning' than I think the novel can sustain, but his general point is useful.

14. Towers, 'Sterne's Cock and Bull Story'; Robert Alter, '*Tristram Shandy* and the Game of Love', *American Scholar* 37 (1968), 316–23; Frank Brady, '*Tristram Shandy*: Sexuality, Morality, and Sensibility', *Eighteenth-Century Studies* 4 (1970), 41–56.

15. For example, Ehlers claims that 'Once we look beyond the Shandean male propaganda, it becomes evident that Sterne's novel is indeed very much of a "woman's book," in which women are invested with considerable, though untapped, restorative powers'; Mrs Shandy's knitting 'indicates not indifference, but love and care; she at least attempts to restore order and creativity to a house visited by death (Bobby's) and plagued by declining potency (Walter's and later Tristram's)' (Leigh A. Ehlers, 'Mrs Shandy's "Lint and Basilikon": The Importance of Women in *Tristram Shandy*', *South Atlantic Review* 46 (1981), 61, 64; see also Ruth Marie Faurot, 'Mrs Shandy Observed', *Studies in English*

Literature, 1500–1900 10 (1970), 579–89). On the other hand, sometimes knitting is just knitting.

16. Perry, 'Words for Sex'; Elizabeth W. Harries, 'Sorrows and Confessions of a Cross-Eyed "Female Reader" of Sterne', in *Approaches to Teaching Sterne's Tristram Shandy*, ed. Melvyn New (New York, NY: Modern Language Association, 1989), 111–17; Barbara M. Benedict, '"Dear Madam": Rhetoric, Cultural Politics, and the Female Reader in Sterne's *Tristram Shandy*', *Studies in Philology* 88 (1992), 485–98.

17. Juliet McMaster, 'Walter Shandy, Sterne, and Gender: A Feminist Foray', in New (ed.), *Critical Essays on Sterne*, 213; Paula Loscocco, 'Can't Live Without 'Em: Walter Shandy and the Woman Within', in New (ed.), *Critical Essays on Sterne*, 241.

18. Here I echo Virginia Mason Vaughan's chapter, 'Racial Discourse: Black and White', in her *Othello: A Contextual History* (Cambridge: Cambridge University Press, 1994): 'I think this play is racist, and I think it is not' (70). Vaughan plays, of course, on Othello to Iago: 'I think my wife be honest, and think she is not; I I think that thou art just, and think thou art not' (III.iii.385–6).

19. Harries, 'Sorrows and Confessions', 117.

20. Thomas, '*Tristram Shandy*'s Consent', 228.

9

CHRISTOPHER FANNING

Sterne and print culture

Although Laurence Sterne would not have used the phrase 'print culture', he had a developed conception of the constellation of socio-economic and aesthetic factors clustered around the print medium, and he understood how to exploit these in an authorial career based on, though extending beyond, his literary work on the page. Sterne's expressions, in his letters and published work, of his awareness of the opportunities made possible by print allow us to define 'print culture' in his own terms. The main categories by which he recognised print culture were both public and private, combining an acute awareness of the market for literary works – the power of public opinion and the tools (patronage, reviews) by which a reading public is created and maintained – with a philosophical conception of the existential implications of printed expression for notions of individuality and original-ity.[1] For Sterne, print culture manifested itself in three basic categories: fame (the social phenomenon of the celebrity), finance (the business of professional authorship), and physicality (the printed artefact). Both the social-cultural aspects of print culture (fame and finance) and the concretely material (physi-cality) mark an intersection of public and private. Not only is the print marketplace a locus of exchange where private written expression is made public; the printed text itself is also, for Sterne, a place where author and reader interact, and a point of contact that reveals the unbridgeable gap between participants in the act of communication.

'I wrote not [to] be *fed*, but to be *famous*'

Sterne is our first author to achieve celebrity status in the modern sense of the term: a popular phenomenon in and of himself, and one who grounds his fame in public performance and market manipulation rather than, like 'the celebrated Mr. Pope' earlier in the century, in commendatory poems, col-lected editions, and claims to canonical status in a classical tradition.[2] The celebrity author is distinct from the author presupposed by the reader of any given book – that sense of an author manifest in a text that has been a concern of literary theory since Foucault and Barthes. Because Sterne was not just an author posited by a text, but himself a celebrity phenomenon in 1760, the public could respond to both the fictional and the real author figures. His book was read by many who met the author, or who wanted to: as Sterne boasted soon after publishing the first volumes of *Tristram Shandy*, 'I … am engaged allready to ten Noble men & men of fashion to dine' (*Letters* 96; see also 102, 104). Conversely, he was known – as an author – by many who never read the book. Indeed, Sterne created for himself something of a fictional persona, signing correspondence with the names of his characters, Tristram and Yorick, and deliberately blurring the lines between his biological self and his literary creations. Together, Laurence Sterne and *Tristram Shandy* garnered much attention. Sterne's association of himself with his mad narrator, or with his jester-cum-parson, brought him a reputation for whimsy and a certain carelessness about the mores of polite society. What had become of the 'authority' of such an author?

When Sterne announced his preference for fame over food (*Letters* 90), he was inverting a statement of Colley Cibber, who, as a way of excusing his writing, insisted he wrote 'more to be Fed, than to be Famous'.[3] This connection is telling of cultural developments over the middle-third of the eighteenth century. Cibber, the poet laureate of the previous generation, had been crowned king of the dunces in the last versions of Alexander Pope's *Dunciad* (1742–3). He was a self-promoter extraordinaire, much to the offence of the Scriblerian satirists (primarily Pope, Jonathan Swift, and John Gay), who ridiculed him as a threat to human culture by means of his pandering (and successful) approach to artistic production – a man who vulgarised the stage, and who changed poetry to a vehicle for flattery rather than moral instruction, all unabashedly in the name of self-interest. What does it mean that Laurence Sterne, a generation later, could both admire and imitate the Scriblerians and yet take on a campaign of public self-promotion like Cibber? This is an indication of shifting assumptions, tastes, and fundamental beliefs about authorship, changes of which Pope and Swift had been aware and afraid. They saw Cibber and Grubstreet hacks in general as enemies of learning and humanistic culture who wrote for no higher end than money or preferment.[4] In their resistance to a model of literature as a consumer commodity, Pope and Swift proclaimed themselves to be anti-materialists in both the philosophical and economic senses, however indebted they were in practice to the literary and commercial techniques of the new print culture.

By the 1760s, in contrast, Sterne was not only much more comfortable with publicity and the validity of public opinion, but also comfortable with the system of consumer-driven literary production. He shows a distinct lack of resistance to what Pope would have labelled the forces of Dulness. 'There is a shilling pamphlet wrote against Tristram.—I wish they would write a hundred such', Sterne writes to a correspondent in May 1760 (*Letters* 107), clearly pleased at this sign of popular approval. And there would be dozens of such responses. Imitations, parodies, outcries, spurious continuations, and publications under the names of Shandean characters proliferated, all attempting to capitalise on the fact that 'Tristram is the Fashion' (*Letters* 102).

In addition to this kind of print-market response were the more formal reviews. These were mixed, some celebrating the wit and oddity of the book, others condemning its bawdiness. And when Sterne's sermons were published as *The Sermons of Mr. Yorick*, many took offence, like Owen Ruffhead in the *Monthly Review*, at his 'mount[ing] the pulpit in a *Harlequin's coat*' (*CH* 77). Less than a year later, after the publication of volumes 3 and 4, Sterne's enthusiasm for any kind of attention was undiminished, especially as it implied financial success: 'One half of the town abuse my book as bitterly, as the other half cry it up to the skies—the best is, they abuse it and buy it, and at such a rate, that we are going on with a second edition, as fast as possible' (*Letters* 129–30). Sterne's sensitivity to his market played a significant role in the development of *Tristram Shandy* over the seven-year period of its publication: not only does Tristram respond to the attacks of the reviewers directly in subsequent volumes, but Sterne can be seen as adjusting and adapting his work to these responses.[5] For example, many reviews noted Sterne's skill in the pathetic, or sentimental, and encouraged him to include more of this (and less bawdry). The shift in emphasis in *Tristram Shandy* towards Uncle Toby – the benevolent, naive, wounded old soldier – indicates that Sterne was listening to his critics. In order to remain 'the Fashion', *Tristram Shandy* had to keep pace with shifts in popular taste. And when popular taste lost interest in the Shandean mode, Sterne had Tristram voice his financial concerns: 'Is it not enough that thou art in debt, and that thou hast ten cart-loads of thy fifth and sixth volumes still—still unsold, and art almost at thy wit's ends, how to get them off thy hands' (*TS* 8.6.663). Certainly Sterne's shift of modes in his final work, *A Sentimental Journey*, may be construed as both a response and an adaptation to the tastes of his reading public: 'If it is not thought a chaste book, mercy on them that read it, for they must have warm imaginations indeed!' (*Letters* 403).

At least in public, Swift and Pope would have condemned all of these concerns as elements of hack work: writing to popular taste for financial gain. Even though Sterne admired the satire of the Scriblerians, who attacked popular authorship so vehemently, he was a full participant in a living print culture as a consumer of popular texts himself. Thomas Keymer has recently argued that Sterne was well-read in ephemeral fictions such as John Kidgell's *The Card* (1755) and the anonymous *Life and Memoirs of Mr. Ephraim Tristram Bates* (1756), as well as in popular works by contemporaries of the 1760s such as James Macpherson's Ossian poems. That these are not the canonical figures of his day is significant, for Sterne's rapid rise to fame gives the lie to the traditional, canonical, Virgilian path of working upward through the classical genres. Indeed, his calculated approach to fame distinctly avoided the literary authorities of mid-century England.

Nevertheless, Sterne did seek out cultural authority of a different kind. Rather than align his work with the most prestigious literature of the moment, he placed himself within a discourse of publicity that was only partly connected to textual production.[6] Before even coming to London in March 1760, he had orchestrated approval of his work (using the first, self-published, York edition of 1759) from David Garrick, the most celebrated actor and theatrical producer of the day, and this became a publicly noted friendship following his arrival in the capital. By the end of May, Sterne had negotiated contracts for – and seen the publication of – London editions of *Tristram Shandy* and *The Sermons of Mr. Yorick*. He had also procured acceptance of his dedication to the Prime Minister, William Pitt, obtained a frontispiece illustration by the renowned artist William Hogarth, and sat for a portrait by Joshua Reynolds that would be engraved for his edition of the *Sermons*, the opening volumes of which boasted a prestigious list of 660 subscribers.

We should return to Sterne's first access to fashionable London life, David Garrick, to assess an essential quality of celebrity: personal presence. Garrick had effected a revolution in acting technique in the 1740s by creating a less formal, more 'natural' style that emphasised the particular details of a character rather than a universal human nature. Twice in the second instalment of *Tristram Shandy* Sterne would invoke Garrick, first placing the actor against the rule-bound grammarians who only consult their watches during Garrick's dramatic pauses: 'But in suspending his voice——was the sense suspended likewise? Did no expression of attitude or countenance fill up the chasm?—— Was the eye silent?' (*TS* 3.12.213). The bookishness of the grammarians is contrasted to Garrick's *embodiment* of sense, something that Sterne valued (as is evident from the rhetoric of his sermons) and sought to translate into printed form in *Tristram Shandy*. The dependence of Garrick's technique on the style of the individual actor (rather than on a stock of codified gestures) blurs the lines between his own self and that of the characters he portrayed; and this confusion leads to his celebrity. Garrick was much sought out off the stage, and was known for 'performing' at non-theatrical social settings, such as a Parisian salon or a London art show.[7] Sterne clearly emulates Garrick's social presence, and sees it as an essential part of true celebrity. This is apparent in Tristram's second invocation: 'O *Garrick!* what a rich scene of this would thy exquisite powers make! and how gladly would I write such another to avail myself of thy immortality, and secure my own behind it' (4.7.333).

'Tall, opake words' and the physicality of print

That Sterne is concerned with the possibilities for personal presence in a text is clear from the great lengths to which he pushed his publishers to play with the *mise en page* (the design and layout) of his work. In a jocoserious letter appended to his first published work of satirical fiction, *A Political Romance*, the author forbids his printer 'to alter or transpose one Word, nor rectify one false Spelling, nor so much as add or diminish one Comma or Tittle, in or to my *Romance*' (*Letters* 68). Such work usually was left to the printer, but Sterne was invested in the minutiae of his text. As he wrote to his prospective London publisher, Robert Dodsley, concerning his own, first, York edition of *Tristram Shandy*, 'I ... shall correct every proof myself, it shall go perfect into the world, and be printed in so creditable a way as to paper, type, &c., as to do no dishonour to you' (*Letters* 80–1).

Tristram Shandy is a veritable museum of typographic idiosyncrasy, particular examples of which I discuss below. However, we must note that this is consistent in all of Sterne's publications. For example, in printing the London edition of his sermons (especially the second set, published in 1766), Sterne attempted to ensure that these dramatic performances would be rendered onto the page. Drawing on the Scriblerian tradition of performative textuality (in which non-verbal elements supplement the verbal meaning of the text) and the already established Shandean style of presentation, Sterne renders the orality of his sermons on the page by the use of white space, expressive dashes, and other techniques of layout.[8] Implicit in the use of these techniques is the recognition that language is material. A print culture only emphasises this as it distances us from the sense of a living author and presents mere matter: black marks on the page, or, as an exasperated Tristram at one point puts it, 'tall, opake words' (*TS* 3.20.235). Sterne will not let his reader forget that 'texts' (an abstract concept) are in reality concrete books, physical things that require tactile handling. A minutely detailed instance of this philosophy occurs when Corporal Trim is instructed to look for 'aught of a sailing chariot' in Stevinus's book. Trim does not use the index, the table of contents, or read through Stevinus for references to the chariot. Instead, he drolly insists on making 'sure work' of the task: 'so taking hold of the two covers of the book, one in each hand, and letting the leaves fall down, as he bent the covers back, he gave the book a good sound shake' (2.15.137–8). If texts are things (objects), they are paradoxical ones because they communicate. They do this through a fiction about the transparent referentiality of abstract words. However, interfering with this fiction, reminding us that communication takes place through physicality, is the *mise en page*; the presence of the page is a counter to the abstract conception of literature.

This also has implications for the idea of authorship. How can the page compensate for the absence of the author at the time of reading? And what is unique to print culture about this concern? Mark Rose has argued that the development of cultural interest in both biographical authors and the creation of psychologically realistic characters in the eighteenth-century novel is a response to the vexed issue of copyright during this period. He suggests that the need to ground copyright in a particular owner of intellectual property gives rise to the development of the value of originality in literary composition (as opposed to neoclassical imitation), and to the notion of personality as something transferable to literature, making a work unique (and hence something that can be owned). Thus copyright debates played a role in creating the romantic idea that the author becomes known through his work.[9] In Rose's view, the author is a construct of a print culture that needs to locate the origins of the text for primarily financial or legal reasons; it is the literary text that performs this construction. For Sterne, however, even as his animated pages offer the idiosyncrasy of the text as a substitute for the personality of the author, the independent existence of the author is never out of sight.

And in this regard, Sterne ultimately seems to resist the openness of the print market; he resists the 'death of the author' implied in a vision of the author as a textual construct. This is manifest in two somewhat contradictory ways: the physicality of his printed books, and a thematic strain of resistance to print itself within *Tristram Shandy*. First, the typographical gestures that Sterne offers in *Tristram Shandy* make his book stand out from the crush of books. Among the more obvious examples are the black page memorialising Yorick (*TS* 1.12.37–8; see Fig. 1); the chapter 'torn out' and represented by a 'chasm of ten pages' (4.25.372); the blank page provided for the reader to draw his own widow Wadman (6.38.567); the diagrams of the narrative line (6.40.570–1; see Fig. 2, discussed below); and the flourish of Trim's stick (9.4.743). More subtly, throughout the nine volumes of the work as a whole, we find a characteristic textual 'feel' – in the ubiquitous asterisks, the generous use of varying dash-lengths, the unconventional deployment on the page of white space (see, for example, 6.18.526–9) and printer's devices (even

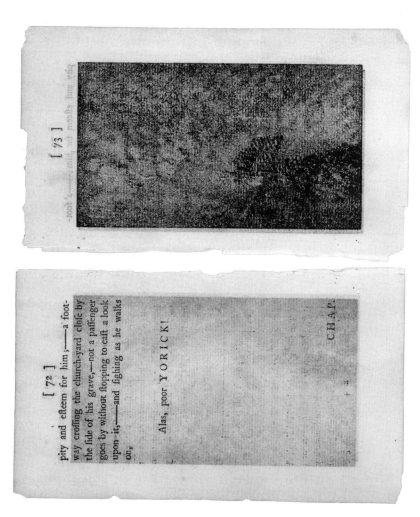

Figure 1 Yorick's death and the black page in volume 1 of *Tristram Shandy*, 2nd edn (1760), pp. 72–3.

C H A P. XL.

I Am now beginning to get fairly into
my work; and by the help of a
vegitable diet, with a few of the cold
seeds, I make no doubt but I shall be
able to go on with my uncle *Toby*'s story,
and my own, in a tolerable straight line.
Now,

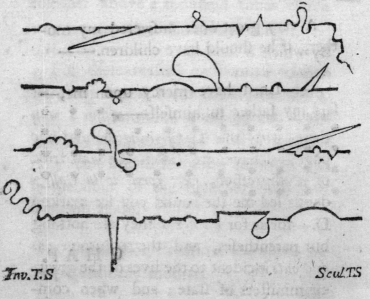

Inv. T.S   *Scul. T.S*

These

Figure 2 Lines of narrative for volumes 1 to 4 of *Tristram Shandy*, from the first edition
of volume 6 (1761), p. 152.

catchwords, which were strictly for the purposes of ensuring continuity of pages at the press).

Although not without precedent, the ostentatious, concentrated, and consistent use of typographic effects is unique to Sterne.[10] His authorial 'personality' is immediately recognisable by sight alone. But this gives rise to questions about originality. The Shandean style proved itself to be quite imitable, as the number of 'literary' responses suggests. Furthermore, as idiosyncratic as the layout of the book is, what does it mean that there were at least five thousand more or less identical copies in circulation by the end of 1760?[11] Here we may turn to Sterne's most famous textual experiment: the marbled page (*TS* 3.36.269–70). The marbled page may be seen as a response to, or even a struggle against, the fixity of print. One expects a printed book to correspond to other copies of the same edition, give or take the odd correction to standing type.[12] The significant feature of marbling in this context is that, as a variable manual process, it produces a different result each time it is done. Thus, unlike printing, the act of marbling changes the design in each copy of *Tristram Shandy*'s third volume.[13] It is as if Sterne – so insistent on the physicality of the text – finds in the uniformity of print an abstraction that represents the absence of the author from the reader. By transcending the idiosyncrasy of his printed presentation in an entire edition with the idiosyncrasy of each individual copy, Sterne has asserted the singularity and originality of his work. And so, despite the apparent comfort of Sterne's sense of himself as an operator within print culture (in his management of fame, finance, and physicality), there remains within *Tristram Shandy* something of a nostalgia for the manual production of manuscript culture: for that presence of the author at the time of inscription that qualifies our sense of Sterne as 'typographic man'.[14]

'Inv.T.S | Scul.T.S': graphism, print and authorship

One consistent motif in *Tristram Shandy* that operates in counterpoint to the bravura performance of textual presence is woven into the work by means of references to the author as a biographical reality. In references to the scene of writing, *Tristram Shandy* explores the philosophical implications of a print culture for ideas concerning personal identity: 'Every line I write, I feel an abatement of the quickness of my pulse, and of that careless alacrity with it, which every day of my life prompts me to say and write a thousand things I should not' (*TS* 3.28.254). Here, in one of several represented scenes of writing, we are presented with a meditation on writing as a manifestation of the individual mind in a physical act, a biological function by which the inner being is expressed and made present to the world, and to the writer's self. As the passage goes on, 'this moment that I last dipp'd my pen into my ink' becomes a confirmation of Tristram's existence in space and time (four specific dates of composition, from 9 March 1759 to 12 August 1766, are given over the course of the work). He is biologically one with his writing, developing the preceding connection of his pulse and his writing into a sanguinary apostrophe: 'spurting thy ink about thy table and thy books' (3.28.254). *Tristram Shandy* is one of the most personalised deployments of print we know, and yet, even as Sterne pushed his printers to heights of expressive idiosyncrasy, he harboured a sense of alienation from print: can the manipulation of cast type in a print shop by a team of journeymen render the authorial self?

The unpronounceable subtitle above comes from the abbreviated phrases beneath Tristram's diagram of his narrative lines (*TS* 6.40.570), signifying that 'Tristram Shandy invented' and 'engraved' these lines. What is the meaning of Sterne's use of print technology in the context of Tristram's many explicit references to technologies other than that of movable type printing: pen, ink and paper, pencil and paintbrush, the pentagraph, coin stamping, marbling and engraving? I refer to these under the heading of 'graphism' to distinguish them from print, for the insistent presence of non-print graphism in the context of the printed work marks an attempt to authorise the printed work – that is, to tie the multiplied and disseminated product to its author or originator. In Fig. 2, the crooked lines draw attention to themselves in their peculiar relationship to print. They are clearly woodcuts that stand out against the movable type of the page, attesting to an older technology, and perhaps alluding to an ornamental calligraphic flourish associated with writing (as with the later flourish of Trim's stick (9.4.743)). Yet, at the same time, they are embedded in a linear text and very carefully set parallel to the lines of type. Their deviance from the straight lines (literal and metaphorical) that Tristram writes about in this chapter and elsewhere is limited by the medium. If the medium limits the expression of individual deviance, what is the interrelationship between developing senses of authorship in the eighteenth-century print market and the sense of agency made available to the author in the material act of inscription? The question is implicit in Tristram's inscription: 'Invenit T.S' suggests both literary senses of 'invention' – the first of the five parts of classical rhetoric, which seeks out existing arguments for deployment – and the modern conception of 'originality'. 'Sculpsit T.S', the personal act of engraving, implies the uniqueness of the artefact (another sense of originality), and its direct connection to the author. How can the act of printing – multiplying a text in the absence of the author, and disseminating it in a different material medium – be an 'authorial' act?

In a study of early modern writing manuals, Jonathan Goldberg draws attention to the relay between the cultural violence enabled by writing (social stratification, control of knowledge) and the physical violence of the material scene of writing: the focus on the knife that sharpens the quill or stylus, and the subsequent ploughing and gouging metaphors used to describe the action of the pen upon paper.[15] Readers of Sterne might find a parallel scene of textual violence where Walter Shandy seeks to 'scratch some better sense' into Erasmus by means of a penknife: 'See, my dear brother *Toby*, how I have mended the sense.—But you have marr'd a word, replied my uncle *Toby*.—My father put on his spectacles,—bit his lip,—and tore out the leaf in a passion' (*TS* 3.37.272). This literal violence has metaphorical application elsewhere in *Tristram Shandy*, as when Tristram rounds on the reviewers of his previous instalment: 'how could you cut and slash my jerkin as you did?——how did you know, but you would cut my lining too?' (3.4.190–1).

The literary 'violence of the letter' that interests Goldberg is the forced conformity of the hand to the rule of writing. The standardisation of hand-writing marks the erasure of the author's personal hand. Goldberg further notes of his sources that 'the printed books realise what was implicit in the writing practices prescribed in the manuals, for if the aim was to produce a hand conformed to a model, printing insured the duplication of the hand'.[16] The effacement of the writer in the act of writing after a model is clinched by the replicating technology of print. Returning to the diagrams of volume 6, consider Tristram's version of Goldberg's thesis. Tristram speaks of the decreasing deviance of his narrative from linear expectations:

> If I mend at this rate, it is not impossible ... but I may arrive hereafter at the excellency of going on even thus;
>
> ———————————————————————————————
>
> which is a line drawn as straight as I could draw it, by a writing-master's ruler, (borrowed for that purpose) turning neither to the right hand or to the left.
> (*TS* 6.40.571–2)

As we know from comments on straight lines elsewhere in *Tristram Shandy*, such a history is 'morally speaking, impossible', for any author of spirit 'will have fifty deviations from a straight line to make with this or that party as he goes along, which he can no ways avoid' (1.14.41). The fact that Tristram does not own his own ruler suggests that he will not conform his hand to the rule, even as he promises to do just that.

But how will he convey his idiosyncratic hand in so regulated a medium as print? Or, how is an author to convey his sense of self in this impersonal form? One of the ways in which Sterne attempts to 'reinscribe' printing – to personalise and authorise it – is by insisting on the scene of writing that stands behind the printed artefact: 'In less than five minutes I shall have thrown my pen into the fire, and the little drop of thick ink which is left remaining at the bottom of my ink-horn, after it' (*TS* 4.32.400). Tristram reminds us and himself, by means of such details, that there is a living being behind these printed words.

And this is not only a comic reminder, for inscription is, as it were, a confirmation of agency and, as such, a means of self-knowledge in the existential sense: a moment of conscious self-identity. The precedent for Sterne's deployment of writing to manifest self-presence may be found in John Locke's philosophical discussion of personal identity. Here, writing becomes a ground for a present identity based in consciousness:

> Had I the same consciousness, that I saw the Ark and *Noah*'s Flood, as that I saw an overflowing of the *Thames* last Winter, or as that I write now, I could no more doubt that I, that write this now, that saw the *Thames* overflow'd last Winter, and that view'd the Flood at the general Deluge, was the same *self* … than that I that write this am the same *my self* now whilst I write … that I was Yesterday.[17]

Writing, for Locke, reveals a sense of continuing self-presence by acting as a sort of mirror; the self is doubled through writing, allowing self-recognition.

Tristram, too, asserts that the activity of writing manifests an author's sense of his existence, for 'every letter I trace tells me with what rapidity Life follows my pen' (*TS* 9.8.754). A subsequent discussion of writer's block confirms the biological connection of life and writing. 'I never stand confering with pen and ink one moment', Tristram boasts, and when other remedies fail:

> I take a razor at once; and having tried the edge of it upon the palm of my hand, without further ceremony, except that of first lathering my beard, I shave it off … for consider, Sir, as every man chuses to be present at the shaving of his own beard (though there is no rule without an exception) and unavoidably sits overagainst himself the whole time it is doing, in case he has a hand in it—the Situation, like all others, has notions of her own to put into the brain.—— (9.13.763)

Tristram finds that the self-presence induced by shaving gives rise to intellectual reflection, which is both a pre- and co-requisite for writing. Through this process of making himself present to himself, he becomes able to extend this reflection into the writing that further confirms his presence: 'A man cannot dress, but his ideas get cloath'd at the same time; and if he dresses like a gentleman, every one of them stands presented to his imagination, genteelized along with him—so that he has nothing to do, but take his pen, and write like himself' (9.13.764). This is an application of Locke's formula for identity: *I write therefore I am*. In dragging one's pen across the page, one is confirmed in one's biological sense of an empirical self – externalised on the page, yet connected to the volition that drives the hand. This is not a connection available to the author of works circulating in print, or at least not without considerable and somewhat paradoxical effort.

In December 1761, Sterne began to autograph every instalment of *Tristram Shandy* (see Fig. 3). This was probably an attempt to protect his copyright, supported by advertisements stating that 'Every book is signed by the Author'. But might we also read this decision as an attempt to ground the printed text in its biological origins? Jacques Derrida has taught us the paradox of originality implicit in the signature – that mark of singularity which must be repeated.[18] Sterne certainly enjoyed such problems, as the various puzzles of identity posed in *Tristram Shandy* suggest, including the unrepeatability of the marbled page and the impasse that arises when, in narrating two separate trips through Auxerre, Tristram finds he has been 'getting forwards in two different journies together, and with the same dash of the pen', and must pause to 'collect myself' before continuing (*TS* 7.28.621–2). However, the signatory act was also a moment to confirm identity for Sterne in several ways. Here, I turn to a well-known anecdote about Sterne's schooldays in the 1720s (well-known because it is the only one he supplied to posterity), in which his Yorkshire schoolmaster

> had the cieling of the school-room new white-washed—the ladder remained there—I one unlucky day mounted it, and wrote with a brush in large capital letters, LAU. STERNE, for which the usher severely whipped me. My master was very much hurt at this, and said, before me, that never should that name be effaced, for I was a boy of genius, and he was sure I should come to preferment—this expression made me forget the stripes I had received—   (*Letters* 3–4)

This is the single anecdote of his youth in the memoir Sterne wrote for his daughter Lydia, suggesting that the mature author recognised the importance of the lesson learned that day decades earlier. There are in fact several lessons to be learned here, for the context in which this memory is produced affects the meaning of the incident. The memoir was begun in 1758 (before Sterne's rise to fame), but this anecdote was added in 1767, at the height of his celebrity, and near the end of his life, as he was aware. In other words, this narrative of primal graphism (the autograph in graffiti) is recalled and written only after Sterne had fulfilled his schoolmaster's prophecy. It is also recounted after Sterne had signed issues of *Tristram Shandy* for six years, to a probable total of some 12,250 signatures.[19]

The anecdote concerns an *act* of writing, and it would appear that it is the *action* of signing his name that is of first importance. Sterne's account draws

L Sterne

THE
LIFE and OPINIONS
OF
TRISTRAM SHANDY, Gent.

CHAP. I.

I CALL all the powers of time and chance, which feverally check us in our careers in this world, to bear me witnefs, that I could never yet get fairly to my uncle Toby's amours, till this very moment, that my mother's *curiofity*,

Vol. IX. B as

attention to the activity of this writing. He does not say 'I wrote my name upon the ceiling'. Rather, he gives us the action letter by letter, printed in capitals in Lydia's 1775 edition of the memoir (the incomplete manuscript lacks this passage). The importance of this act of writing is shown in its production of two kinds of self-confirmation for the boy, by which I mean the confirmation of his existence to himself: first, in body, with the whipping given by the usher ('stripe' is probably from the Germanic *strippen*, to flog, but also suggests the graphic); second, in mind or soul, with the master's declaration of the boy's genius. Both acts correlate the marks made with the maker, their referent, the signatory Laurence Sterne. This is Sterne's primal scene of writing. It asserts his existence in the same way that the signatures in *Tristram Shandy* draw attention to Laurence Sterne, who may or may not be identical with the Tristram who so carefully describes his scenes of writing. It is this Laurence Sterne who decides to relate the anecdote in 1767, in a world very different from that of the schoolboy. The unity of authorship with the act of writing has dissolved over the intervening years. Sterne the literary celebrity has seen his name fly out of his control – has seen published spurious continuations of his work, and, in one case, has even read a report of his own death; he has lost the feel of the pen moving across the pages of which he is supposedly the author. Does the anecdote of the schoolboy reassert his sense of himself as a writer? Surely he recognised that the anecdote would not have been called for if he were not a public figure. Just as the rebellious lines of narrative in volume 6 are subject to the rule of print, and are interpretable only in relation to straight lines, so the value of the writer – the act of writing itself, even as it confirms the writer's self-identity – is found in the circulation of print.

The real historical biological boy writing his name from the ladder is produced to testify to the existence of an aging and decaying Laurence Sterne. However, the anecdote would not exist for us without the demand for such a concrete detail as an author. Ironically, this demand is created by the intervening figure of a fictional Tristram Shandy, who himself attempts to confirm his reality by means of writing:

> It is not half an hour ago, when (in the great hurry and precipitation of a poor devil's writing for daily bread) I threw a fair sheet, which I had just finished, and carefully wrote out, slap into the fire, instead of the foul one.
>
> Instantly I snatch'd off my wig, and threw it perpendicularly, with all imaginable violence, up to the top of the room—indeed I caught it as it fell—but there was an end of the matter; nor do I think any thing else in *Nature*, would have given such immediate ease. (*TS* 4.17.349–50)

This image of the writer evokes many of the facets of Sterne's involvement with print culture. It is a scene of writing placed in a Grubstreet context of writing for bread, where the pressure of the press causes the hurry and precipitation of the error. It represents a failure to fit the biological human element into the mechanised system of print. And yet Tristram's recovery in this scene re-humanises the author. Every one of us has done the equivalent of tossing our wig at the frustrations of writing, and hence we will recognise the author in the work, even as we realise the impossibility of so discovering the 'real' Laurence Sterne.

NOTES

1. A convenient summary of print culture conditions is found in John Brewer, *Pleasures of the Imagination: English Culture in the Eighteenth Century* (London: Harper Collins, 1997), 125–97; see esp. 148–51.

2. For different views of Pope's celebrity, see James McLaverty, *Pope, Print, and Meaning* (Oxford: Oxford University Press, 2001), esp. 50–68, and Helen Deutsch, *Resemblance and Disgrace: Alexander Pope and the Deformation of Culture* (Cambridge, MA: Harvard University Press, 1996), 17–23.

3. Colley Cibber, *A Letter from Mr. Cibber to Mr. Pope* (1742), 9, quoted in *Letters* 92.

4. See, in general, Brean Hammond, *Professional Imaginative Writing in England, 1670–1740: 'Hackney for Bread'* (Oxford: Clarendon Press, 1997).

5. Anne Bandry has suggested that, in subsequent volumes of *Tristram Shandy*, Sterne adopted ideas from some of his imitators ('Imitations of *Tristram Shandy*', in *Critical Essays on Laurence Sterne*, ed. Melvyn New (New York, NY: G. K. Hall, 1998), 39–52). Thomas Keymer offers a more broadly theoretical approach to the serialisation of *Tristram Shandy* in *Sterne, the Moderns, and the Novel* (Oxford: Oxford University Press, 2002), 85–149.

6. For a fuller account of this phenomenon, including the role of Garrick, see Peter M. Briggs, 'Laurence Sterne and Literary Celebrity in 1760', *Age of Johnson* 4 (1991), 251–80.

7. On the physiology of the passions and the codification of gesture in the period, see Alan T. McKenzie, *Certain, Lively Episodes: The Articulation of Passion in Eighteenth-Century Prose* (Athens, GA: University of Georgia Press, 1990); McKenzie offers telling anecdotes about Garrick's offstage demonstration of his gestural technique for conveying different emotions at 1–5.

8. See Christopher Fanning, 'On Sterne's Page: Spatial Layout, Spatial Form, and Social Spaces in *Tristram Shandy*', *Eighteenth-Century Fiction* 10 (1998), 429–50; also 'Small Particles of Eloquence: Sterne and the Scriblerian Text', *Modern Philology* 100 (2003), 360–92. Sterne's attention to minutiae did not diminish, and there is evidence that, in 1767, he requested changes to the lengths of the dashes in volumes 5 and 6: see Melvyn New's introduction to the Florida edition (*TS* 835–7).

9. Mark Rose, *Authors and Owners: The Invention of Copyright* (Cambridge, MA: Harvard University Press, 1993), 113–29.

10. On the use of book format in novels prior to Sterne's, see Janine Barchas, *Graphic Design, Print Culture, and the Eighteenth-Century Novel* (Cambridge: Cambridge University Press, 2003).

11. Exact print-runs of the opening volumes are uncertain, but Kenneth Monkman proposes a figure of between 200 and 500 copies for Sterne's York edition, and 5,000 copies for the first London edition ('Bibliography of Early Editions of *Tristram Shandy*', *The Library*, 5th series 25 (1970), 11–39). There were also two further London editions and three Dublin editions in 1760.

12. Fixity is one of the key features of print for Elizabeth Eisenstein, *The Printing Press as an Agent of Change: Cultural Transformations in Early Modern Europe*, 2 vols. (Cambridge: Cambridge University Press, 1979), I, 113–26. Adrian Johns has argued that 'fixity' is a construct created by publishers themselves (*The Nature of the Book: Print and Knowledge in the Making* (Chicago, IL: University of Chicago Press, 1998), esp. 10–32 and 628–38), but it was certainly an expectation among readers.

13. For a full description of the laborious (and costly) process of marbling, see Diana Patterson, 'Tristram's Marblings and Marblers', *Shandean* 3 (1991), 70–97.

14. The phrase is from Marshall McLuhan's pioneering study of print culture, *The Gutenberg Galaxy: The Making of Typographic Man* (Toronto, ON: University of Toronto Press, 1962).

15. Jonathan Goldberg, *Writing Matter: From the Hands of the English Renaissance* (Stanford, CA: Stanford University Press, 1990), esp. 57–108.

16. Goldberg, *Writing Matter*, 136.

17. John Locke, *An Essay Concerning Human Understanding*, ed. Peter H. Nidditch (Oxford: Clarendon Press, 1975), 340–1 (2.27.§16). There has been much debate over the seriousness or otherwise of Sterne's use of Locke; for a balanced account, see Peter M. Briggs, 'Locke's *Essay* and the Tentativeness of *Tristram Shandy*', *Studies in Philology* 82 (1985), 494–517.

18. Jacques Derrida, 'Signature Event Context', in his *Limited Inc*, trans. Samuel Weber and Jeffrey Mehlman (Evanston, IL: Northwestern University Press, 1988), 1–23.

19. See Kenneth Monkman's 'Bibliographical Descriptions' in the Florida edition (*TS* 907–38), which give the following figures for the signed volumes: volume 5, first edition, 4,000 copies; volume 5, second edition, 750 copies; volume 7, 4,000 copies; volume 9, 3,500 copies (noting that at least one surviving copy of volume 9 lacks Sterne's signature).

10

PETER DE VOOGD

Sterne and visual culture

We will never know his name, and can only guess at his motives. He was probably a sailor, who possessed a copy of W. W. Ryland's stipple engraving (1779) after Angelica Kauffman's painting of 'Maria – Moulines', and had time on his hands. He cut out Maria's face, coloured it in, stitched it on an oval piece of canvas, and skilfully embroidered the rest with wool and silk: her white dress, her dog Sylvio, a brook, and a poplar tree (see Fig. 4). His 'woolwork' is unusual in that it does not depict a ship or naval scene, as is normally the case in this curious genre (woolwork being a type of woven or embroidered picture widely produced by sailors in the period, usually of their own vessels). And although this is a rare and early example, it is not the only one. At least one similar woolwork has recently been auctioned on the eBay website, and has an intriguing series of three finely-wrought silk embroidered pictures with cutwork appliqués, which tell the entire story that inspired them, from Maria sitting by the roadside in *A Sentimental Journey* to Yorick discovering her there and escorting her into Moulines. Sterne would have been pleased to find his '*Work of Redemption*' (*Letters* 399) so popular in this humble species of folk art.

He would also have been intrigued by the art form, and by the way in which his deliberate set-piece of sentimental writing had been translated into a visual medium, for he had a vivid interest in the relationship between word and image. From the very start of his writing career, he was aware of the self-promoting value of graphic representation in the business of marketing his work. On arriving in London to see how the first two volumes of *Tristram Shandy* were doing, he asked William Hogarth to design a frontispiece for the second (first London) edition of his book, using Richard Berenger, a close friend of Garrick and an acquaintance of Hogarth, as an intermediary. In his letter to Berenger, he asks 'for no more than ten Strokes of *Howgarth's* witty Chissel, to clap at the Front of my next Edition of *Shandy*', and specifies the subject: 'the loosest Sketch in nature of Trim's reading the sermon to my father & my uncle Toby' (*Letters* 99, 101). The remarkable result of this

Figure 4 Anonymous woolwork based on the stipple engraving by William Wynne Ryland
(1779) of Angelica Kauffman's painting 'Maria – Moulines' (1777).

request from an obscure clergyman from the north of England to one of the most famous artists of the day was the frontispiece to volume 1 (engraved by Simon François Ravenet, Hogarth's favourite engraver and a leading book illustrator of the period), the second state of which, with clock and hat added, adorned all subsequent London printings and was frequently adopted in other editions. Hogarth also designed a frontispiece for volume 4, depicting the christening of baby Tristram, and can thus be listed as Sterne's first illustrator. His two frontispieces (see Fig. 5) fixed the visual features of Shandy Hall's inhabitants until the present day, not only by virtue of their inclusion in many of the most prominent editions of *Tristram Shandy*, but also because other illustrators have tended to follow Hogarth's designs when representing the sermon-reading and christening scenes.

Later that spring, Sterne managed to persuade Sir Joshua Reynolds to paint his portrait. Now in the National Portrait Gallery and known as the Lansdowne portrait, this splendid oil shows Sterne in full clerical garb, gazing at the viewer, resting his right elbow on a table with writing implements and the manuscript of *Tristram Shandy*, and leaning his head on his right hand.

Figure 5 William Hogarth's frontispieces to the second edition (1760) of *Tristram Shandy*, volumes 1 and 2 (Trim reading the sermon), and to the first edition (1761) of volumes 3 and 4 (Tristram's baptism), engraved by Simon-François Ravenet.

His other hand rests almost jauntily on his hip, and his clerical bob-wig is slightly askew. The painting was exhibited at the Society of Artists in 1761, where a visitor observed that Sterne appears 'in as facetious a humour as if he would tell you a story of Tristram Shandy',[1] and was engraved in mezzotint for mounting and framing by Edward Fisher and again by S. W. Reynolds. A line engraving was made by Ravenet to serve as frontispiece to the two volumes of Sterne's sermons published in May under the somewhat scandalous title of *The Sermons of Mr. Yorick*, when many readers took offence at Sterne's use of his jesting Yorick persona in a sacred context. This portrait was to lead a life of its own, reappearing and subtly changing in numerous editions, both British and foreign. It came to stand model for a significant number of illustrations in which Sterne's fictional characters, notably Yorick, are given his own features, thus registering, though also oversimplifying, an association of identities that Sterne had established himself. Indeed, his face as represented by Reynolds crops up in the most unexpected places, such as a plate in George Henry Millar's *New, Complete and Universal System of Geography* (1783, facing II, 671), with the caption 'The Beggars asking Alms of Sterne, at Montreuil in France'. Thus, from the beginning, Sterne's work and persona were associated with, and promoted by, the two greatest living British painters, at a point in the history of book illustration when very few novels were illustrated at all.[2]

The second person to illustrate Sterne's work was Sterne himself, a fact sometimes overlooked, but there is no doubt that he designed the curious squiggles – captioned 'Inv. T. S | Scul. T. S' (*TS* 6.40.570–1) – in volume 6, the woodcut depicting Corporal Trim's flourish in volume 9, the coat of arms in *A Sentimental Journey*, and of course that 'motly emblem of my work!', the hand-marbled leaf in volume 3 of *Tristram Shandy* (3.36.269–70), which in early editions cleverly subverts the basic principle of the printed book as identical reproduction. The two marbled pages, with their margins and page-numbers, are unique 'texts' that turn each copy of *Tristram Shandy* into an individual work of art.[3]

The visual quality of much of Sterne's writing – both in the highly pictorial descriptions of characters and scenes and in the allusions to artists and contemporary aesthetic theory – has often been noted. Commentators on his narrative technique regularly note his distinctive use of the indescribability trope ('words cannot paint...') and the visual imperative, and it is striking how frequently the reader is urged to 'behold' or 'observe', to 'picture' or 'see' a scene. Of particular relevance in this context is the point in *Tristram Shandy* at which the reader is openly invited to produce an illustration to the text on a page left blank for the purpose in volume 6. Here the reader is asked to imagine the widow Wadman, and to 'call for pen and ink—here's paper ready to your hand. ——Sit down, Sir, paint her to your own mind——as like your mistress as you can——as unlike your wife as your conscience will let you' (*TS* 6.38.566). The blank page is a logical complement to the black and marbled pages, another witness to the impossibility of perfect communication in language, which may be why no early reader is known to have taken up Tristram's challenge in any surviving copy.

Few contemporary novelists were so frequently portrayed as Sterne. Even before he shot to fame, George Romney is said to have painted him (a portrait now unfortunately lost), and we know of an early caricature in oil of Sterne in a harlequin's costume by Thomas Bridges, owned by a Dr James Atkinson in York, who showed it to the collector Thomas Frognall Dibdin in 1838. The painting has now disappeared, but Dibdin had an engraving made, a double picture of Bridges as mountebank and Sterne as his apprentice. When famous, Sterne was painted by Sir Joshua Reynolds, Benjamin West, Thomas Patch, Carmontelle (Louis Carrogis), and John Hamilton Mortimer; Joseph

Nollekens sculpted a life-size bust.[4] Sterne obviously realised that portraits were important for the marketing of his work, and his letters contain numerous references to copies of his own likeness that were made, given to friends, or shown to others, as well as references to portraits of people he knew and liked, such as Commodore and Mrs James, close friends of his last years, at whose house he first met Eliza Draper, the young woman he fell in love with in 1767, and whose portrait he bandied about in public and immortalised in the opening pages of *A Sentimental Journey*.

Equally striking is Sterne's theoretical and technical know-how. His satire of connoisseurs in *Tristram Shandy* indicates his intimate knowledge of contemporary aesthetic terminology, and the same is clear from his extended play on Hogarth's treatise, *The Analysis of Beauty* (1753), in the opening volumes of the work. He also clearly expects his readers to pick up allusions to specific works of art, as when Father Lorenzo in *A Sentimental Journey* is described in terms of a painting by the Italian baroque master Guido Reni. Sterne listed painting as one of his hobbies, and John Croft, whose inimical character sketch is one of the few we have, confirms that he liked to paint; 'he had a good Idea of Drawing, but not the least of mixing his colours', is Croft's characteristic comment.[5] Towards the end of his life, Sterne was still riding this hobby-horse when he 'presented [Mrs James] ... with colours, and an apparatus for painting, and gave her several lessons before I left town' (*Letters* 412).

Finally, of course, there is Sterne's active involvement in the practical design of his books, his insistence that layout, typeface, and format were essential contributors to meaning and effect, the fact that he personally oversaw the production of his texts, and the probability that he composed them with an eye to the exact appearance of the words on the page (see ch. 9 of this work). Read from a painterly point of view, his novels and sermons appear to contain many discrete 'scenes', composed as tableaux, often with an over-supply of gratuitous visual detail, or using the technique of freeze-framing the action, as when the Shandy brothers take several chapters to descend a staircase. (It is this sequence (*TS* 4.9–13.335–43) that inspired Patrick Caulfield, commissioned to design a tapestry for the British Library at St Pancras in 1994, in his monumental 'Pause on the Landing', now displayed in the hall of the library's conference centre.) When we think of *Tristram Shandy*, we see the Shandy brothers in the parlour, talking and smoking pipes; when we think of *A Sentimental Journey*, we see Yorick and Father Lorenzo exchanging snuff boxes in front of the remise door. It is not to be wondered at that Sterne has become one of the most illustrated writers of English literature.

For the history of the reception of a literary work, illustrations are an important source, as Robert Halsband demonstrated in his groundbreaking history of Alexander Pope's *The Rape of the Lock* (1714). David Blewett, who does something similar for *Robinson Crusoe* (1719), justly remarks that 'the repeated illustration of the same scene in successive illustrated editions or...the simultaneous existence of several rival editions with illustrations of the same scene...reinforces the importance and power of those scenes, fixing them in the memory, like a device of rhetoric, while also building up a collective visual comment'.[6] Sterne is an ideal subject for reception history of this kind, as both the most published and the most illustrated novelist of the eighteenth century; the frequency as well as consistency of illustrations of his works over time enable us to trace in detail the fluctuations of his critical reception. The English-language editions alone yield well over 1,300 different illustrations, and the field is so vast that it must be subdivided. In what follows, I take into account paintings and prints, book illustrations, and artefacts illustrating *Tristram Shandy* and *A Sentimental Journey*, and trace the ways in which these have both reflected and influenced changing responses to, and understandings of, Sterne's literary output. Because these two works were (and are) differently received, it will be necessary to distinguish between them; in this, as in other respects, his writing has, as he famously puts it, '*more handles than one*' (*Letters* 411).

Tristram Shandy

In true Shandean fashion, the earliest known paintings based on *Tristram Shandy* are known only by name. Painted in 1761 and 1762 by George Romney, who knew Sterne when he lived in York, these canvases represented the death of Le Fever, Dr Slop's encounter with Obadiah, Uncle Toby and Obadiah in the garden, and the introduction of Slop to the Shandy brothers. The last survives in the form of an engraving reproduced in William Hayley's *Life of George Romney* (1809), and shows, in a crowded frame, the Shandy brothers and Obadiah realistically portrayed, with a caricatured Dr Slop. Another early series of four images did survive in its entirety, designed in 1772 by the amateur draughtsman Henry William Bunbury. 'The Overthrow of Dr. Slop', 'The Battle of the Cataplasm', 'The Siege of Namur' (Fig. 6), and 'The Damnation of Obadiah' were engraved and published by James Bretherton in 1773, reprinted in 1799 by S. W. Fores, and lithographed in 1815–17; at least one Dublin piracy is known. Bretherton and Fores dealt in large numbers, and sets, coloured and uncoloured, still turn up for sale with some regularity. 'The Battle of the Cataplasm' was copied as a frontispiece in a 1779 Dublin printing of *Tristram Shandy*, but otherwise these designs were used exclusively in the print trade. For Bunbury, *Tristram Shandy* was clearly, above all, a comic novel: both in his choice of subjects and in the caricaturing

Figure 6 Henry William Bunbury, 'The Siege of Namur' (designed 1772, engraved 1773).

tendency of his designs, Bunbury opted for farce as opposed to humour, portraying Sterne's characters as conspicuously mad.[7]

The same is true of the series of twelve prints designed by Robert Dighton in 1784 and published by Carington Bowles in 1785 under the title 'Prints, representing the most interesting, sentimental, and humorous Scenes, in Tristram Shandy'. Like Bunbury, Dighton was free to use his own format, working as he did for the print trade as opposed to a book publisher. He opted for landscape folio, an unusual and 'wide' horizontal format, which allowed him to include copious detail. Dighton obviously knew the designs of three fellow illustrators, all of whom worked for the book trade. These were Michael Angelo Rooker, Thomas Stothard, and Daniel Dodd, who had designed plates for three editions of Sterne a few years beforehand: the 1780 *Collected Works* brought out by a consortium of booksellers led by William Strahan, the 1781 reprint of Sterne's novels in Harrison's *Novelist's Magazine*, and Joseph Wenman's cheap edition (also 1781) in his *Complete Circulating Library* series. To these can be added a series of designs by John Nixon, of which only a few were actually worked out, for the tenth (1787) and later editions of *The Beauties of Sterne*, a popular compilation published by George Kearsley in 1782, and the illustrations designed by Richard Corbould and others for Cooke's *Novelist's Pocket Library* series in the 1790s.[8]

There can be little doubt that these mass-produced and frequently reprinted plates shaped readers' reactions to Sterne's strange novel. It is striking how often illustrators were drawn to the same passages: Hogarth and Bunbury set the pattern, and beyond them there is considerable overlap in subject matter, with a strong emphasis on the pathetic story of Le Fever and on the comic subplots of Uncle Toby, Corporal Trim, and the widow Wadman. The illustrations thus further the sense of *Tristram Shandy* as a curious collection of memorable scenes, an effect reinforced by *The Beauties of Sterne*, which anthologised the separate scenes, emphasising the humorous and sentimental features of the curtailed selections. Noteworthy as well as exceptional is a rare version of *Tristram Shandy* published around 1785 under the fictitious imprint 'Amsterdam: for P. van Slaukenberg, 1771', which contains fourteen sexually explicit illustrations with captions from the text such as 'The duce take that slit' and 'Tom's had more gristle in it'.⁹

Other than the examples noted above, very few paintings were based on *Tristram Shandy*, even if one also includes George Stubbs's 1762 painting of a racehorse owned by Viscount Bolingbroke, called Tristram Shandy, which ran at Newmarket in the 1760s. The Royal Academy exhibited only two (rather insignificant) canvases in the eighteenth century, by William Hincks and Henry Singleton, both inspired by Le Fever's story. The relative unpopularity of *Tristram Shandy* with illustrators would change in the next century, with Charles Robert Leslie's painting 'Uncle Toby and the Widow Wadman', first exhibited in the Royal Academy in 1831, of which at least three versions exist. Leslie's image became a bestseller, and engravings after it were sold all over Europe; 'Phiz', illustrating Dickens's *Dombey and Son* (1848), shows one hanging on the wall in Dombey's dining room (ch. 26). From the mid century, it began appearing on the lids of Staffordshire pots containing 'Russian Bear's Grease', a perfumed hair treatment, and it turns up thereafter in equally unexpected places, including bookmarks issued in the early twentieth century by the Scottish Widows Fund, an Edinburgh-based mutual life office, and the logo of the Australian breakfast cereals firm founded in 1893 as the Uncle Tobys Company.¹⁰ Thus Tristram came to be overshadowed by his sentimental uncle, a fact illustrated by popular nineteenth-century American editions, which took for their frontispiece a striking portrait of Toby by Felix Octavius Darley, who emphasises his benevolence. The contrast with the demented war-gamer of Bunbury's illustrations is remarkable.

The most recent adaptations of *Tristram Shandy* in visual media, by the cartoonist Martin Rowson and the film maker Michael Winterbottom, follow the pictorial tradition by curtailing Sterne's text considerably. Rowson's cartoon version of 1996 skips most of the later volumes of Sterne's book, putting in their stead brilliant modern equivalents for Sterne's self-conscious play on contemporary modes of narration: thus we get 'Oliver Stone's *Tristram Shandy*: From a Place called Namur to Hell and Back', starring, among others, 'Meryl Streep as "Trim"'. More recently still, Michael Winterbottom's motion picture *Tristram Shandy: A Cock and Bull Story* (2006) inserts highlights from Sterne's novel in a narrative frame that foregrounds the rivalries of the two main comic actors and the problems of financing the film.[11] Both adaptations focus on a selection of set pieces, and stress the wildly digressive nature of the narrative, representing Sterne's text in a caricaturing sequence of frames and scenes. Interestingly, both these reworkings of *Tristram Shandy* ignore the sentimental and moral aspects of Sterne's text, and instead emphasise the bawdy and scatological potential.

A Sentimental Journey

A Sentimental Journey yields a very different picture. Bunbury's 'The Departure of La Fleur from Montreuil', which he exhibited at the Royal Academy in 1779, is characteristic: unlike his caricaturing *Tristram Shandy* prints, this one is soft-toned and sentimental. It was stipple-engraved by Thomas Watson in 1781 and, to judge from the bilingual caption (English and French), produced for the international market; at least one Dublin piracy used it as a frontispiece. The popularity of *A Sentimental Journey* is further attested by the survival of an illustrated fan from 1796 (fans based on fashionable novels had been a phenomenon since Richardson's *Pamela* half a century beforehand), the continuous plated double paper leaf of which contains three stipple etched and engraved scenes in oval cartouches. Entitled 'Yorick & The Monk', 'La Fleur & Madame de L***', and 'Yorick & The Glovers Wife', all three scenes are realistically depicted.[12]

The Royal Academy exhibited some thirty-five paintings and engravings based on the *Journey* between 1768 and 1820. Favourite subjects were the captive in his cell, the peasant mourning his dead ass, Yorick and the monk exchanging snuff boxes, and similar sentimental scenes and vignettes that offered themselves readily for illustration. A good example of the way in which Sterne generated illustrations by using pictorial language is found in the episode captioned 'The Captive. Paris', in which Yorick literally imagines the captive's 'picture' and describes the setting, posture, and even the lighting of 'the portrait' (*SJ/BJ* 97–8). The most popular subject, however, was Maria of Moulines, who sat for almost one third of all illustrations. Abandoned by her lover, and deeply melancholic, Maria had first appeared in volume 9 of *Tristram Shandy*, when Tristram finds her sitting by a brook under a poplar tree, playing her shepherd's flute and accompanied by a little goat – an animal that somewhat detracts from the sentimental dignity of the scene. Towards the end of *A Sentimental Journey*, Yorick, too, meets Maria:

> When we had got within half a league of Moulines, at a little opening in the road leading to a thicket, I discovered poor Maria sitting under a poplar—she was sitting with her elbow in her lap, and her head leaning on one side within her hand—a small brook ran at the foot of the tree ... She was dress'd in white, and much as my friend described her, except that her hair hung loose, which before was twisted within a silk net.—She had, superadded likewise to her jacket, a pale green ribband which fell across her shoulder to the waist; at the end of which hung her pipe.—
> $\hfill$ (*SJ/BJ* 150)

Since meeting Tristram, Maria goes on to tell Yorick, in a passage poised between pathos and absurdity, that her goat has left her, to be replaced by a dog called Sylvio; tears are shed, Maria reveals a handkerchief embroidered with a capital S (S for Sylvio, or perhaps even for Shandy or Sterne), and Yorick accompanies her to Moulines. The episode was anthologised widely, appearing prominently in compilations such as *The Beauties of Sterne* (1782, with numerous reprintings well into the nineteenth century) and *Gleanings from the Works of Laurence Sterne* (1796), and it shows Sterne's management of his own reputation at its most astute. The reference to *Tristram Shandy* is an early example of product placement, the S on the handkerchief underscoring the possible identification of Sterne with his characters, and even suggesting an element of autobiography in the fiction; small wonder that travellers went on sentimental pilgrimages to Moulines in the hope of meeting Maria, or that texts appeared under titles like *The Letters of Maria, with an Account of her Death in the Castle of Valerine* (1790). As a stimulus to visual representation, the passage also hands the illustrator useful specifications such as the poplar tree, while also offering, in its delicate innuendoes and hints of self-mockery, considerable freedom of artistic choice.

The first Maria painting was exhibited in 1773 by George Carter, who created at least six paintings based on *A Sentimental Journey*, and painted his daughter in the attitude of Maria; it was mezzotinted a year later. Fourteen other Marias were exhibited between 1774 and 1792, of which ten went into mass production as prints. David McKitterick has pointed out that, although oil paintings took pride of place at the Royal Academy, 'their reputation and their influence depended on the trade in reproductive engravings'.[13] Too little is known of the precise scope of the print trade of the period, but the market was expanding rapidly, free-standing prints were sold in great numbers, and many of these illustrations will have entered the cultural memory of readers in much the way that modern paperback cover images become associated with, and condition response to, the text within. It may well have been these mostly

Figure 7 Angelica Kauffman, 'Maria – Moulines' (1777; engraved by W. W. Ryland, 1779).

very sentimental illustrations, rather than Sterne's decidedly ambiguous text, that fixed his late eighteenth-century reputation as an exponent of pure sensibility.

Of the many Marias, Angelica Kauffman's 'Maria – Moulines', one of several produced by the artist, exhibited in 1777 and engraved in 1779 by William Wynne Ryland (see Fig. 7), became in due course the best known, a process fuelled in the 1780s when Josiah Wedgwood began using Lady Templetown's design 'Poor Maria' for his jasperware tea service, so disseminating her image on candlesticks, cameo brooches, bud vases, and other consumer articles.[14] This image of Maria was so well known that, as late as 1833, the political cartoonist John Doyle ('HD'), who worked for *Punch* and designed a series of political cartoons for the publisher Thomas McLean, could use it to attack Queen Adelaide, the unpopular wife of William IV, who was held responsible for the 'Coercion Acts' passed to suppress Irish popular protest at the time (see Fig. 8). Here the

Figure 8 John Doyle, 'A Study for Sterne's Maria' (1833), caricaturing Queen Adelaide.

Queen is portrayed in the attitude of Kauffman's Maria, with all the usual attributes: a poplar tree, a white dress, a pipe on a string, a running brook, and a small animal, in this case a lamb with 'Irish Coercion' shorn into its fleece.[15] Doyle states in his caption that he has taken the liberty to change Maria's dog into a lamb (perhaps to introduce connotations of fleecing), and this suggests that he may have been unaware of the earlier Maria scene in *Tristram Shandy*, involving a goat. It is clear enough that his cartoon has nothing directly to do with Sterne's work, just as not all owners of Wedgwood china would have been aware of the provenance of

Figure 9 Edward Edwards's illustration of Yorick and Maria, engraved by Peltro Williams Tompkins, for the reprint of *A Sentimental Journey*, published in 1780 by William Strahan and others.

the 'Poor Maria' design on their table; the image had become dissociated from its source, a piece of cultural property in common.

The first book illustration featuring Maria was by Edward Edwards, for Strahan's *Sentimental Journey* and the important ten-volume *Works* of 1780 (see Fig. 9). Curiously, both Yorick and Maria are depicted here as members of

Figure 10 William Bromley's engraving of Yorick and Maria, from a design by M. Archer, for the Creswick edition (1794) of *A Sentimental Journey*.

the affluent middle class. The handkerchief is very much in the centre of the picture; Yorick is watchful, Maria demure, Sylvio at ease at her feet, the carriage ready, and the spectator at a distance, viewing the theatrical scene from the other side of the brook. Fourteen years later, William Bromley depicted the departure of Yorick and Maria to Moulines for the Creswick edition, which came out in three different formats in 1794, when the sentimental vogue was at its height. This frontispiece (see Fig. 10) yields a very different picture: Yorick, clearly a clergyman, supports a visibly distressed and wan Maria, his hand on his feeling heart, his attempt to establish eye contact frustrated by her downward glance. The scene invites in the spectator an empathetic reaction, and it is no coincidence that Maria became a favourite frontispiece subject or title-page vignette of several editions, not necessarily of *A Sentimental Journey*, during the period. Thus she appears as frontispiece in the frequently reprinted anthology by William Enfield, *The Speaker* (1801), and elsewhere, in the role of emotional trigger: the spectator (and reader of compilations like *The Beauties of Sterne*) was confirmed in possessing a proper 'heart of sensibility' (to use the idiom of the sentimental vogue) on sympathetically viewing this picture of Maria's 'virtue in distress'. There are over forty known illustrations, English as well as Continental, all conjuring up the same picture of a benevolent, if slightly ineffectual, Yorick, from whom a mentally distressed Maria elicits emotional support. In his detailed study of the cult surrounding this figure, Blake Gerard suggests three different phases in the history of Maria illustrations: her first appearance as a figure of mourning (c. 1770–1810) overlaps with representations of her rescue by Yorick (c. 1790–1830), and is gradually supplanted by images of Maria as lost to this world, a madwoman whom Gerard labels 'Maria as Other' (c. 1840–88).[16] This last category suggests a fascinating link with the popularity in Victorian culture of the Ophelia figure, and more generally with the love-mad heroine in Victorian fiction, whose characteristics Helen Small has traced in part to 'the spectacle of feminine derangement' offered by Sterne's Maria and exploited by Kauffman and her imitators.[17] When one surveys all illustrations, however, this neat schema does not quite work out: different 'readings' of the episode coexist at all times, and the only clear development is the gradual disappearance of sentimentalism, the concomitant change in the role played by Maria in the picture, and the reappearance of her goat.

The last, and lasting, picture of Maria is Maurice Leloir's full page illustration (1884), which was used well into the 1920s in editions of *A Sentimental Journey* in France, Germany, Spain, Britain, and North America (see Fig. 11). The landscape has become domesticated (note the prominent gate), Yorick has been defrocked again, Maria shows little interest in him and seems not to notice his handkerchief; her hand rests on the head of Sylvio, who has turned into a retriever. This is but one of twelve full-page illustrations (with 220 smaller images scattered throughout the text). From the middle of the nineteenth century, Maria's dominance waned, and other subjects, with more obvious erotic charge, began to take over: Gilbert Stuart Newton's 'Yorick and the Grisette', and particularly Frith's paintings 'Feeling the Pulse' (1842) and 'The Gloves, Paris' (1843), set a new model, which became almost standard in the great outburst of expertly illustrated and beautifully produced editions in the 1920s and 1930s, in which Yorick's flirtations are evidently of

Figure 11 Maurice Leloir's illustration of Yorick and Maria, from Emile Blémont's French translation of *A Sentimental Journey* (Paris: Librairie artistique, 1884).

greater interest than the sensibilities of Maria. In particular, the episodes entitled 'The Fille de Chambre. Paris' (*SJ/BJ* 87–90), 'The Temptation. Paris', and 'The Conquest' (*SJ/BJ* 121–4) are singled out by illustrators such as Véra Willoughby, Norah McGuinness, and Valenti Angelo.[18]

Sterne scholarship has always been a divided field, and debates have tended to veer between two extremes. One emphasises the fact that the Revd L. Sterne was a clergyman and a Latitudinarian divine, and reads him as a moralist and satirist; the other points out that an eighteenth-century Anglican churchman need not have been personally pious, and stresses the libertine side of Lory Sterne, a member of the rakish Demoniacs club, a crony of the notorious freethinker John Wilkes, a womaniser and sentimentalist who sympathised with the *philosophes*, and was received in the *salon* of the atheist d'Holbach. The history of Sterne illustrations shows that visual interpretation of the text has been as varied as its critical reception. The shorter and more accessible *Sentimental Journey* has been vastly more illustrated than *Tristram Shandy*, but whereas the latter has been almost exclusively rendered as a funny and at times farcical work, rather than as a serious satire, the former has been ambiguously interpreted from the start, as a repository of alternative possibilities, sentimental, satirical, or sexual.

NOTES

1. *Reynolds*, ed. Nicholas Penny (London: Weidenfeld, 1986), 199–200.
2. A rare contemporaneous case is Smollett's *Sir Launcelot Greaves* (1760–1), the earliest novel to be published as an illustrated magazine serial: see Robert Folkenflik, 'Tobias Smollett, Anthony Walker, and the First Illustrated Serial Novel in English', *Eighteenth-Century Fiction* 14 (2002), 507–32.
3. See Diana Patterson, 'Tristram's Marblings and Marblers', *Shandean* 3 (1991), 70–97; Peter de Voogd, 'Laurence Sterne, the Marbled Page, and the "Use of Accidents"', *Word & Image* 1 (1985), 279–87.
4. For a complete and generously illustrated list, see Arthur H. Cash's appendix on 'Portraits of Sterne', in his *Laurence Sterne: The Early and Middle Years* (London: Methuen, 1975), 299–316; the engraved version of the Bridges caricature is Plate II.
5. John Croft, 'Anecdotes of Sterne Vulgarly Tristram Shandy', in *The Whitefoord Papers*, ed. W. A. S. Hewins (Oxford: Clarendon Press, 1898), 231.
6. David Blewett, *The Illustrations of Robinson Crusoe, 1719–1920* (Gerrards Cross: Colin Smythe, 1995), 15; see also Robert Halsband, *The Rape of the Lock and Its Illustrations, 1714–1896* (Oxford: Clarendon Press, 1980).
7. For Romney, see T. C. Duncan Eaves, 'George Romney: His *Tristram Shandy* Paintings and Trip to Lancaster', *Huntington Library Quarterly* 7 (1944), 321–6; for Bunbury, see Peter de Voogd, 'Henry William Bunbury, Illustrator of *Tristram Shandy*', *Shandean* 3 (1991), 138–44.
8. See Peter de Voogd, 'Robert Dighton's Twelve *Tristram Shandy* Prints', *Shandean* 6 (1994), 87–98; W. G. Day, 'Michael Angelo Rooker's Illustrations to *Tristram Shandy*', *Shandean* 7 (1995), 30–42; David McKitterick, 'Tristram Shandy in the Royal Academy: A Group of Drawings by John Nixon', *Shandean* 4 (1992), 85–110. Catherine Gordon's overview, '"More than One Handle": The Development of Sterne Illustration, 1760–1820', *Words: Wai-te-Ata Studies in Literature* 4 (1974), 47–58 has been superseded by W. B. Gerard and Brigitte Friant-Kessler, 'Towards a Catalogue of Illustrated Laurence Sterne', *Shandean* 16 (2005), 19–70, continued in *Shandean* 17 (2006), 35–79, 18 (2007), 56–87, and 19 (2008), 90–130; see also the 'Short Catalogue of Visual Representations of the Work of Laurence Sterne, 1760–2005' appended to Gerard's monograph *Laurence Sterne and the Visual Imagination* (London: Ashgate, 2006), 179–231.
9. See Brigitte Friant-Kessler, '"Curious Cuts" and Sterne in the *Catena Librorum Tacendorum*', *Shandean* 15 (2004), 117–34.

10. See W. G. Day, 'Charles Robert Leslie's *My Uncle Toby and the Widow Wadman*: The Nineteenth-Century Icon of Sterne's Work', *Shandean* 9 (1997), 83–108.

11. Martin Rowson, *The Life and Opinions of Tristram Shandy, Gentleman* (London: Picador, 1996), Frame 56; see also Rowson's commentary in 'Hyperboling Gravity's Ravelin: A Comic Book Version of *Tristram Shandy*', *Shandean* 7 (1995), 62–86. For a good account of Winterbottom's film, see Patrick Bullard's review in the *Times Literary Supplement* for 10 February 2006.

12. For further description and a facsimile of this fan, see Peter de Voogd, 'Sterne All the Fashion: A Sentimental Fan', *Shandean* 8 (1996), 133–6; on the *Pamela* fan, see Thomas Keymer and Peter Sabor, *Pamela in the Marketplace: Literary Controversy and Print Culture in Eighteenth-Century Britain and Ireland* (Cambridge: Cambridge University Press, 2005), 143–6.

13. McKitterick, 'Tristram Shandy in the Royal Academy', 87.

14. W. B. Gerard, 'Sterne in Wedgwood: "Poor Maria" and the "Bourbonnais Shepherd"', *Shandean* 12 (2001), 78–88.

15. See Peter de Voogd, 'John Doyle's "Study of Maria"', *Shandean* 14 (2003), 135–8.

16. W. B. Gerard, '"All that the heart wishes": Changing Views toward Sentimentality Reflected in Visualizations of Sterne's Maria, 1773–1888', *Studies in Eighteenth-Century Culture* (2004), 231–69; a revised version is in Gerard's *Laurence Sterne and the Visual Imagination*, 135–73.

17. Helen Small, *Love's Madness: Medicine, the Novel, and Female Insanity, 1800–1865* (Oxford: Oxford University Press, 1996), 13.

18. See Paul Goring, 'Illustration of *A Sentimental Journey* in the 1920s', *Shandean* 6 (1994), 54–65.

11

MELVYN NEW

Sterne and the modernist moment

'To define——is to distrust', as Tristram triumphantly informs Eugenius, although he immediately realises he has a victory without laurels: 'I triumph'd over him as I always do, like a fool' (*TS* 3.31.258). Similarly, I have foolishly managed over the past fifteen years to write about Sterne and modernist authors without ever defining modernism or postmodernism. I have, for example, written about Sterne and Proust, Sterne and Nietzsche, Sterne and Svevo,[1] but have continued to believe all along that Sterne is neither proto-modernist nor proto-postmodern, neither an anticipation of Joycean stream of consciousness nor a foretaste of a Derridean breakdown between signified and signifier (which, assuredly, first happened in Eden, not in Paris). Rather, Sterne, like all great artists, was a writer of his own time and place; all that we can really mean when we assign a prophetic aura to his work is that authors of a later period have read Sterne in ways that we must now take seriously, their powerful lenses proving to be filters we are unable to avoid. As I expressed it in explaining Proust's influence on Sterne: 'twentieth-century readers, reading the best that has been produced in their own century, come to earlier literature through that experience and cannot free their reading from it'.[2]

With this in mind, let me define *modernism* in the narrowest possible sense, keeping in mind that by *modernism* I mean *modernism*, and 'nothing more, or less', as Sterne says about defining the word *nose* (*TS* 3.31.258). It was a condition of Western thought that started with Nietzsche, but perhaps earlier with Kierkegaard, and perhaps before that with Hume and Kant – a condition that some believe ended with the anointing of postmodernism and Derrida at Johns Hopkins University in 1968, although here, again, precursors might be discovered, every messiah having had his John the Baptist. Still others would argue that postmodernism was merely a contrarian moment, fuelled by politics, in a modernist age, and that, this moment having passed, we continue to be modernists into the twenty-first century, like Jews holding fast to Torah and Talmud, unswayed by false messiahs and new testaments. In short, by *modernism*, I mean the question that should stand uppermost in our consideration of what it means to be human in our own time: how is it possible in this most hair-raising of eras to still stand erect? 'What a life of it has an author, at this pass!' (*TS* 3.33.262).

Put alternatively, we might suggest that the singular aim of postmodernism was to demonstrate the flaws of modernist thought by means of a philosophical-linguistical-sociological (and, thinking of *Tristram Shandy* (1.21.72), all other categories of thought 'ending ... in *ical*') assault on its aesthetic and metaphysical (counter-materialist) tendencies. To reassert, then, the meaning of *modernism*, we should allow the aesthetic and metaphysical to speak for themselves. More narrowly formal definitions have their uses, and to think of modernist narration in terms of its characteristic disruptions of temporal sequence, narrative framing, and the realist illusion is at least to approach the affinity with Sterne acknowledged by writers such as Joyce, and subsequently adumbrated by critics.[3] Yet modernism begins by placing the very concept of definition itself under question, and its manifestations – in works of literature, music, art – are everywhere a warning against the definitional process, the defining of matter by form. For this reason, I will eschew generalisations and instead examine very closely two representative excerpts from two modernist fictions; what is most worth observing about Sterne in proximity to the artists of the modern era will, it is hoped, emerge from this examination.

The first passage, pertinently enough since I have invoked an image of the modernist as persistent Jew, is to be found in *Street of Crocodiles* (1934) by Bruno Schulz (1894–1942), a Polish Jew shot to death in his home town, Drogobych, by the Gestapo.[4] The second passage is from Virginia Woolf's *Mrs Dalloway*, published some nine years before *Street of Crocodiles*. Needless to say, Woolf was not a Jew (though married to one), but the persistence with which she cleaves to the notion that her formal innovations in the face of modern dilemmas had to be steeped in familiarity with her aesthetic past will here suffice for what I will suggest is one of modernism's most paradoxical characteristics: a persistent metaphysical engagement with the past, whatever the present or the future might hold. Woolf greatly admired Sterne, and indeed wrote an introduction to a new edition of *A Sentimental Journey* three years after writing *Mrs Dalloway*.[5] Schulz, on the other hand, gives no explicit indication that he had read Sterne, but he did read and translate Kafka, who certainly read Nietzsche, who called Sterne 'the most liberated spirit who ever wrote' – only three degrees of separation.[6]

Bruno Schulz was an art teacher at a local high school for all of his adult life. *Street of Crocodiles*, a collection of loosely connected short stories, was published when he was forty, followed by a second collection, *Sanatorium under the Sign of the Hourglass*, in 1937; he was supposedly working on a novel, *The Messiah*, when he was killed in 1942. Like Tristram, the narrator of the stories in *Street of Crocodiles* has a theory-driven father, Jacob, 'that incorrigible improviser, that fencing-master of imagination ... that metaphysical conjurer' (Schulz 24). His primary theory is nothing less than a new thesis of creation, unfolded in two linked stories, 'Tailors' Dummies' and 'A Tractate on Tailors' Dummies, or The Second Book of Genesis'.[7] Jacob formulates not only a commentary on Schulz's own disorienting and magnificently innovative fictions, but also a useful window through which to view whatever we eventually come to define as modernism.

The 'Dummies' are connected to Jacob's dry-goods shop, and serve for the fitting and cutting of garments; for Jacob, however, it is not the garments but the remnants that become the foundation of his theory, the 'heap of cuttings, of motley rags and pieces ... the thousand scraps, the frivolous and fickle trimmings' (Schulz 27). If this notion moves us closer to the world of *Tristram Shandy* (where the planet itself is said to be made of the 'shreds and clippings of the rest' (*TS* 1.5.8), where a marbled page serves as a 'motly emblem' of the work (3.36.268), and where Uncle Toby's virtue is finally reduced to 'nothing but *empty bottles, tripes, trunk-hose*, and *pantofles*' (9.22.777)), so does Jacob's concomitant interest in the seamstresses (*grissets*) drop us into the very middle of *A Sentimental Journey*, Yorick, and the beautiful grisset in Paris. Responding to the 'magnetism of his strange personality', the young women allow Jacob to 'study the structure of their thin and ordinary little bodies', to feel their pulses, so to speak. On one particular occasion, the theory is formulated: 'pulling Pauline's stocking down from her knee and studying with enraptured eyes the precise and noble structure of the joint', Jacob revises Genesis: 'If ... I were to attempt a criticism of creation, I would say "Less matter, more form!" Ah, what relief it would be for the world to lose some of its contents. More modesty in aspirations, more sobriety in claims' (Schulz 29). Sterne makes the same point in using a sentence from Epictetus as his title-page motto for volumes 1 and 2 of *Tristram Shandy*: 'We are tormented with the opinions we have of things, and not by things themselves.'

Like Walter Shandy, Jacob lives in an intellectualised universe where matter matters most. Both are driven by a persistent urge to find the proper forms (their theories) for all that matters (and for all matter), and, most significantly, to reduce or dismiss whatever matter they cannot contain within their forms as matter that doesn't matter, the refuse of their lives. For both Walter and Jacob, the overflow of matter is a cause of constant alarm, and while they both might sensibly wish for relief from the agitations of theorising, both remain insensibly mounted and a-gallop on the hobby-horses of their *form*ulations. Sterne and Schulz, however, remain sceptical concerning this world of thought and *form*ation, and acutely aware that 'Pauline's white calf', released 'from the prison of her stocking' (Schulz 29), has the capacity to *de*form and *re*form the world. In that single insight, I would locate one of the hinges upon which Sterne opened his own door to modernism.

Jacob struggles to elucidate his theory in his 'Tractate', reminiscent of *Slawkenbergius's Tale* on the one hand, the *Tristrapaedia* on the other: 'Matter grows under our hands.—Let no man say,—"Come—I'll write a *duodecimo*"' (*TS* 5.16.446). The monism of 'thinking matter', one of the heresies of rationalism in Sterne's century, is for Schulz the 'Great Heresy', and for Jacob, 'Our Heresiarch', who mesmerises his small audience with his 'dangerous charm', his insistence that 'matter has been given infinite fertility, inexhaustible vitality, and, at the same time, a seductive power of temptation which invites us to create as well ... The whole of matter pulsates with infinite possibilities' (Schulz 30). Even without informing spirit, in other words, matter is already alive and fecund in itself. Schulz's portrayal of this matter as feminine is mirrored by Sterne's association of masculinity with Walter, the *philosophus gloriosus* (formalism), with Toby, the *miles gloriosus* (militarism, triumphalism), and, significantly enough in both instances, with impotence, which, in James A. Work's succinct formulation, 'hovers like a dubious halo over the head of every Shandy male, including the bull'.[8]

As Jacob spins his theory, its dangers become more and more apparent. Matter is

> pliable like a woman, submissive to every impulse, it is a territory outside any law, open to all kinds of charlatans and dilettanti, a domain of abuses and of dubious demiurgical manipulations. Matter is the most passive and most defenseless essence in [the] cosmos. Anyone can mold it and shape it; it obeys everybody. All attempts at organising matter are transient and temporary, easy to reverse and to dissolve.
>
> (Schulz 30)

The further one carries the theory, the more appalling it becomes, the passivity of matter suggesting that each new formalism can be freely imposed on it, that between Hegel and Heidegger (to invoke the philosophical bookends of modernism), the reduction of all matter to a new formalism, ever and always in the name of history and the reality of things (what 'really *matters*'), was not only acceptable but demanded: 'Homicide is not a sin. It is sometimes a necessary violence on resistant and ossified forms of existence which have ceased to be amusing' (30). Or, as Jacob concludes, with the blindness of Uncle Toby pursuing the 'great ends of [his] creation' as he delivers his apologetical oration in defence of warfare (*TS* 6.32.557), 'here is the starting point of a new apologia for sadism' (Schulz 31).

Modernism, I suggest, is an aesthetic (and metaphysical) attempt to confront the *sadism* inherent in the mind's encounter with matter. Put in Sterne's language, with a nod toward Keats, could we ride our hobby-horses 'peace-ably and quietly along the King's high-way', and not compel others to 'get up behind [us]' (*TS* 1.7.12), could we celebrate the infinitude of matter without any 'irritable reaching after fact and reason', we could indeed celebrate a world of rich fecundity without guilt or shame or tartuffery.[9] And indeed, 'They order ... this *matter* better in France', a land of *grissets* and *filles de chambre* (*SJ/BJ* 3; my italics). That is not, however, the world in which we find ourselves, and the forms by which we attempt to control matter's infi-niteness, even when they begin 'in jest', always end 'in downright earnest' (*TS* 1.19.61). This entire passage from *Tristram Shandy* is worth contemplating as an indication of the incipient 'sadism' of Walter's theorising: 'he was serious;—he was all uniformity;—he was systematical, and, like all system-atick reasoners, he would move both heaven and earth, and twist and torture every thing in nature to support his hypothesis' (1.19.61). As the twentieth century bears witness, formalisms always begin with a rhetorical demonstra-tion (Walter) and always – at least in our cultural memory – end in warfare (Toby).

Clearly, however, this cannot be the only view of formalism entertained by Sterne, or by modernists, both being so often brilliant formalists themselves. Art is, after all, a complicating rather than a simplifying discourse, the antithesis of the political. Modernist aesthetics is intensely aware of its own implication in the containment of matter. Here is a description of Jacob, a fragment broken loose from a story written by a Polish Jew in 1934:

> As my father proceeded from these general principles of cosmogony to the more restricted sphere of his private interests, his voice sank to an impressive whisper, the lecture became more and more complicated ... and the conclusions which he reached became more dubious and dangerous ... He half-closed one eye, put two fingers to his forehead while a look of extraordinary slyness came over his face. He transfixed his listeners with these looks ... (Schulz 31)

Is there anyone who has read *Tristram Shandy* who will not here recognise Walter Shandy, a fragment within a novel written by an Anglican cleric between 1759 and 1767? The mind creates the formal linkage, binds the two figures and two fragments together, and then prepares to publish its insight to the world: 'What could be wanting in my father but to have wrote a book to publish this notion of his to the world? Little boots it to the subtle speculatist to stand single in his opinions,----unless he gives them proper vent' (*TS* 1.19.63). We do not, as yet, destroy those who disagree with us about such literary links (the *matters* of literature do not seem to *matter* very much), but as the nation of Israel (Jacob) discovered, transfixing listeners (the act of conversion) is the beginning of the justification of conviction, control, sadism, and war.

Modernism – in its complicated aesthetic engagement with formalism, in its ironies and self-conscious scepticism that turns most evidently on its own doubts, its own heresies, its own relationship with its heritage – is a desire to *deconvict* the world. Sterne may be considered one of those authors who first suggested that such an irenic or pacific vision might possibly be more Christian than the doctrinalism that his world inherited; he called such doctrinalism 'polemical divinity', but significantly enough, when asked to define it, Yorick pulls out a copy of Rabelais and reads a page (*TS* 5.28.462–29.464): there has perhaps never been an era in which the 'modernist' urge to *deconvict* has not been accompanied by the counter-urge to re*form* the world to the shape of one's own *convictions*. Precisely for this reason, such sceptical foresight – or insight – into the habitual tenacity of human beings with 'important' ideas ought not be labelled 'modernism', which only celebrates yet another formalism, that of precursiveness. It is more useful, perhaps, to suggest that, in the infinitude of matter's potential, Schulz is the lens through which we can locate the modernist moment in Sterne, just as Sterne is the lens through which the modernist moment in Rabelais comes to light – and to fruition. Hence, the modernist, as opposed to the postmodernist, has no predominant instinct to destroy the forebears (the art of politics), but rather, as with Sterne, a paradoxical embrace of the past alongside both innovation and a highly individualised, not to say idiosyncratic, vision: the unexpected always depends on the expected.

One more point may help to complicate further this shared moment between Sterne and Schulz. As noted, Jacob's entire theory begins with a woman's body, and, indeed, it also collapses in the same encounter. The women of his audience discover how easy it is to break his spell, and in a gesture rich with scriptural significance, one of the girls moves 'her chair forward and, without getting up from it, lifted her dress to reveal her foot tightly covered in black silk, and then stretched it out stiffly like a serpent's head' (Schulz 33). In case we miss his point, Schulz repeats the image: 'Adela's outstretched slipper trembled slightly and shone like a serpent's tongue. My father rose slowly, still looking down, took a step forward like an automaton, and fell to his knees. The lamp hissed in the silence of the room ... whispers of venomous tongues floated in the air, zigzags of thought' (34). As with Sterne, human sexuality – the crevice in the fireplace, Slawkenbergius's nose, the cursed slit in the petticoat, the making of sausages, and countless other images, male and female – calls formalism back to matter, the infinite fertility of matter, and the inadequacy of human efforts to subdue it. We can return to the Garden for our explanation, or we can accept, with Rabelais and Sterne,

Freud and Proust, Nietzsche and Schulz (that is, with modernists of every era), that the human mind, that fortress of conviction and certainty, is always and everywhere vulnerable to the zigzaggery of sexuality's – the body's – approaches.

Hence, it should not surprise us that when Tristram encounters the fact that 'matter and motion are infinite', it is embedded within Trim's funeral oration *and* a discussion of his persuasive genius. Death, along with impotence, hovers over both Shandy Hall and Toby's bowling green, but it is important to Sterne's ultimately Christian vision that love and sexual desire hover there as well. Where Sterne differs from his era, perhaps, is in his willingness to entertain the possibility that this overlapping, here on earth and in the constant interplay of human interaction, is preparatory to salvation.[10] That Trim's oration is pieced together from the Book of Common Prayer is telling; but it is equally noteworthy that Trim, alongside his mourning, offers us a lesson in persuasiveness – and seduction. The dropping of his hat as an emblem of death works precisely because we are 'not stocks and stones ... but men cloathed with bodies, and governed by our imaginations' (*TS* 5.7.431–2). For Sterne, this vulnerability marks the pathway of persuasiveness, and he opens to the reader, much as Schulz would do almost two centuries later, the dangerous landscape of modernity:

> Ye who govern this mighty world and its mighty concerns with the *engines* of eloquence,—who heat it, and cool it, and melt it, and mollify it,——and then harden it again to *your purpose*——
>
> Ye who wind and turn the passions with this great windlass,—and, having done it, lead the owners of them, whither ye think meet—
>
> Ye, lastly, who drive——and why not, Ye also who are driven, like turkeys to market, with a stick and a red clout—meditate—meditate, I beseech you, upon *Trim*'s hat.   (*TS* 5.7.433)

The world of twentieth-century political positiveness, whether from the right or from the left, and the instruments of its persuasiveness, from oratory, rhetoric, and propaganda to torture and warfare, are here foreshadowed with a deftness of touch that almost seems, again, a justification for sadism; in the space between 'eloquence' and 'a stick and a red clout', one can locate perhaps every historical event of a most anguished century.

Sterne refuses, however, to let this vision dominate his text. The courting of Susannah turns vulnerability into a relationship that Sterne will not allow us to ignore, much less to condemn: the persuasion or seduction to human sexuality. As he talks about death and corruption, Trim directs his speaking toward Susannah: 'What is the finest face that ever man looked at!—I could hear *Trim* talk so for ever, cried *Susannah*,—what is it! (*Susannah* laid her

Figure 12 Bruno Schulz, 'Sleeping Adela and Edzio' (c. 1934).

hand upon *Trim*'s shoulder)—but corruption?——*Susannah* took it off' (*TS* 5.9.435). Our most profound theories and thoughts – even those offered as an alternative Genesis, or as reparation for the sin and death entailed by the Fall therein – are tinged with what it means to be human, to have 'this delicious mixture' (5.9.435) within us.[11] These 'threads of love and desire ... entangled with the piece' (*SJ/BJ* 124) must always be acknowledged, not as matter to be overcome, not as sin, or disease, or madness, but as the site of love and caring, that single gesture of openness toward a fellow creature that might deconvict the world of its certainties, that might disarm its violence, and that might, just possibly, have saved us from the twentieth century. *Modernism* is that single gesture defined aesthetically, and while both Sterne and Schulz acutely (and humorously) chronicle the opposing human embrace of closure (close-mindedness), they continue to dream, each in his own way, of the harmonies that could change the world. It is certainly no accident that both authors image themselves, finally, as a human being stretching across an abyss in search of the bodily matter of the human being on the other side (see Fig. 12).[12]

Virginia Woolf was a close and appreciative reader of Sterne, but for our present purpose, I want to concentrate on one particular passage in *Mrs Dalloway* that is, to my mind, Woolf's most poignant illustration of what I take modernism to be – and of the demons it was designed to confront. If Jacob and Walter Shandy can be reduced to one formal construct, so might an even more unlikely pairing – the highly successful Harley Street physician, Sir William Bradshaw, and the Yorkshire sesquipedalian, Dr Slop – be reduced to another, at least insofar as both represent the ultimate weapon in the reduction of matter to form, the advent of science and technology. Perhaps no image in literature is more pregnant with the dangers of the finite mind (and its yearnings for conviction) than Dr Slop's forceps, designed to engage matter with precisely the right force, but sufficiently flawed, despite its set screws and other mechanical precautions, that one's nose is in constant danger. Needless to say, his other 'instruments of delivery' are instruments of death, instruments, significantly enough, that impale and carve the infant skull for its easier removal from the womb.

I have, on occasion, considered Sterne a satirist in the tradition of Swift, Pope, and the Scriblerians, but nothing he ever wrote is equal to the savage indignation informing Woolf's portrait of Sir William. She begins with a slight undercurrent of irony at his expense: 'a heavy look, a weary look (the stream of patients being so incessant, the responsibilities and privileges of his profession so onerous), which weariness, together with his grey hairs, increased the extraordinary distinction of his presence and gave him the reputation ... not merely of lightning skill and almost infallible accuracy in diagnosis, but of sympathy; tact; understanding of the human soul'.[13] His diagnosis of Septimus Warren Smith marks the conviction of true science: 'He could see the first moment they came into the room (the Warren Smiths they were called); he was certain directly he saw the man; it was a case of extreme gravity. It was a case of complete breakdown – complete physical and nervous breakdown ... he ascertained in two or three minutes (writing answers to questions, murmured discreetly, on a pink card)' (Woolf 81). The repressed anger in this description is obvious enough, but at its core is Woolf's own engagement with history, as we recall how and why Septimus has become a challenge to the medical profession (even if only a three-minute challenge), a victim of that warfare Uncle Toby practises so benignly (in the eyes of many a Tobyphile, at any rate) on his bowling green; in fact, is Woolf not recalling Sterne aurally when she defines Septimus's war as 'the European War–that little *shindy* of schoolboys with gunpowder'?[14]

Against the 'heroism' of warfare, the human attempt to subdue matter to its own dimensions, as Swift would have it,[15] Septimus has an alternative vision, that he has 'committed an appalling crime and been condemned to death by human nature' (Woolf 82). We might well ask, what is the *matter* with Septimus, the primary medical (and psychiatric) question, but Septimus already knows that, as a defender of what *mattered* to some people, he has destroyed – and seen destroyed – what *mattered* to others. The aborting of the infinite fecundity of matter, the inability after the fact to keep straight the difference between what matters (what we preserve) and what did not seem to matter (what we discard, destroy), that is his disease – the matter of (and with) his mind. Sir William's diagnosis is, it would seem, wonderfully correct: 'he was not mad, was he? Sir William said he never spoke of "madness"; he called it not having a sense of proportion' (82).

Is it possible that modernism, as both form and matter, can be defined simply by its lack of Sir William's 'sense of proportion'? Similarly, is Sterne's purchase on modernism the fact that his eponymous hero is not born until the third volume, and is only five years of age when the ninth volume concludes – epical signifiers of disproportion? Obviously so, but with one vital qualification if we are to distinguish between modernism and postmodernism, each of which might claim 'lack of proportion' as its *raison d'être*, each of which lays claim to Sterne (if not to Woolf) as its prescient ancestor. Woolf can, perhaps, help us locate the distinction.

Sir William is, I would suggest, Woolf's own prescient ancestor of postmodernism, for his worship of proportion – 'Proportion, divine proportion, Sir William's goddess' (Woolf 84) – is ultimately science's response to the world's formlessness, to the lamentable fecundity of matter that calls forth the mind's unceasing efforts – by means of forms, formulas, formulations – to exercise sufficient control. If Sir William attempts to 'cure' the world of its 'prophetic Christs and Christesses, who prophesied the end of the world, or the advent of God' (Woolf 84–5), by prescribing a glass of milk and better sleeping habits, so too has postmodernism attempted, at long last, to relieve the world of 'Christ (a common delusion)' (84), insofar as Christ, in John's gospel formulation, is the Word, the Logos, the guarantee that there is, after all, some relationship between our words and the world – or, as Sterne's Yorick would have it, between a mother and her son, despite the best reasonings of canon law and visitation diners (*TS* 4.30.393–4). If Sir William finds madness in the 'advent of God', so the postmodernist finds it there as well, although 'God' is not as useful a theoretical word as 'truth', 'determinacy', 'certainty' (that is, 'untruth, 'inde-terminacy', 'uncertainty') or any of the other evasions of late twentieth-century dogmatism. What unites the doctor and the theorist, in other words, is their absolute embrace of positive knowledge, not as an alternative possibility within matter's fecundity, but as the signifier of matter's impotence in the hands of science and the theoretical, the power of the human mind.

In both instances, however, it is not the content of the theory that matters (after all, as Woolf astutely notes, 'we know nothing about – the nervous system, the human brain' (Woolf 84)), but the reductive systemisation that makes possible the Harley Street professionalism of the physician, the aca-demic institutionalisation of the theorist: the certainties of the politician. For 'Proportion has a sister', Woolf writes, less smiling, more formidable, a Goddess even now engaged – in the heat and sands of India, the mud and swamp of Africa, the purlieus of London, wherever, in short, the climate or the devil tempts men to fall from the true belief which is her own ... Conversion is her name and she feasts on the wills of the weakly, loving to impress, to impose, adoring her own features stamped on the face of the populace. At Hyde Park Corner on a tub she stands preaching ... How he would work – how toil to raise funds, propagate reforms, initiate institutions! But Conversion, fastidious Goddess, loves blood better than brick, and feasts most subtly on the human will.[16]

It is modernism's acutely nervous foreshadowing of the 'Goddess of Conversion' – a foreshadowing arising, perhaps, from the events ticking all across Europe and Asia from the mid nineteenth century to the Doppelganger explosions of communism and fascism – that separates modernism from postmodernism. As modernism wanes, 'conversion' re-enters the marketplace of ideas as a new mode of orthodoxy and respectability, the non-aesthetics of a world in which everything is political; it is a world Sterne, Schulz, and Woolf deplored. Indeed, Sterne's own nervous foreshadowing of the decline of Christian thought – 'I hesitate not one moment to affirm, that in half a century, at this rate, we shall have no souls at all; which being the period beyond which I doubt likewise of the existence of the Christian faith, 'twill be one advantage that both of 'em will be exactly worn out together' (TS 7.14.595) – ties him far more closely to the modernist than to the postmodernist. We see this not only in his creation of Walter Shandy, that great converter through logic and argumentation, but even more so in his figure of Uncle Toby, whose bowling-green activities bespeak a world at war, much in the same way that Sir William in Harley Street and the preacher on his tub at Hyde Park Corner (Sterne's great progenitor Swift is surely summoned by that image) reinscribe for Woolf (and Septimus) the horrors of war. To suggest that Septimus's guilt is madness, as Sir William does, is perhaps the mirror image of the suggestion that Uncle Toby is innocent; in both instances, we fail to recognise the impetus that drives both Sterne and the modernist artist: a dread of the orthodox, the straight line, the insistence of form over matter, the reformation of matter by way of conforming it to the dimensions of one's own science, one's own theories, one's own militant occupation of the seemingly empty spaces of the world, otherwise known as what 'matters' to other people.

It is to Sterne's credit that he never confuses the straight line of orthodoxy with that mode of Christianity that lovingly embraces all that cannot be known or contained. Schulz, with his strong acquaintance with kabbalistic Judaism, shares that same sense of religion, not as definitive truth but as infinite possibility. It is not, finally, Christianity that modernism seeks to recover (as a careful reading of the greatest of modernist poets, T. S. Eliot, would show), but art and metaphysics, both of which were most overtly manifested in Western thought in the wake of ineffable monotheism.

Bruno Schulz, Virginia Woolf, and Laurence Sterne would not necessarily agree with this *formulation* of their work, or the notion of modernism it entails. In responding to the exercise of finding the modernist connection in Sterne, I have already accepted the postulate that some 'sense of proportion' exists between the two, that it would require only a proper ordering of observations and insights to 'solve' the equation, repair our previous lack of knowledge, cure our ignorance. I suspect, however, they would – in their own unique voices – ask me to dismount my hobby-horse. Or perhaps – if I have been able to capture the modernist spirit in any way – they might see in my zig-zag approach to the question not Uncle Toby's tactical march to the very centre of the place (which, we note, may prove a place of impotence after all), but the paths of a maze (another Shandean image) from which neither I nor my reader can emerge with any positive sense of the ground traversed, much less a sense of proportion or convertible knowledge. Life and art converted into knowledge: the devastating path of conversion upon which Hegel set us in the interval between Sterne, who foresaw his visionary scheme (our systems of knowledge, Tristram declares (*TS* 1.21.72), have 'gradually been creeping upwards towards that Ακμὴ of their perfections, from which ... we cannot possibly be far off'), and Schulz and Woolf, who had to live with its con-sequences. All three authors worked to invert that seeming inevitability of matter subdued to knowledge, all three in their own ways (and it is, I would maintain, a modernist credo – if modernists had credos) worked to convert knowledge back into art and thus into life. In that celebration of art (and life), Sterne joined with Schulz and Woolf to shape a modernist possibility: ☞ 'But this is not matter of SYSTEM; ... nor is it matter of BREVIARY——for I make no man's creed but my own——nor matter of FACT——at least that I know of; but 'tis matter copulative and introductory to what follows' (8.8.665). That this is the eighth and last paragraph in the eighth chapter of the eighth volume of *Tristram Shandy* is probably – but not assuredly – an accident; the modernist mind can leave it at that.

NOTES

1. See Melvyn New, 'Proust's Influence on Sterne: A Remembrance of Things to Come', *Modern Language Notes* 103.5 (1988), 1031–55; *Tristram Shandy: A Book for Free Spirits* (New York, NY: Twayne, 1994); 'Three Sentimental Journeys: Sterne, Shklovsky, Svevo', *Shandean* 11 (1999), 126–34; 'Reading Sterne through Proust and Levinas', *Age of Johnson* 12 (2001), 329–60.
2. New, 'Proust's Influence', 1053.

3. For the broad spectrum of twentieth-century authors interested in Sterne, see the essays collected in *Laurence Sterne in Modernism and Postmodernism*, eds. David Pierce and Peter de Voogd (Amsterdam: Rodopi, 1996); also the bibliography of works cited. Pierce's introduction to this volume cites Joyce's famous invocation of Sterne to explain his attempt 'to build many planes of narrative with a single esthetic purpose' in *Finnegans Wake* (10).
4. *Street of Crocodiles* is quoted from *The Complete Fiction of Bruno Schulz*, trans. Celina Wieniewska (New York, NY: Walker, 1989), hereafter cited parenthetically as 'Schulz'. For Schulz's life, see Jerzy Ficowski, *Regions of the Great Heresy: Bruno Schulz, A Biographical Portrait*, trans. Theodosia Robertson (New York, NY: Norton, 2003).
5. See Miriam L. Wallace, 'Thinking Back Through Our Others: Rereading Sterne and Resisting Joyce in *The Waves*', *Woolf Studies Annual* 9 (2003), 193–220; while the essay itself is an example of postmodernism run amok, the quotations garnered from Woolf's essays and manuscripts concerning Sterne are well worth recovering.
6. On Nietzsche and Sterne, see Duncan Large, '"The Freest Writer": Nietzsche on Sterne', *Shandean* 11 (1999), 9–29. The phrase 'freest writer' is from *Human, All Too Human* (1886), quoted by Large, at 11: 'How, in a book for free spirits, could there be no mention of Laurence Sterne, whom Goethe honoured as the freest spirit of his century! Let him accept the honour here of being called the freest writer of all time, in comparison with whom all others seem stiff, square, intolerant, and boorishly direct.' New also discusses this passage at length (*Book for Free Spirits*, 15–17, 113–18).
7. The translation reads 'Treatise', but as others have noted, 'Tractate', with its allusiveness to talmudic commentary, is perhaps a more telling rendition.
8. See James A. Work's edition of *Tristram Shandy* (New York, NY: Odyssey Press, 1940), lx.
9. *Letters of John Keats*, ed. H.E. Rollins, 2 vols. (Cambridge, MA: Harvard University Press, 1958), I, 192 (21 December 1817). For Sterne's understanding of tartuffery, a mode of domineering hypocrisy that pervades his satire, see New, *Book for Free Spirits*, 113–34.
10. See, in particular, Sermon 29, 'Our conversation in heaven', and New's discussion of it as a commentary on *A Sentimental Journey* (*SJ/BJ* 273–5).
11. Cf. *SJ/BJ* 116: 'But there is nothing unmixt in this world; and some of the gravest of our divines have carried it so far as to affirm, that enjoyment itself was attended even with a sigh—and that the greatest *they knew of*, terminated *in a general way*, in little better than a convulsion.' For a discussion of this passage, and its roots in Montaigne (another modernist), see *SJ/BJ* 346–7, n. to 116.7–11; see also 124 ('The Conquest').
12. See the concluding aposiopesis of *A Sentimental Journey*: 'so that when I stretch'd out my hand, I caught hold of the Fille de Chambre's / END OF VOL. II.' (*SJ/BJ* 165); also *The Drawings of Bruno Schulz*, ed. Jerzy Ficowski (Evanston, IL: Northwestern University Press, 1990), esp. 'The Book of Idolatry', 52–107.
13. Virginia Woolf, *Mrs Dalloway*, ed. David Bradshaw (Oxford: Oxford World's Classics, 2000), 81; hereafter cited parenthetically as 'Woolf'.
14. Woolf 81; my italics. Cf. Toby's 'apologetical oration': 'If, when I was a school-boy, I could not hear a drum beat, but my heart beat with it——was it my fault?' (*TS* 6.32.555).

15. 'For what man in the natural state or course of thinking, did ever conceive it in his power to reduce the notions of all mankind exactly to the same length, and breadth, and height of his own? Yet this is the first humble and civil design of all innovators in the empire of reason' (Jonathan Swift, *A Tale of a Tub and Other Works*, eds. Angus Ross and David Woolley (Oxford: Oxford University Press, 1986), 80).

16. Woolf 85; cf. *TS* 2.5.106: 'When a man gives himself up to the government of a ruling passion,——or, in other words, when his HOBBY-HORSE grows head-strong,——farewell cool reason and fair discretion.' Once again, we find Swift's *Tale of a Tub* underlying the notion: 'But when a man's fancy gets *astride* on his reason, when imagination is at cuffs with the senses, and common understanding as well as common sense, is kicked out of doors; the first proselyte he makes is himself, and when that is once compassed, the difficulty is not so great in bringing over others' (*Tale* 82). Swift's proselyte and Woolf's converter meet, I would maintain, not only in Walter's study, but on Toby's bowling green as well: warfare is, after all, persuasion by other means.

12

DONALD R. WEHRS

Postcolonial Sterne

Sterne occupies a central place in postcolonial studies, a field that traces the evolution of Western colonialist thought as well as its contestation in post-colonial literatures. By likening Toby's fixation upon the wars of William and Anne, through which England laid claim to world power, to Walter's delight in philosophical systemisations through which he hopes to 'govern' other people and the future, Sterne seems to identify political and intellectual sources of Britain's imperialism, and subject them to satirical critique. In later decades, Sternean sentimentalism entered into abolitionist (anti-slavery) discourse by suggesting that affective, divinely-inspired recognitions of ethical bonds reveal all intellectualised justifications of inhumanity to be impositions upon others and ourselves. In our own era, Shandean themes and character types, which underscore how easily, persistently, and inventively human subjectivity may assume forms complicit with imperialistic power relations, become recurrent preoccupations within contemporary postcolonial fiction.

Sterne and abolition

As early as his sermon on 'Job's account of the shortness and troubles of life, considered', published in 1760, Sterne anticipated abolitionist thought. Although this sermon conventionally decries slavery as a postlapsarian evil, and its frame of reference is classical rather than Caribbean (*Sermons* 10.99), it prompted an ex-slave, Ignatius Sancho, to urge Sterne to 'give half an hours attention to slavery (as it is at this day undergone in the West Indies)'; handled in Sterne's manner, the subject would 'ease the Yoke of many, perhaps occasion a reformation throughout our Islands' (*Letters* 282–3). Sterne replied that he was writing 'a tender tale of the sorrows of a friendless poor negro girl', which, if he could fit it into his work, would be 'at the service of the afflicted' (*Letters* 287). The scene in question, which duly appeared in volume 9 (1767) of *Tristram Shandy*, was later incorporated into an abolitionist pamphlet, and Thomas Clarkson, the first historian of abolitionism, noted its influence: 'Sterne, in his account of the Negro girl in his Life of Tristram Shandy, took decidedly the part of the oppressed Africans. The pathetic, witty, and sentimental manner, in which he handled this subject, occasioned many to remember it, and procured a certain portion of feeling in their favour.'[1] Clarkson attributes the political efficacy of Sterne's scene to its aesthetic sophistication, which goes beyond the lament of the earlier sermon.

Toby and Trim's conversation about 'a poor negro girl' (*TS* 9.6.747) employed in the Lisbon shop owned by Tom's Jewish widow showcases an interweaving of affect and irony that, by this stage in *Tristram Shandy*, had become almost a trademark. Here, Trim's insistence upon 'circumstances in the story of that poor friendless slut that would melt a heart of stone' ('slut' is non-pejorative here, as was common in the period) unites appeal to sentiment with a reminder of how much Toby enjoys images affording aesthetic contemplation of his own good nature. Unusually for its time, *Tristram Shandy* highlights the proximity of aestheticising perception to colonising cognition even as it insists, in opposition to Hobbes, Mandeville, and French materialists, that affections, sympathy, and benevolence are irreducible to egoism.

Like many eighteenth-century Anglican divines, Sterne draws upon Augustinian critiques of Stoicism, as in Sermon 15, 'Job's expostulation with his wife' (*Sermons* 15.140–9), to rebut egoist-materialist philosophy. Augustine maintains that were the mind untouched by any emotion whatsoever, its insensitivity ('*hunc stuporem*') would leave us morally defective due to lacking compassion – a quality he defines as 'a kind of fellow-feeling in our hearts for another's misery, which compels us [*compellimur*] to come to his help'.[2] In this spirit, Sterne's self-reflexive sentimental mode, thematising the reader's vulnerability to affect, attests to the 'compelled' character of a compassion that not only discloses the impress of divine goodness upon created being, but also regulates how scripture should be read – how the sense governing revealed discourse should be construed. Moved by the affecting image of the African girl, Trim is led to ask if '[a] Negro has a soul?', prompting from Toby the response that, 'I suppose, God would not leave him without one, any more than thee or me', to which Trim returns in agreement: 'It would be putting one sadly over the head of another' (*TS* 9.6.747). Goodness of heart lets Toby and Trim intuit interpretative principles traceable to Erasmus, whose Augustinian affirmation of natural compassion combines with a sacred hermeneutics, a mode of interpreting scripture, that was soon to be integral to abolitionist polemic. Noting that there are scriptural passages that seem to conflict with Christ's call for universal love, Erasmus recommends construing them allegorically, lest Biblical literalism foster theological deprecations of ethical sense.³ Latitudinarian divines insisted that just such absurdities follow from Catholic and Dissenter literalisms. Sterne underlines the importance of this tradition of ethical regulation of scriptural sense to his fiction by attributing to Yorick his own rejection of 'this principle that there *can* be religion without morality' (*Sermons* 27.266) or 'religion without mercy' (*TS* 2.17.163; see also *TS Notes* 284–5).

The same principle, that ethical sense should govern Biblical interpretation because Christ's universalising of neighbourly love stands as the first and highest commandment, underlies Quobna Ottobah Cugoano's claim in *Thoughts and Sentiments on the Evils of Slavery* (1787), that after the Christian revelation, all that remains of 'the law' are 'the ever abiding obligations, and ever binding injunctions of moral rectitude, justice, equity and righteousness'. This principle also gives rise to the Revd William Hughes's insistence in 1788 that 'the obligation that all men are under to do all possible good to their fellow-creatures, of whatever nation or religion', lies at the core of 'the new convenant'.⁴

Likewise refusing theological interpretations at odds with ethical sense, Toby and Trim apprehend slavery and racial oppression as effects of histories of violence without providential or moral sanction. That the poor girl 'has no one to stand up for her', Toby insists, 'recommends her to protection—and her brethren with her' (*TS* 9.6.748). Toby's chivalric locutions affiliate benevolent impulses with Don Quixote's notion of a knight-errantry 'established, to defend damsels, shelter widows, and succor orphans and those in need'.⁵ For Sterne and his audience, as the merging of Quixote's image with Yorick's indicates (1.10.18–24), quixotism denotes less madness than sublime idealistic ignorance of the world's baseness (a pattern also observable in Fielding's Abraham Adams in *Joseph Andrews* and Fielding's play of 1734, *Don Quixote in England*). By construing this baseness as something that *might* be reformed, the politics entailed by Erasmian sacred hermeneutics suggests that, in endeavouring to 'make the world see its error' in mocking knight-errantry,⁶ Quixote presents a naïve prototype of modern, ethical, and Christian identities.

Much contemporary critical theory questions whether cultural discourse ever motivates progressive political change. For instance, by figuring Africans as victims (symbolically female) and Europeans as their (male, martial) rescuers, Sterne may seem to consolidate the trope of European males 'saving' non-Western women that, as Gayatri Chakravorty Spivak has argued, helped to justify imperialism.⁷ Sterne's irony may critique such ideological work, however, by encouraging readers to distance their own hermeneutics from Toby's and Trim's naïve consumption of the scene. Certainly, Sterne furthers the cause of abolition by suggesting that compassion is a moral imperative uniting service to others with the expression of one's best self. Moreover, by insisting that the misery of slavery derives from loss of a liberty 'whose taste is grateful, and ever wilt be so, till Nature herself shall change' (SJ/BJ 96), Sterne suggests that liberty is integral to humanity. This is also implied by his comic explorations of how people's inalienable liberty baffles and delights us, exposing every colonising thought and feeling to mocking reproach. To the extent that such portraits persuade, they make abolitionist politics an ethical imperative.

Current historical research suggests that the discourse of abolitionism did indeed motivate change. Whereas Eric Williams postulated in 1944 that capitalists turned against the slave trade because it became less profitable than wage labour, and David Brion Davis argued in 1975 that abolitionism diverted attention from domestic injustice, scholarship since the 1980s reveals that the slave trade and slave-produced commodities became more, not less, profitable as the eighteenth century progressed, and that domestic social-reform rhetoric imitated and appealed to abolitionist discourse.[8] One must ask why so many diverse people bound their moral identities to the act of opposing lucrative, well-established practices. Part of the answer seems to lie in Sterne's influential blending of Erasmian sacred hermeneutics with satire against colonising consciousness and evocations of compelled compassion.

Sterne and postcolonial fiction

A seemingly very different Sterne recurs in postcolonial fiction. If one argues, with Edward Said and Homi Bhabha, that Enlightenment empiricism and universalism led to colonising 'naturalisations' in which historically con-structed and contested ways of seeing, valuing, and knowing are presented as self-evident facts of nature, then the 'naturalising' conventions of realistic fiction may appear complicit with pseudo-scientific discourses that sustain racism and imperialism.[9] Sterne's metafictional self-reflexivity, his play with semantic uncertainties of reference, and his staging of conceptual heterogene-ities (as when he fuses 'innocent' and sexual connotations) may thus be taken as undermining the claims and exposing the interests of colonialist discourse.

If we follow Richard A. Lanham in reading Sterne as offering 'games of pleasure' whose artificial structures grant us a solace otherwise unavailable, we may see Sterne anticipating the romantic neo-idealism that Malcolm K. Read attributes to Jorge Luis Borges, who by 'dispens[ing] with the whole notion of referents' escapes the dissatisfactions and inadequacies of language while exposing the epistemological naïveté of conventional notions of referentiality.[10] Sterne's epistemological critique of Enlightenment myth-making seems so consonant with the fiction of Borges that one may speak of joint influence (upon Carlos Fuentes and Cabrera Infante, for example), despite Borges' slight engagement with Sterne, which occurred largely through friendship with Alfonso Reyes, Sterne's Spanish American translator.[11]

If we, on the other hand, take a darker (existentialist or materialist) view of such estrangements from shared experience and public life, hobby-horsical self-enclosure issues less in sunny vistas of free play than in toxic solitudes. Although such solitudes are found in Borges,[12] they are central to Gabriel García Márquez's Macondo, the 'city of mirrors (or mirages)' ['*ciudad de los espejos (o los espejismos)*'][13] chronicled in *One Hundred Years of Solitude* (1967). By dramatising a historical process that 'wrings out' the affective susceptibilities and the valorisation of liberty and charity that make Walter and Toby irreducible to their manias, García Márquez, and later Salman Rushdie, Carlos Fuentes, and Peter Carey, follow Günter Grass's *The Tin Drum* [*Die Blechtrommel*] (1959) in transposing horrific national history into a dark comic epic of stunted development and self-entrapping defence mechanisms.[14] Grass gives narrative expression to dark postmodern readings of history that, rather than following the 'games of pleasure' side of post-modernism, view cultural history as generating totalities that co-opt and disarm all alternatives.

In *The Tin Drum*, the Sternean trope of seeking refuge from the violence of history in hobby-horsical self-enclosures governs all characterisation. Oskar's story begins when his grandfather, Joseph Koljaiczek, who is pursued by police for setting fire to a sawmill after being assaulted by his boss for painting a fence white and red (the national colours of then partitioned Poland), hides under Oskar's grandmother's 'wide skirts'. Linking capitalism (the sawmill) to imperialistic nationalism (Prussian control of eastern Poland), Grass establishes postmodern fiction's pivotal contrast between all-enveloping, soulless systems and resistances that, like the stereotype of Polish romantic individualism, are anarchic and self-marginalising. Oskar's magical attributes – wilful dwarfism, obsessive drumming, glass-shattering voice – repudiate, as does Koljaiczek's nationalism, a colonised and colonising socio-political world, but his character blends Toby-like withdrawal with Walter-like irritation to produce a negatively generated, problematic identity.[15] Just as Walter and Toby shape Tristram, literally, so Oskar's putative fathers – the dull but reliable German Matzerath and the idealistic but ineffectual Pole Bronski – mimic flawed national stereotypes in such a way as to reinforce his own indifference and leave his mother, like Mrs Shandy and Widow Wadman, unsatisfied.

John Reddick distinguishes between a 'brainbox' Oskar lacking affect, and a 'tears' Oskar, whose emotional susceptibility opens him up to victimisation by the world he portrays.[16] Although intermittently shaken by guilt over his 'monstrousness', Oskar is as aware as Tristram and Yorick of how easily guilt feelings collude with the colonising uses of others.[17] In Sterne, however, recognising the ubiquity of Augustinian self-love yields the tolerant attitude to others that is famously epitomised when Toby releases (as opposed to killing) a fly that torments him, on the principle that 'This world surely is wide enough to hold both thee and me' (*TS* 2.12.131). In Grass, when Oskar's drumming effects in others the same narcissistic regressions that characterise himself, he becomes a postwar celebrity. However, as his pathological pursuit of Sister Dorothea attests, assuaging trauma through evading ethical maturity comes at a fearsome price. All instinct to connect with others is deformed into 'fascistic' possessiveness, and so the feminine, the sexual, and the material, already disturbing for Sterne's male characters, elicit paranoiac dread, epitomised by Oskar's fear of being devoured by the Black Witch, a malevolent fairytale figure evocative of death, meaninglessness, and blind materiality (Grass 577–89/482–91).

In *One Hundred Years of Solitude*, García Márquez traces hobby-horses back to their quixotic inspiration, and Spanish American culture back to conjunctions of quixotic idealisation and proto-scientific, proto-imperialistic totalisation. Like Grass in the case of Oskar, he links José Arcadio Buendía's descent into learned folly to his habits 'of walking through the house without paying attention to anyone' (García Márquez 14/62) – habits expressing an irritated withdrawal from the disorderly intercourse that, as the conversations between Walter and Toby stress, works to sustain sociability. Depicting multiple variants of such withdrawal, and ever greater hostility across the generations to whatever disturbs systemic purity and order, García Márquez suggests that anti-social aspects of quixotic-theoretical-idealising Western subjectivity come, at least in Spanish American contexts, to engender such antipathy to the pluralistic and the material that its ultimate fruit is an apocalyptical closure of regenerative possibilities. Walter's fantasies of order, and his grudge against the material, especially the sexual, underlie Fernanda del Carpio's sterilising mania for purity of blood and ideology, just as Toby's consoling compulsive sieges underlie Colonel Aureliano Buendía's obsessive fashioning of little gold fishes.

In *Midnight's Children* (1980), Rushdie recasts in Indian subcontinental terms Grass's compromised resistance and García Márquez's familial eradication and cultural sicknesses unto death. Here Saleem's genealogical and cultural heterogeneity links 'hybridity', the refusal of 'a standard code in the language and any monocentric view of human experience', with generic, conceptual 'impurity' in Shandean discourse.[18] By portraying himself as 'falling apart', as 'literally disintegrating',[19] Saleem evokes Tristram, who ascribes his temperament to a conception that 'scattered and dispersed the animal spirits' (*TS* 1.1.2). The fact that Saleem's death echoes Tristram's conception implies their crucial difference, however – a difference that may suggest thematic as well as formal grounds for Rushdie's well-known remark that, were he to award medals for narrative technique, he would accept the silver, but confer the gold upon Sterne.[20] Whereas both Tristram and his text *live from* heterogeneities in principle self-sustaining enough to 'be kept a-going these forty years, if it pleases the fountain of health to bless me so long' (1.22.82), both Saleem and the India he embodies 'com[e] apart at the seams' (Rushdie 36) because both are born into worlds hostile to pluralism.

On the one hand, *Midnight's Children* and Saleem blend East and West, Muslim and Hindu, in a modernist redemptive paradigm inaccessible to the characters or their world. On the other, like Oskar, Saleem is congenitally estranged from the pluralisms that his discourse affirms. The idea of a 'new India', the nation state conceived by Nehru, whose letter Saleem takes as evidence of a messianic destiny, proves quixotic because antipathy to pluralism is so integral to the novel's world that it forces Oskar's fate of deformity, immaturity, and self-division upon Saleem.

This resistance to reform governs the disjunction between Saleem as Tristram-like narrator and as Oskar-like character. Whereas Oskar's withdrawal into a clothes closet is motivated by others' images of his own self-involved indifference (Grass 155/124), the 'nearlynine' Saleem hides in a washing-chest to evade postcolonial pressures, to be 'concealed from the demands of parents and history' (Rushdie 173, 177). In both cases, the shelter taken from trauma through infantile regression is compromised by the witnessing of maternal sexual secrets. Oskar sees his mother with Bronski; Saleem overhears his mother naming her lover and watches her undress: 'And now – O shameless mother! Reveler of duplicity, of emotions which have no place in family life; and more: O brazen unveiler of Black Mango!' (Rushdie 183). While Saleem's Tristram-like cadences seem to mock the scandalised patriarchal misogyny that he rehearses, his actions are either, as here, complicit in cultural violence – 'lust for revenge upon [his] perfidious mother' prompts him to expose another adulterous wife to her husband's murderous rage – or ineffectual, as when he is sterilised at the hands of the Widow (Indira Gandhi), Rushdie's analogue to the Black Witch, whose tyrannical rule, devouring midnight's children, constitutes a 'sperectomy: the draining-out of hope' (Rushdie 288, 503).

Carlos Fuentes' *Cristóbal Nonato* (1987) discovers its descent from Sterne, *Don Quixote*, and Erasmus while seeking less bleak conclusions from analogous readings of Spanish American history.[21] Alongside a Hispanic postmodernism that (as one critic puts it) conceives 'Spanish American cultural discourse as intrinsically beholden to hegemonic values and concerns',[22] *Tristram Shandy* exemplifies roads not taken. Fuentes monumentalises Spain's fateful rejection of pluralism in *Terra Nostra* (1975), where the expulsion of Jews and Moors and the embrace of a 'purity' allying empire and Inquisition induce a stasis symbolised in the work by a structure in which each chapter retells the same story. Fuentes thus reconstitutes the novel as a system of reciprocal forces rather than a centre of narrative causality ('*como sistema de fuerzas recíprocas y ya no como centro de una causalidad narrativa*').[23] He locates the alternative to ideological and psychic self-enclosure in Erasmus, who by 'relativiz[ing] the pretended absolutes' of both imposed dogmas and 'the empire of the self' offers a potential touchstone for Spanish American culture; unhappily, however, 'Erasmianism sifted through Spain' has lost the self-critical edge that distinguishes resistance from quixotic illusions of 'emancipated uniqueness'.[24] To avoid the problem evident in Hispanic 'total' novels such as *Terra Nostra*, in which 'a critical apparatus promoting plurality and tolerance' is undercut by totalising narrative content,[25] Fuentes refigures Spanish American cultural history in Shandean terms. Magically taking in 'the essence' of the world around him *in utero*, Christopher's digressive playfulness portends progressive education, *Bildung*, symbolised by moving towards a birth that is emblematic of Mexico's possible rebirth.

Christopher's discourse, like Tristram's, centres upon hobby-horsical relatives. For Christopher, however, a homicidal family drama discloses the fragmenting of psychic space into 'labyrinths of solitude'[26] that underwrite the privatising of public spheres: the leasing of some parts of the country to US oil interests; the transformation of other parts into autonomous tourist playgrounds. Moreover, the act of hiding beneath various 'wide skirts' stunts all social defence mechanisms against postmodern co-option. Noting that it is not 'action nor statistics' but 'imagination and symbols' that will eradicate discontent (Fuentes 29/37), the government minister Robles Chacón 'packages' a random secretary as 'Mamadoc', a commercialised Virgin/Mother/Sex Symbol, to be 'Mother Doctor of all Mexicans!' (34–5/43). Whereas tension between Walter and Toby is balanced by exasperated affection, Christopher's uncles Don Homero Fagoaga and Don Fernando Benítez, the former devoted to a linguistic 'purity' reflective of ultra-conservatism, the latter seeking among isolated Indians a 'pure' Mexico uncontaminated by Europeans, view each other with a fratricidal loathing emblematic of all Mexico's competing totalisations. Just as the uncles' 'civil war', and Don Homero's efforts first to brainwash and then to murder Christopher's father, Angel, recast as carnival the material of historical tragedy, so Angel's naming his wife in his own image as Angeles, his being dwarfed by the burden of family history, and her corresponding lack of a past of her own, parody themes of conquest, colonisation, and sexism. Angeles resembles not just Mrs Shandy but also García Márquez's Santa Sofía de la Piedad, who epitomises self-effacing Hispanic women by magically seeming not to exist except when needed. Likewise, the monopolistic businessman-politician Ulises López recalls Fuentes' Artemio Cruz and other 'big men' whose personal histories reflect national betrayal.[27]

In Fuentes, anarchic violence assumes the cold calculation of terrorism: Angel and Angeles direct impoverished youths to murder tourists in Acapulco (Fuentes 204/226); the frustrated writer Matamoros Moreno, having already organised a gang rape of Angel and Angeles (252–3/276–7), becomes a populist 'Ayatollah', and sponsors a mob assault that murders Ulises López and his family (431–440/458–67). Such violence, though directed against morally bankrupt caricatures, associates anarchic revolt with colonising and sexually pathological power relations, and consolidates hegemony: Robles Chacón uses the massacres and Matamoros to eliminate his rival. While it has been argued that, from the novel's exuberant Shandean language, a new Mexico might be born,[28] the disjunction between that language and the events that occasion it suggests that Christopher, like Oskar and Saleem, is affectively deficient, thus representing the limitations imposed by the world of the novel.

No Black Witch or Widow, however, has the last word. Having found in all 'counterforce' only 'corruption, injustice, stupidity, egoism, arrogance, disdain, and hunger', unborn Christopher and his parents seek refuge in 'the New World of Pacífica', a Pacific Rim economic-political order defined by 'the maximum conjunction of labor, technical know-how, and political will in human history', and so a potential escape from 'the tyrannical Atlantic', a potential saving of 'the West from itself by teaching it once again to deny power to power' (Fuentes 512–13/544). The novel's *Bildung* should culminate in apocalyptic transformation, with Shandean discourse pulling Spanish American civilisation back onto the Erasmian-Cervantean tracks from which it was tragically diverted – tracks that unite an Erasmian anti-dogmatic universalising ethical sense with a Cervantean hermeneutics of allowing particulars to generate meaning out of their own internal coherence and integrity.[29] The stress placed by Fuentes on Cervantes' role in inaugurating the internally self-governing communicative strategies of modern aesthetic discourse is consistent with the emphasis of Diana de Armas Wilson and others upon the presciently postcolonial implications of *Don Quixote*, unmasking as it does a chivalric discourse mobilised to describe and justify conquest in the Americas.[30] On the one hand, Fuentes' turn to Sterne highlights his extravagant ambition: when Sterne evokes Erasmian-Cervantean theological-hermeneutical contexts, he appeals to central currents of his own culture, but Fuentes, on his own account, appeals to the marginal and abjected. On the other hand, announcing a global economy that displaces 'power' with 'well-being' (516/547), Pacífica may allow Shandean pluralism to break free of Spanish America's nightmarish history. Aesthetically, the novel's ending seems unearned, but in shifting to the reader responsibility for the world into which Christopher will be born, Fuentes evokes Sternean play with blank pages to affirm a freedom subversive of dark postmodern readings of history.

Peter Carey's *The Unusual Life of Tristan Smith* (1995) transposes Shandean fiction into a meditation upon complicity and resistance between the fictional states of hegemonic Voorstand and peripheral Efica, evocative of the United States and Australia. Carey's counterfactual reality is an ideal space for exploring the compromised position of settler societies produced by totalising ethnocentric imaginations that have swept aside precolonial 'facts'. Despite nominal political independence, Efica's culture echoes the hegemonic Voorstand Sirkus – a combination of Disney, Wild West, circus, and Vegas spectacle – in a slightly different Efican Sirkus. Resistance itself becomes an institutionalised repertoire of performances, epitomised by the theatre company run by Tristan's mother, Felicity, herself a Voorstand émigrée, as a 'radical' alternative to Sirkus. It offers, besides 'colloquial Shakespeare', a 'sort of agitprop, part circus, part soapbox', designed to attack, as Tristan assures his imagined Voorstand reader, 'our country's craven relationship with yours'.[31]

The novel's first half, set in Efica, rearticulates a pattern now familiar in postcolonial Shandean narrative: a 'monstrous' child is born of multiple fathers (the callow actor Bill Millefleur, the ex-criminal production manager Wally, and the businessman intellectual Vincent). But rather than personifying a nation's botched conception and stunted growth, Tristan is the consequence of a maternal revolt that is both sublime and hobby-horsical. Dominating her three consorts, Felicity assumes political-cultural agency through a theatre intended to be an anticolonial counterforce. As a refuge for obsessive 'acting out', however, the theatre resembles Toby's bowling green, and as an ideological vehicle, it becomes, like Walter's disquisitions, a tireless endeavour to fit experience into a system.

The story of Tristan's generation from the theatre is enfolded in the story of the theatre's collapse as a political community. Accommodating Tristan becomes so onerous that the actors rebel, forcing aside the fiction that the troupe is a 'collective'. When challenged, Felicity can banish all who oppose 'her vision' because she owns the theatre: 'It was hers in her secret heart, and not because it was her money that had purchased it, but because she had made it, dreamed it, spun it out of herself' (Carey 107, 108–9). This collapse suggests that what the novel's world produces (the monstrous/magical child) undermines its survival, but Tristan's tone recalls Tristram's elegiac cadences in the later volumes of *Tristram Shandy*, rather than the cold satire of Oskar, Saleem, and Christopher. Instead of linking the postcolonial to an affectively stunted familial, social realm, Carey suggests that extravagant love, symbolised by the 'mad' devotion inspired by Tristan, renders unsustainable all alternative visions that, by resembling the hobby-horses of Toby and Walter, betray their 'private ownership'. That Felicity can be both 'strident and humourless' and 'a softly spoken woman with warm eyes' (9) suggests the kind of saving graces that redeem Toby and Walter, but in Carey such transcendence, by 'breaking up' our hobby-horses, exposes us to postcolonial political violence. Felicity becomes a politician, which makes her a threat to Voorstand's hegemony; the secret police expose her to scandal over the married Vincent, then murder her in a way that can be passed off as a politically useful suicide (222–3). Carey recycles the dark postmodern plot with a vengeance.

The novel's second half, describing the adult Tristan's clandestine journey to Voorstand, reiterates postmodern fears of all-enveloping systems (the mission is compromised because Tristan's nurse is really a cross-dressing secret agent). It also reflects concerns that resistance must dissipate into co-option. Exposed to the seductive power of the Voorstand Sirkus, Tristan takes advantage of his ability to fit inside a mechanic doll of the Sirkus character Bruder Mouse, and assumes colonising, mystifying attributes; he becomes a celebrity through 'oracular pronouncements' while pursuing 'long-curbed sexual urges' with the 'agoraphobic millionaire, Peggy Kramer'.[32] Peggy's seduction by Bruder Mouse, like Widow Wadman's obsession with Toby, links vulnerability to one's own (concupiscent) imagination with vulnerability to cultural fictions (in the Widow's case, notions about retired military gentlemen). 'Tristan's deception proves to be as captivating as the propaganda of the Voorstand Sirkus', as Christer Larsson notes: as a result, when Tristan reveals 'his true face', Peggy sees 'the Hairy Man', displacing 'Bruder Mouse with a less appealing mythological figure', whereas Tristan is 'torn from his fantasy' by seeing 'how repulsed Peggy Kram is by his appearance';[33] this aligns his position with that of Toby at the end of *Tristram Shandy*. That Tristan, unlike Toby, 'comes very close to achieving evil'[34] suggests not just the fragility of postcolonial resistance, but its paucity of resources for avoiding replication of the forces it would oppose. Carey points out that Tristan is 'lucky' rather than 'saved by his own moral wisdom and goodness', and that at best he has 'a will toward goodness' arising from sources alien to Voorstand-Efican politics, for he 'has been loved. There has been a passionate effort to love him.'[35] The implication is that redemption from postmodern postcolonial nightmares lies in recovering something like that impress of divine goodness which, for all the postmodern disruptions of *Tristram Shandy*, sets Sterne's characters apart from their totalising, self-enclosing propensities.

Sterne and postcolonial criticism

The career of Shandean postcolonial fiction suggests both the opportunities and the limitations of employing postcolonial criticism to reread Sterne. One approach emphasises Sterne's Irishness, despite his permanent departure from Ireland as a child and his family's English roots. Noting the paradox that Toby, 'a paragon of sentimentalism, is forever whistling "Lillabullero", a song which his author must have known is actually a mocking Williamite satire of Gaelic Jacobite hopes', Terry Eagleton argues that *Tristram Shandy* reflects Irish experience and sensibility in being 'a tale of the battered and blighted, of impotence and disfigurement'.[36] He thus rereads as effects of England's earliest forays into colonialism features of the text that existentialist criticism of an earlier generation had ascribed to absurdity and randomness. Joan Meyler takes this approach further, reading *Tristram Shandy* as 'an allegory of the history of Ireland', and Tristram, like Saleem, as the nation's 'anthropomorphised map'.[37] While such interpretations affiliate Sterne with resistance to colonialism, the identification of his characters with the ideal of 'English liberty', and the relationship between this cause and military and commercial expansionism, complicate the politics of Sterne's fiction. Relevant in this context is Nicholas Visser's observation that the money and freely disposable time that Walter has for system-spinning comes from 'the Turkey trade', and that the date of Tristram's birth, coinciding with William of Orange's landing in England on the anniversary of Guy Fawkes Day, is not fortuitous: 'Writing during the peak of Whig power, Sterne, in *Tristram Shandy*, looks back to the founding period of that power, between 1688 and 1714.'[38] Thomas Keymer points out how Toby's sieges recall Andrew Marvell's portrait in *Upon Appleton House* of the parliamentarian general Sir Thomas Fairfax's re-enactments in his garden of the 1644 battle of Marston Moor, so that Sterne, embedding civil war horrors in bowling green games, unites 'Cervantic ... mock-heroic deflation', which reduces the conquering hero to a comic monomaniac, with pointed explorations of 'the moral and psychological status of his traumatized veteran'.[39]

Too often, however, postcolonial criticism draws unwarranted conclusions based on outmoded paradigms. Visser, for instance, argues that to address 'the full richness of *Tristram Shandy*, we would do as well to read Immanuel

Wallerstein as Roland Barthes'.[40] The implication is that Wallerstein's treatment of the West as centre of a world system that co-opts non-Western 'peripheries' will illuminate *Tristram Shandy*'s participation in Western-dominated global capitalism. However, empirical economic and historical studies have largely discredited Wallerstein's and similar 1970s paradigms.[41] Perhaps a postcolonial Sterne's richest promise lies in its capacity to disclose transhistorical dynamics of colonising and resistance. Keymer notes that the 'grim continuity between partisan struggle and global war' that ties Fairfax and Toby together is co-extensive with 'putting private pleasure – and private pleasure that is personally debilitating – above' the interests of human survival.[42] Sterne might see colonising tendencies as consequences of Augustinian original sin; we might view them as effects of endemic egoism or of the evolutionary binding of attention and emotion to self-interested calculation.[43] Because of, rather than despite, these differences, the openness of Sterne's work to postcolonial analysis may move postcolonial theory beyond its current preoccupations with Western historicity and toward more complex ethical assessments.

NOTES

1. Charlotte Sussman, *Consuming Anxieties: Consumer Protest, Gender, and British Slavery, 1713–1833* (Stanford, CA: Stanford University Press, 2000), 145; Thomas Clarkson, *The History of the Rise, Progress, and Accomplishment of the Abolition of the African Slave-Trade by the British Parliament*, 2 vols. (1808), I, 60–1.

2. Augustine, *City of God*, trans. Henry Bettenson (Harmondsworth: Penguin, 1972), 565, 349; *City of God, Books XII–XV*, trans. Philip Levine, Loeb Classical Library (Cambridge, MA: Harvard University Press, 1966), 314; *City of God, Books VIII–XI*, trans. David S. Wiesen, Loeb Classical Library (Cambridge, MA: Harvard University Press, 1968), 168.

3. See Erasmus, *Enchiridion militis christiani* [*The Handbook of the Christian Soldier*], in *The Collected Works of Erasmus, Volume 66: Spiritualia*, ed. John W. O'Malley (Toronto, ON: University of Toronto Press, 1988), 68; Shimon Markish, *Erasmus and the Jews*, trans. Anthony Olcott (Chicago, IL: University of Chicago Press, 1986), 43. In *The Praise of Folly* (1509), Erasmus extends Lucianic satire to any hermeneutics that would estrange theology from ethics.

4. Quobna Ottobah Cugoano, *Thoughts and Sentiments on the Evil of Slavery* (New York, NY: Penguin, 1999), 34; William Hughes, *An Answer to the Rev. Mr. Harris's 'Scriptural Researches on the Licitness of the Slave-Trade'* (1788), 5.

5. Miguel de Cervantes, *Don Quijote*, trans. Burton Raffel, ed. Diana de Armas Wilson (New York, NY: Norton, 1999), 60 / *Don Quijote de la Mancha*, ed. Martín de Riquer (Barcelona: Editorial Juventud, 1955), 106.

6. Cervantes, *Don Quijote*, 367/547.

7. Gayatri Chakravorty Spivak, 'Can the Subaltern Woman Speak?', in *The Post-Colonial Studies Reader*, eds. Bill Ashcroft, Gareth Griffiths, and Helen Tiffin (London: Routledge, 1995), 24–8.

8. See Eric Williams, *Capitalism and Slavery* (Chapel Hill, NC: University of North Carolina Press, 1944); David Brion Davis, *The Problem of Slavery in the Age of Revolution, 1770–1823* (Ithaca, NY: Cornell University Press, 1975). For more recent scholarship, see esp. Leo d'Anjou, *Social Movements and Cultural Change: The First Abolitionist Revisited* (New York, NY: Aldine de Gruyter, 1996); David Eltis, *Economic Growth and the Ending of the Transatlantic Slave Trade* (New York, NY: Oxford University Press, 1987); Seymour Drescher, *Capitalism and Antislavery: British Mobilization in Comparative Perspective* (New York, NY: Oxford University Press, 1987).

9. See Edward W. Said, *Culture and Imperialism* (New York, NY: Knopf, 1993); Homi Bhabha, *Nation and Narration* (London: Routledge, 1990); Emmanuel Chukwudi Eze, *Achieving our Humanity: The Idea of the Postracial Future* (New York, NY: Routledge, 2001), 3–111.

10. Richard A. Lanham, *Tristram Shandy: The Games of Pleasure* (Berkeley, CA: University of California Press, 1973); Malcolm K. Read, *Jorge Luis Borges and his Predecessors: or, Notes Toward a Materialist History of Linguistic Idealism* (Chapel Hill, NC: University of North Carolina Press, 1993), 83. This argument would link Sterne to the 'games-playing' side of Nakokov, Barthelme, and Kundera.

11. Marcos-Ricardo Barnatan, *Borges: Biografía total* (Madrid: Ediciones Temas de Hoy, 1995), 256–7.

12. See 'Las ruines circulares', in Luis Jorge Borges, *Ficciones* (Buenos Aires: Emecé, 1956 [1944]), 61–9.

13. Gabriel García Márquez, *One Hundred Years of Solitude*, trans. Gregory Rabassa (New York, NY: Bard, 1970), 383 / *Cien años de soledad* (Madrid: Espasa-Calpe, 1982 [1967]), 448, hereafter cited parenthetically as 'García Márquez'.

14. See Carrie Dawson, '"Who Was that Masked Mouse?": Imposture in Peter Carey's *The Unusual Life of Tristan Smith*', *Southern Review* 30 (1997), 208; Linda Hutcheon, *The Politics of Postmodernism* (London: Routledge, 1989), 104; Patricia Merivale, 'Saleem Fathered by Oskar: *Midnight's Children*, Magic Realism, and *The Tin Drum*', in *Magical Realism: Theory, History, Community*, eds. Lois Parkinson Zamora and Wendy B. Faris (Durham, NC: Duke University Press, 1995), 329–45.

15. See Jürgen Rothenberg, *Günter Grass: Das Chaos in verbesserter Ausführung* (Heidelberg: Carl Winter Universitätsverlag, 1976), 10.

16. John Reddick, *The "Danzig Trilogy" of Günter Grass: A Study of The Tin Drum, Cat and Mouse, and Dog Years* (New York, NY: Harcourt Brace Jovanovich, 1974), 58–82.

17. Günter Grass, *The Tin Drum*, trans. Ralph Manheim (New York, NY: Vintage, 1961, 1962), 138, 201, 333–7 / *Die Blechtrommel* (Darmstadt: Luchterhand, 1974 [1959]), 171, 247, 403–7; hereafter cited parenthetically as 'Grass'.

18. Bill Ashcroft, Gareth Griffiths, and Helen Tiffin, *The Empire Writes Back: Theory and Practice in Post-Colonial Literatures* (London: Routledge, 1989), 41.

19. Salman Rushdie, *Midnight's Children* (New York, NY: Penguin, 1980), 36; hereafter cited parenthetically as 'Rushdie'.

20. See Walter Göbel and Damian Grant, 'Salman Rushdie's Silver Medal', in *Laurence Sterne in Modernism and Postmodernism*, eds. David Pierce and Peter de Voogd (Amsterdam: Rodopi, 1996), 87.

21. Carlos Fuentes, *Christopher Unborn*, trans. Alfred MacAdam and Carlos Fuentes (New York, NY: Farrar, Straus, Giroux, 1989), 134–5 / *Cristòbal Nonato* (México: Fondo de Cultura Económica, 1987), 152, hereafter cited parenthetically as 'Fuentes'; see Santiago Juan-Navarro, 'The Dialogical Imagination of Salman Rushdie and Carlos Fuentes: National Allegories and the Scene of Writing in *Midnight's Children* and *Cristòbal Nonato*', *Neohelicon* 20 (1993), 257–312, esp. 306–8.

22. Carlos J. Alonso, 'The Mourning After: García Márquez, Fuentes and the Meaning of Postmodernity in Spanish America', *Modern Language Notes* 109 (1994), 266.

23. Quoted in Sergio López Mena, 'Lectura y recuperación de *Tierra nostra*, un acto de justicia', in *Carlos Fuentes: Perspectivas críticas*, ed. Pol Popovic Karic (México: Siglo Veintiuno, 2002), 141.

24. Carlos Fuentes, *Terra Nostra*, trans. Margaret Sayers Peden (New York, NY: Farrar, Straus, Giroux, 1976), 770; *Terra Nostra* (Barcelona: Seix Barral, 1975), 774.

25. Mark Anderson, 'A Reappraisal of the "Total" Novel: Totality and Communicative Systems in Carlos Fuentes' *Terra Nostra*', *Symposium: A Quarterly Journal in Modern Literatures* 57 (2003), 75.

26. See Octavio Paz, *El Laberinto de la Soledad* (México: Fondo de Cultura Económica, 1959 [1950]).

27. See Carlos Fuentes, *La Muerte de Artemio Cruz* (México: Fondo de Cultura Económica, 1962).

28. See Julio Ortega, '*Christopher Unborn*: Rage and Laughter', trans. Carl Mentley, *Review of Contemporary Fiction* 8 (1988), 285–91; Kristine Ibsen, 'Narrative Perspectives and the Role of the Reader in Fuentes's *Cristòbal*', *Romance Notes* 33 (1993), 313–17.

29. For the connection between Erasmian critiques of dogmatism and egoism and Cervantes' literary hermeneutics, see Carlos Fuentes, *Cervantes o la crítica de la lectura* (Madrid: Alcala de Henares, 1994 [1976]).

30. See Diana de la Armas Wilson's introduction to *Don Quijote*, xii–xv.

31. Peter Carey, *The Unusual Life of Tristan Smith* (New York, NY: Knopf, 1995), 9; hereafter cited parenthetically as 'Carey'.

32. Peter Pierce, 'Captivity, Captivation: Aspects of Peter Carey's Fiction', in *'And What Books Do You Read?': New Studies in Australian Literature*, eds. Irmtraud Petersson and Martin Duwell (Queensland: University of Queensland Press, 1996), 147.

33. Christer Larsson, *'The Relative Merits of Goodness and Originality': The Ethics of Storytelling in Peter Carey's Novels* (Uppsala: Uppsala University Press, 2001), 131.

34. Interview, in 'Peter Carey on *The Tax Inspector* and *The Unusual Life of Tristan Smith*: A Conversation with Ray Willbanks', *Antipodes: A North American Journal of Australian Literature* 11 (1997), 15.

35. *Ibid.*, 15.

36. Terry Eagleton, *Crazy John and the Bishop, and Other Essays on Irish Culture* (Notre Dame: University of Notre Dame Press, 1998), 82, 133.

37. Joan Meyler, 'The "Body National" and the "Body Natural": *Tristram Shandy*'s History of Ireland', *Irish Studies Review* 11 (2003), 137.

38. Nicholas Visser, '*Tristram Shandy* and the Straight Line of History', *Textual Practice* 12 (1998), 491, 499.
39. Thomas Keymer, *Sterne, the Moderns, and the Novel* (Oxford: Oxford University Press, 2002), 209.
40. Visser, '*Tristram Shandy* and the Straight Line', 499.
41. See esp. Frederick Cooper, 'Africa and the World Economy', in Frederick Cooper *et al.*, *Confronting Historical Paradigms: Peasants, Labor, and the Capitalist World System in Africa and Latin America* (Madison, WI: University of Wisconsin Press, 1993), 84–201.
42. Keymer, *Sterne, the Moderns*, 214.
43. For the former alternative, see Emmanuel Levinas, *Otherwise Than Being, or Beyond Essence*, trans. Alphonso Lingis (Pittsburgh, PA: Duquesne University Press, 1981); for the latter, Patrick Colm Hogan, *The Mind and Its Stories: Narrative Universals and Human Emotion* (Cambridge: Cambridge University Press, 2003).

FURTHER READING

Scholarly editions of *Tristram Shandy*, the *Sermons*, and *A Sentimental Journey* in the standard Florida Edition of the Works of Laurence Sterne, six vols. to date (Gainesville, FL: University Presses of Florida, 1978–) are listed in the List of abbreviations at the start of the book; *The Letters of Laurence Sterne*, eds. Melvyn New and Peter de Voogd, two vols., is forthcoming in the same series. There are good paperback editions of *Tristram Shandy* by Ian Campbell Ross (Oxford: Oxford University Press, 1983), Melvyn New (London: Penguin, 2003), and Robert Folkenflik (New York, NY: Random House, 2004). Tim Parnell's Oxford World's Classics edition of *A Sentimental Journey and Other Writings* (Oxford: Oxford University Press, 2003) also includes *A Political Romance*, the *Journal to Eliza*, and selected sermons; an excellent alternative, though lacking *A Political Romance*, is *A Sentimental Journey and Continuation of the Bramine's Journal, with Related Texts*, eds. Melvyn New and W. G. Day (Indianapolis, IN: Hackett, 2006). Two specialist periodicals contain valuable material, a few examples of which are listed below: the *Shandean*, a volume devoted annually since 1989 to scholarly research on Sterne, and the semi-annual *Scriblerian*, which since 1986 has carried reviews and digests of new work plus updates to the Florida annotations.

Biography and reference

Bosch, René, *Labyrinth of Digressions: Tristram Shandy as Perceived and Influenced by Sterne's Early Imitators*. Amsterdam: Rodopi, 2007.

Bowden, Martha F., *Yorick's Congregation: The Church of England in the Time of Laurence Sterne*. Newark, NJ: University of Delaware Press, 2007.

Cash, Arthur H., *Laurence Sterne: The Early and Middle Years*. London: Methuen, 1975.

    Laurence Sterne: The Later Years. London: Methuen, 1986.

Curtis, Lewis Perry, *The Politicks of Laurence Sterne*. London: Oxford University Press, 1929.

Gerard, W. B., *Laurence Sterne and the Visual Imagination*. Aldershot: Ashgate, 2007.

Gerard, W. B., and Brigitte Friant-Kessler, 'Towards a Catalogue of Illustrated Laurence Sterne', *Shandean* 16 (2005), 19–70, continued in *Shandean* 17 (2006), 35–79, 18 (2007), 56–87, and 19 (2008), 90–130.

Howes, Alan B., ed., *Sterne: The Critical Heritage*. London: Routledge, 1974.

    Yorick and the Critics: Sterne's Reputation in England, 1760–1868. New Haven, CT: Yale University Press, 1958.

New, Melvyn, 'Sterne, Laurence (1713–1768)', in *Oxford Dictionary of National Biography*. Oxford: Oxford University Press, 2004 [online edition by subscription at www.oxforddnb.com/view/article/26412, last accessed 15 January 2009].

New, Melvyn, *et al.*, 'Scholia to the Florida Edition of the Works of Sterne, from the *Scriblerian* 1986–2005', *Shandean* 15 (2004), 135–64.

Patrick, Duncan, 'Character and Chronology in *Tristram Shandy*: Four Papers and a Chronological Table', *Shandean* 14 (2003), 39–69 and 15 (2004), 31–56.

Ross, Ian Campbell, *Laurence Sterne: A Life*. Oxford: Oxford University Press, 2001.

Voogd, Peter de and John Neubauer, eds., *The Reception of Laurence Sterne in Europe*. London: Thoemmes Continuum, 2004.

Criticism

Introductory studies

Byrd, Max, *Tristram Shandy*. London: Unwin Hyman, 1985.

Iser, Wolfgang, *Laurence Sterne: Tristram Shandy*. Cambridge: Cambridge University Press, 1988.

Kraft, Elizabeth, *Laurence Sterne Revisited*. New York, NY: Twayne, 1996.

New, Melvyn, *Tristram Shandy: A Book for Free Spirits*. New York, NY: Twayne, 1994.

Pfister, Manfred, *Laurence Sterne*. London: Northcote House / British Council, 2001.

Whittaker, Ruth, *Tristram Shandy*. Milton Keynes: Open University Press, 1988.

Monographs

Campbell, Duncan, *The Beautiful Oblique: Conceptions of Temporality in Tristram Shandy*. Bern: Peter Lang, 2002.

Cash, Arthur Hill, *Sterne's Comedy of Moral Sentiments: The Ethical Dimension of the Journey*. Pittsburgh, PA: Duquesne University Press, 1966.

Hammond, Lansing Van der Heyden, *Laurence Sterne's Sermons of Mr. Yorick*. New Haven, CT: Yale University Press, 1948.

Holtz, William V., *Image and Immortality: A Study of Tristram Shandy*. Providence, RI: Brown University Press, 1970.

Keymer, Thomas, *Sterne, the Moderns, and the Novel*. Oxford: Oxford University Press, 2002.

Lamb, Jonathan, *Sterne's Fiction and the Double Principle*. Cambridge: Cambridge University Press, 1989.

Lanham, Richard A., *Tristram Shandy: The Games of Pleasure*. Berkeley, CA: University of California Press, 1973.

Loveridge, Mark, *Laurence Sterne and the Argument about Design*. London: Macmillan, 1982.

Moglen, Helene, *The Philosophical Irony of Laurence Sterne*. Gainesville, FL: University of Florida Press, 1975.

New, Melvyn, *Laurence Sterne as Satirist: A Reading of Tristram Shandy*. Gainesville, FL: University of Florida Press, 1969.

Stedmond, John M., *The Comic Art of Laurence Sterne: Convention and Innovation in Tristram Shandy and A Sentimental Journey*. Toronto, ON: University of Toronto Press, 1967.

Swearingen, James A., *Reflexivity in Tristram Shandy: An Essay in Phenomenological Criticism*. New Haven, CT: Yale University Press, 1977.

Tadié, Alexis, *Sterne's Whimsical Theatres of Language: Orality, Gesture, Literacy*. Aldershot: Ashgate, 2003.

Traugott, John, *Tristram Shandy's World: Sterne's Philosophical Rhetoric*. Berkeley, CA: University of California Press, 1954.

Watts, Carol, *The Cultural Work of Empire: The Seven Years' War and the Imagining of the Shandean State*. Edinburgh: Edinburgh University Press, 2007.

Collections of essays

Cash, Arthur H., and John M. Stedmond, eds., *The Winged Skull: Papers from the Laurence Sterne Bicentenary Conference*. London: Methuen, 1971.

Keymer, Thomas, ed., *Laurence Sterne's Tristram Shandy: A Casebook*. New York, NY: Oxford University Press, 2006.

Myer, Valerie Grosvenor, ed., *Laurence Sterne: Riddles and Mysteries*. London: Vision, 1984.

New, Melvyn, ed., *Approaches to Teaching Sterne's Tristram Shandy*. New York, NY: Modern Language Association, 1989.

Critical Essays on Laurence Sterne. New York, NY: G. K. Hall, 1998.

Tristram Shandy: Contemporary Critical Essays. New York, NY: St Martin's Press, 1992.

Pierce, David, and Peter de Voogd, eds., *Laurence Sterne in Modernism and Postmodernism*. Amsterdam: Rodopi, 1996.

Traugott, John, *Laurence Sterne: A Collection of Critical Essays*. Englewood Cliffs, NJ: Prentice Hall, 1968.

Walsh, Marcus, ed., *Laurence Sterne*, Longman Critical Readers. Harlow: Longman, 2002.

Articles and chapters

Allen, Dennis W., 'Sexuality/Textuality in *Tristram Shandy*', *Studies in English Literature 1500–1900* 25 (1985), 651–70.

Alter, Robert, 'Sterne and the Nostalgia for Reality', in his *Partial Magic: The Novel as a Self-Conscious Genre*. Berkeley, CA: University of California Press, 1975, 30–56.

Battestin, Martin C., 'A Sentimental Journey and the Syntax of Things', in *Augustan Worlds: New Essays in Eighteenth-Century Literature*, eds. J. C. Hilson, M. M. B. Jones, and J. R. Watson. Leicester: Leicester University Press, 1978, 223–39.

'Sterne among the Philosophes: Body and Soul in *A Sentimental Journey*', *Eighteenth-Century Fiction* 7 (1994), 17–36.

Booth, Wayne C., 'Did Sterne Complete *Tristram Shandy*?' *Modern Philology* 47 (1951), 172–83.

'The Self-Conscious Narrator in Comic Fiction before *Tristram Shandy*', *PMLA* 67 (1952), 163–85.

Brady, Frank, '*Tristram Shandy*: Sexuality, Morality, and Sensibility', *Eighteenth-Century Studies* 4 (1970), 41–56.

Briggs, Peter, 'Laurence Sterne and Literary Celebrity in 1760', *Age of Johnson* 4 (1991), 251–80.

'Locke's *Essay* and the Tentativeness of *Tristram Shandy*', *Studies in Philology* 82 (1985), 494–517.

Brissenden, R. F., 'The Sentimental Comedy: *Tristram Shandy*', in his *Virtue in Distress: Studies in the Novel of Sentiment from Richardson to Sade*. London: Macmillan, 1974, 187–217.

Brown, Homer Obed, 'Tristram to the Hebrews: Some Notes on the Institution of a Canonic Text', *Modern Language Notes* 99 (1984), 727–47. Revised in his *Institutions of the English Novel: From Defoe to Scott*. Philadelphia, PA: University of Pennsylvania Press, 116–37.

Brown, Marshall, 'Sterne's Stories', in his *Preromanticism*. Stanford, CA: Stanford University Press, 1991, 261–300.

Burckhardt, Sigurd, '*Tristram Shandy*'s Law of Gravity', *ELH* 28 (1961), 70–88.

Cash, Arthur H., 'Sterne, Hall, Libertinism, and *A Sentimental Journey*', *Age of Johnson* 12 (2001), 291–327.

Chadwick, Joseph, 'Infinite Jest: Interpretation in Sterne's *A Sentimental Journey*', *Eighteenth-Century Studies* 12 (1978–9), 190–205.

Day, W. G., 'Sterne's Verse', *Shandean* 14 (2003), 9–37.

DePorte, Michael V., 'Sterne: The Eccentric Journey', in his *Nightmares and Hobbyhorses: Swift, Sterne, and Augustan Ideas of Madness*. San Marino: Huntington Library, 1974, 107–35.

Descargues, Madeleine, '*Tristram Shandy* and the Appositeness of War', *Shandean* 12 (2001), 63–77.

Donoghue, Frank, '"I wrote not to be fed but to be famous": Laurence Sterne', in his *The Fame Machine: Book Reviewing and Eighteenth-Century Literary Careers*. Stanford, CA: Stanford University Press, 1998, 56–85.

Downey, James, '*The Sermons of Mr. Yorick*: A Reassessment of Hammond', *English Studies in Canada* 4 (1978), 193–211.

During, Simon, 'Taking Liberties: Sterne, Wilkes and Warburton', in *Libertine Enlightenment: Sex, Liberty and Licence in the Eighteenth Century*, eds. Peter Cryle and Lisa O'Connell. Basingstoke: Palgrave, 2004, 15–33.

Dussinger, John A., 'The Sensorium in the World of *A Sentimental Journey*', *Ariel* 13 (1982), 3–16.

'Yorick and the "Eternal Fountain of our Feelings"', in *Psychology and Literature in the Eighteenth Century*, ed. Christopher Fox. New York, NY: AMS Press, 1987, 259–76.

Eagleton, Terry, 'The Good-Natured Gael', in his *Crazy John and the Bishop, and Other Essays on Irish Culture*. Cork: Cork University Press, 1998, 68–139.

Ellis, Markman, '"The House of Bondage": Sentimentalism and the Problem of Slavery', in his *The Politics of Sensibility: Race, Gender, and Commerce in the Sentimental Novel*. Cambridge: Cambridge University Press, 1996, 49–86.

Fairer, David, 'Sentimental Translation in Mackenzie and Sterne', *Essays in Criticism* 49 (1999), 132–51.

Fanning, Christopher, 'On Sterne's Page: Spatial Layout, Spatial Form, and Social Spaces in *Tristram Shandy*', *Eighteenth-Century Fiction* 10 (1998), 429–50.

'Sermons on Sermonizing: The Pulpit Rhetoric of Swift and of Sterne', *Philological Quarterly* 76 (1997), 413–36.

'Small Particles of Eloquence: Sterne and the Scriblerian Text', *Modern Philology* 100 (2003), 360–92.

'"The Things Themselves": Origins and Originality in Sterne's Sermons', *Eighteenth Century: Theory and Interpretation* 40 (1999), 29–45.

'"This Fragment of Life": Sterne's Encyclopaedic Ethics', *Shandean* 13 (2002), 55–67.

Gibson, Andrew, '*Tristram Shandy*', in his *Reading Narrative Discourse: Studies in the Novel from Cervantes to Beckett*. London: Macmillan, 1990, 60–77.

Ginzburg, Carlo, 'A Search for Origins: Re-reading *Tristram Shandy*', in his *No Island Is an Island: Four Glances at English Literature in a World Perspective*. New York, NY: Columbia University Press, 2000, 43–67.

Harries, Elizabeth W., 'Sterne's Novels: Gathering up the Fragments', *ELH* 49 (1982), 35–49. Revised in her *The Unfinished Manner: Essays on the Fragment in the Later Eighteenth Century*. Charlottesville, VA: University Press of Virginia, 1994, 41–55.

Hartling, Shannon, 'Inexpressible Sadness: Sterne's Sermons and the Moral Inadequacies of Politeness in *Tristram Shandy*', *Christianity and Literature* 55.4 (2006), 495–510.

Hawley, Judith, 'The Anatomy of *Tristram Shandy*', in *Literature and Medicine During the Eighteenth Century*, eds. Marie Mulvey Roberts and Roy Porter. London: Routledge, 1993, 84–100.

Hunter, J. Paul, 'Clocks, Calendars, and Names: The Troubles of Tristram and the Aesthetics of Uncertainty', in *Rhetorics of Order/Ordering Rhetorics in English Neoclassical Literature*, eds. J. Douglas Canfield and J. Paul Hunter. Newark, NJ: University of Delaware Press, 1989, 173–98.

'From Typology to Type: Agents of Change in Eighteenth-Century English Texts', in *Cultural Artifacts and the Production of Meaning: The Page, the Image, and the Body*, eds. Margaret J. M. Ezell and Katherine O'Brien O'Keefe. Ann Arbor, MI: University of Michigan Press, 1994, 41–69.

'Response as Reformation: *Tristram Shandy* and the Art of Interruption', *Novel* 4.2 (1971), 132–46.

Jefferson, D. W., '*Tristram Shandy* and the Tradition of Learned Wit', *Essays in Criticism* 1 (1951), 225–48.

Kay, Carol, 'Sterne: Scenes of Play', in her *Political Constructions: Defoe, Richardson, and Sterne in Relation to Hobbes, Hume, and Burke*. Ithaca, NY: Cornell University Press, 1988, 195–246.

Keymer, Thomas, 'Sterne and Romantic Autobiography', in *The Cambridge Companion to English Literature from 1740 to 1830*, eds. Thomas Keymer and Jon Mee. Cambridge: Cambridge University Press, 2004, 173–93.

Kim, James, '"Good Cursed, Bouncing Losses": Masculinity, Sentimental Irony, and Exuberance in *Tristram Shandy*', *The Eighteenth Century: Theory and Interpretation* 48 (2007), 3–24.

King, Ross, '*Tristram Shandy* and the Wound of Language', *Studies in Philology* 92 (1995), 291–310.

Kraft, Elizabeth, 'Laurence Sterne and the Ethics of Sexual Difference: Chiasmic Narration and Double Desire', *Christianity and Literature* 51 (2002), 363–85.

Lamb, Jonathan, 'Language and Hartleian Associationism in *A Sentimental Journey*', *Eighteenth-Century Studies* 13 (1980), 285–312.

'Sterne and Irregular Oratory', in *The Cambridge Companion to the Eighteenth-Century Novel*, ed. John Richetti. Cambridge: Cambridge University Press, 1996, 153–74.

'Sterne, Sebald, and Siege Architecture', *Eighteenth-Century Fiction* 19 (2006), 21–41.

'Sterne's System of Imitation', *Modern Language Review* 76 (1981), 794–810.

'Sterne's Use of Montaigne', *Comparative Literature* 32 (1980), 1–41.

'The Job Controversy, Sterne, and the Question of Allegory', *Eighteenth-Century Studies* 24 (1990), 1–19.

Lawlor, Clark, 'Consuming Time: Narrative and Disease in *Tristram Shandy*', *Yearbook of English Studies* 30 (2000), 46–59.

Loscocco, Paula, 'Can't Live Without 'Em: Walter Shandy and the Woman Within', *The Eighteenth Century: Theory and Interpretation* 32 (1991), 166–79.

Loveridge, Mark, 'Stories of Cocks and Bulls: The Ending of *Tristram Shandy*', *Eighteenth-Century Fiction* 5 (1992), 35–54.

Lovesey, Oliver, 'Divine Enthusiasm and Love Melancholy: *Tristram Shandy* and Eighteenth-Century Narratives of Saint Errantry', *Eighteenth-Century Fiction* 16 (2004), 373–99.

Lupton, Christina, '*Tristram Shandy*, David Hume and Epistemological Fiction', *Philosophy and Literature* 27 (2003), 98–115.

Lynch, Jack, 'The Relicks of Learning: Sterne among the Renaissance Encyclopedists', *Eighteenth-Century Fiction* 13 (2000), 1–17.

MacKenzie, Scott R., 'Homunculus Economicus: Laurence Sterne's Labour Theory of Literary Value', *Eighteenth-Century Fiction* 18 (2005), 49–80.

McGlynn, Paul D., 'Sterne's Maria: Madness and Sentimentality', *Eighteenth-Century Life* 3 (1976), 39–43.

McMaster, Juliet, '"Uncrystalized flesh and blood": The Body in *Tristram Shandy*', *Eighteenth-Century Fiction* 2 (1990), 197–214. Revised in her *Reading the Body in the Eighteenth-Century Novel*. Basingstoke: Palgrave, 2004, 25–41.

'Walter Shandy, Sterne, and Gender: A Feminist Foray', *English Studies in Canada* 15 (1989), 441–58.

Markley, Robert, 'Sentimentality as Performance: Shaftesbury, Sterne, and the Theatrics of Virtue', in *The New Eighteenth Century: Theory, Politics, English Literature*, eds. Felicity Nussbaum and Laura Brown. London: Methuen, 1987, 210–30.

'*Tristram Shandy* and Narrative Middles: Hillis Miller and the Style of Deconstructive Criticism', *Genre* 17 (1984), 179–90.

Miller, J. Hillis, 'Narrative Middles: a Preliminary Outline', *Genre* 11 (1978), 375–87.

Moglen, Helene, '(W)holes and Noses: The Indeterminacies of *Tristram Shandy*', *Literature and Psychology* 41 (1995), 44–79. Revised in her *The Trauma of Gender: A Feminist Theory of the English Novel*. Berkeley, CA: University of California Press, 2001, 87–108.

Moss, Roger B., 'Sterne's Punctuation', *Eighteenth-Century Studies* 15 (1981), 179–200.

Mullan, John, 'Laurence Sterne and the "Sociality" of the Novel', in his *Sentiment and Sociability: The Language of Feeling in the Eighteenth Century*. Oxford: Clarendon Press, 1988, 147–200.

New, Melvyn, 'Proust's Influence on Sterne: A Remembrance of Things to Come', *Modern Language Notes* 103.5 (1988), 1031–55.

'Reading Sterne through Proust and Levinas', *Age of Johnson* 12 (2001), 329–60.

'Sterne and the Narrative of Determinateness', *Eighteenth-Century Fiction* 4 (1992), 315–29.

'Sterne, Warburton, and the Burden of Exuberant Wit', *Eighteenth-Century Studies* 15 (1982), 245–74.

'The Dunce Revisited: Colley Cibber and Tristram Shandy', *South Atlantic Quarterly* 72 (1973), 547–59.

Norton, Brian Michael, 'The Moral in Phutatorius's Breeches: *Tristram Shandy* and the Limits of Stoic Ethics', *Eighteenth-Century Fiction* 18 (2006), 405–23.

Ostovich, Helen, 'Reader as Hobby-horse in *Tristram Shandy*', *Philological Quarterly* 68 (1989), 325–42.

Parker, Fred, '*Tristram Shandy*: Singularity and the Single Life', in his *Scepticism and Literature: An Essay on Pope, Hume, Sterne, and Johnson*. Oxford: Oxford University Press, 2003, 190–231.

Parnell, Tim, 'A Story Painted to the Heart? *Tristram Shandy* and Sentimentalism Reconsidered', *Shandean* 9 (1997), 122–35.

'Laurence Sterne and the Problem of Belief', *Shandean* 17 (2006), 121–39.

'Swift, Sterne, and the Skeptical Tradition', *Studies in Eighteenth-Century Culture* 23 (1994), 220–42.

Patterson, Diana, 'Foliation Jokes in *Tristram Shandy*', *1650–1850: Ideas, Aesthetics, and Inquiries in the Early Modern Era* 6 (1999), 163–83.

Perry, Ruth, 'Words for Sex: The Verbal-Sexual Continuum in *Tristram Shandy*', *Studies in the Novel* 20 (1988), 27–42.

Petrakis, Byron, 'Jester in the Pulpit: Sterne and Pulpit Eloquence', *Philological Quarterly* 51 (1972), 430–47.

Porter, Roy, '"The whole secret of health": Mind, Body, and Medicine in *Tristram Shandy*', in *Nature Transfigured: Science and Literature 1700–1900*, eds. John Christie and Sally Shuttleworth. Manchester: Manchester University Press, 1989, 61–84.

Putney, Rufus, 'The Evolution of *A Sentimental Journey*', *Philological Quarterly* 19 (1940), 349–69.

Rabb, Melinda Alliker, 'Engendering Accounts in Sterne's *A Sentimental Journey*', in *Johnson and His Age*, ed. James Engell. Cambridge, MA: Harvard University Press, 1984, 531–58.

Regan, Shaun, 'Novelizing Scriblerus: *Tristram Shandy* and (Post-) Scriblerian Satire', *Shandean* 17 (2006), 9–33.

'Print Culture in Transition: *Tristram Shandy*, the Reviewers, and the Consumable Text', *Eighteenth-Century Fiction* 14 (2002), 289–309.

'Translating Rabelais: Sterne, Motteux, and the Culture of Politeness', *Translation and Literature* 10 (2001), 174–99.

Rodgers, James, 'Sensibility, Sympathy, Benevolence: Physiology and Moral Philosophy in *Tristram Shandy*', in *Languages of Nature: Critical Essays on Science and Literature*, ed. L. J. Jordanova. New Brunswick, NJ: Rutgers University Press, 1986, 117–58.

Rogers, Pat, 'Ziggerzagger Shandy: Sterne and the Aesthetics of the Crooked Line', *English* 42 (1993), 97–107.

Rosenblum, Michael, 'The Sermon, the King of Bohemia, and the Art of Interpolation in *Tristram Shandy*', *Studies in Philology* 75 (1978), 472–91.

Ross, Ian Campbell, 'When Smelfungus Met Yorick: Sterne and Smollett in the South of France, 1763', in *Tobias Smollett, Scotland's First Novelist: New Essays in Memory of Paul-Gabriel Boucé*, ed. O M Brack. Newark, NJ: University of Delaware Press, 2007, 74–93.

Rothstein, Eric, '*Tristram Shandy*', in his *Systems of Order and Inquiry in Later Eighteenth-Century Fiction*. Berkeley, CA: University of California Press, 1975, 62–108.

Rowson, Martin, 'A Comic Book Version of *Tristram Shandy*', *Shandean* 14 (2003), 104–21.

'Hyperboling Gravity's Ravelin: A Comic Book Version of *Tristram Shandy*', *Shandean* 7 (1995), 62–86.

Seelig, Sharon Cadman, 'Sterne, *Tristram Shandy*: The Deconstructive Text', in her *Generating Texts: The Progeny of Seventeenth-Century Prose*. Charlottesville, VA: University of Virginia Press, 1996, 128–54.

Seidel, Michael, 'Gravity's Inheritable Line: Sterne's *Tristram Shandy*', in his *Satiric Inheritance, Rabelais to Sterne*. Princeton, NJ: Princeton University Press, 1979, 250–62.

'Narrative Crossings: Sterne's *A Sentimental Journey*', *Genre* 18 (1985), 1–22.

Shankman, Steven, 'Participation and Reflective Distance: The End of Laurence Sterne's *A Sentimental Journey* and the Resistance to Doctrine', *Religion and Literature* 29 (1997), 43–61.

Shklovsky, Viktor, 'The Novel as Parody: Sterne's *Tristram Shandy*', in his *Theory of Prose*. Elmwood Park, IL: Dalkey Archive Press, 1991, 147–70.

Spacks, Patricia Meyer, 'The Beautiful Oblique: *Tristram Shandy*', in her *Imagining a Self: Autobiography and Novel in Eighteenth-Century England*. Cambridge, MA: Harvard University Press, 1976, 127–57.

'*Tristram Shandy* and the Development of the Novel', in her *Novel Beginnings: Experiments in Eighteenth-Century English Fiction*. New Haven, CT: Yale University Press, 2006, 254–76.

Steele, Peter, 'Sterne's Script: The Performing of *Tristram Shandy*', in *Augustan Studies: Essays in Honor of Irvin Ehrenpreis*, eds. Douglas Lane Patey and Timothy Keegan. Newark, NJ: University of Delaware Press, 1985, 195–204.

Stevenson, John Allen, 'Sterne: Comedian and Experimental Novelist', in *The Columbia History of the British Novel*, eds. John Richetti *et al*. New York, NJ: Columbia University Press, 1994, 154–80.

Stewart, Carol, 'The Anglicanism of *Tristram Shandy*: Latitudinarianism at the Limits', *British Journal for Eighteenth-Century Studies* 28 (2005), 239–50.

Stout, Gardner D., Jr, 'Yorick's Sentimental Journey: A Comic "Pilgrim's Progress" for the Man of Feeling', *ELH* 30 (1963), 395–412.

Thomas, Calvin, '*Tristram Shandy*'s Consent to Incompleteness: Discourse, Disavowal, Disruption', *Literature and Psychology* 36 (1990), 44–62.

Van Sant, Ann Jessie, 'Locating Experience in the Body: The Man of Feeling', in her *Eighteenth-Century Sensibility and the Novel: The Senses in Social Context*. Cambridge: Cambridge University Press, 1993, 98–115.

Voogd, Peter J. de, '*Tristram Shandy* as Aesthetic Object', *Word & Image* 4 (1988), 383–92.

Watt, Ian, 'The Comic Syntax of *Tristram Shandy*', in his *The Literal Imagination: Selected Essays*. Seattle, WA: University of Washington Press, 2002, 126–42.

Wehrs, Donald R., 'Sterne, Cervantes, Montaigne: Fideistic Skepticism and the Rhetoric of Desire', *Comparative Literature Studies* 25 (1988), 127–51.

Zimmerman, Everett, '*Tristram Shandy* and Narrative Representation', *The Eighteenth Century: Theory and Interpretation* 28 (1987), 127–47. Revised in his *The Boundaries of Fiction: History and the Eighteenth-Century British Novel*. Ithaca, NY: Cornell University Press, 1996, 179–204.

INDEX

Cambridge Companions to…

AUTHORS

TOPICS